EYE ON THE DIAMONDS

EYE ON THE DIAMONDS

Terry Crawford-Browne

PENGUIN BOOKS

PENGUIN BOOKS

Published by the Penguin Group
Penguin Books (South Africa) (Pty) Ltd, Block D, Rosebank Office Park,
181 Jan Smuts Avenue, Parktown North, 2193, Johannesburg, South Africa
Penguin Group (USA) Inc, 375 Hudson Street, New York, New York 10014, USA
Penguin Group (Canada), 90 Eglinton Avenue East, Suite 700, Toronto, Ontario,
Canada M4P 2Y3 (a division of Pearson Penguin Canada Inc)
Penguin Books Ltd, 80 Strand, London WC2R 0RL, England
Penguin Ireland, 25 St Stephen's Green, Dublin 2,
Ireland (a division of Penguin Books Ltd)
Penguin Group (Australia), 250 Camberwell Road, Camberwell, Victoria 3124,
Australia (a division of Pearson Australia Group Pty Ltd)
Penguin Books India Pvt Ltd, 11 Community Centre,
Panchsheel Park, New Delhi – 110 017, India
Penguin Group (NZ), 67 Apollo Drive, Mairangi Bay, Auckland 1310, New Zealand
(a division of Pearson New Zealand Ltd)

Penguin Books (South Africa) (Pty) Ltd, Registered Offices:
Block D, Rosebank Office Park, 181 Jan Smuts Avenue, Parktown North,
2193, Johannesburg, South Africa

www.penguinbooks.co.za

First published by Penguin Books (South Africa) (Pty) Ltd 2012

Copyright © Terry Crawford-Browne, 2012

All rights reserved
The moral right of the author has been asserted

ISBN 978-0-14-353010-7

Cover by Publicide
Printed and bound by Interpak Books, Pietermaritzburg

FSC
www.fsc.org
FSC® C105736

The mark of
responsible forestry

IN MEMORIAM

Bheki Jacobs, who died in September 2008 at the age of forty-six, was one of the most remarkable figures to come out of the liberation struggle. Jacobs was 'the native who caused all the trouble', the man ultimately responsible for the fact that we have an arms deal scandal.

Information – its gathering, interpretation and dissemination – was Jacobs's life-blood, a craft he pursued brilliantly and ceaselessly, even when he was partly paralysed by the cancer that killed him.

Key amongst his clients, Jacobs suggested, was 'the chief': Thabo Mbeki. The Presidency denied any relationship with Jacobs. The reason for the fallout seems to have been the arms deal. Jacobs's comrades insist he blew the whistle on the arms deal because of a deep frustration that the ANC was betraying its most sacred principles. In this, as in much else, it seems he has been proved right.

Of course, he was one of the first to grasp how the headlong plunge into business would corrupt the ANC, how its internal politics would become a savage contest for resources, and just how early in its victory the party would lose its way.

Above all, what astonished me was his ability to keep in his head a sprawling, immensely detailed circuit diagram of economic and political power in South Africa. Sometimes that made him sound like a wild conspiracy theorist.

But he was so often proved right that I eventually (slowly) learned that when members of the ruling elite have a paranoid and conspiratorial world view, they act conspiratorially and, as a result, conspiracy theory becomes crucial to understanding their behaviour.

Bheki Jacobs is gone, but the South Africa he saw emerging behind the bright platitudes of the 1990s is now manifest all around us. Being right was no comfort to him.

Extracts from an Obituary by Nic Dawes, editor of the *Mail & Guardian*.

Nic Dawes, 'Master of Information', *Mail & Guardian*, September 16, 2008.

CONTENTS

PREFACE

A pacifist's journey

The international war business, and the corruption it unleashes, is out of control. Financial and political elites in Britain and the United States, in collusion with dictatorships in Middle Eastern and African client states, are determined to maintain their hold over oil and other natural resources. The American and British governments are the world's self-appointed policemen. In pursuit of wars and profit, countries and people are deemed mere 'collateral damage'.

The twentieth century was the bloodiest in history. Killing people for profit in the twenty-first century has already become a game described as a PlayStation mentality. As if acting out a Hollywood movie, the 'enemy' is eliminated by a young computer technician sitting thousands of kilometres away in air-conditioned comfort. The 9/11 attack on the World Trade Center in New York was an opportunity for which the war business had been waiting.

President Dwight Eisenhower in 1961 warned of the 'rise of the military-industrial complex' and the dangers it posed for the international community. The 'cost of war' project at Brown University in the USA estimates that since 9/11 the wars in Afghanistan, Iraq and Pakistan have cost almost a quarter of a million lives and up to US$4 trillion. Almost eight million people have been displaced as refugees.[1]

Diamonds are a metaphor for greed, that most destructive of humanity's failings, fed by the vanity of women and the depravity of men. Global money

---

1 'Costs of War', Eisenhower Research Project at the Watson Institute for International Studies, Brown University, June 29, 2011.

laundering is a major security problem, and is now estimated to exceed US$1 trillion annually.

British royalty and American actresses promote gem diamonds. Organised crime and mobsters appreciate that blood diamonds provide the ultimate money laundering opportunities. Supplies of industrial diamonds are critical to the twenty-first century war business but De Beers, which dominated the diamond cartel for more than a century, is fast losing control to far more ruthless Israeli players.

Cheap boart – industrial diamonds – is an essential element for precision machine tools, high energy lasers and drones. The politically turbulent Congo produces seventy-five per cent of the world's supply. Up to ten million people have died there in 'Africa's First World War', killed by the lust for natural resources required by the 'first world's' military-industrial complex. Iraq, Afghanistan and Pakistan are already devastated by an arrogant notion that 'American global leadership is good for America and good for the world'.

Add in religion with sex, oil, money, diamonds and war, and the combinations are explosive. The new empire of a Judaic-Christian alliance between Zionist Israelis and an estimated fifty million American Christian Zionists could lead to the Earth's destruction. An Israeli confrontation with Iran could escalate into a nuclear conflagration from China across Asia and Africa to Nigeria.

Eye On The Diamonds is a sequel to *Eye On The Money* published by Umuzi in 2007. It continues in chapters one, seven and ten with the arms deal saga, which for years has dominated South Africa's political landscape. In response to the author's public interest application, the Constitutional Court in November 2011 issued a consent order to President Jacob Zuma's appointment of a judicial commission of inquiry. The investigation into South Africa's arms deal scandal will be continued in *Eye On The Gold*, and on the pending collapse of the US dollar.

The focus on diamonds links the colonial and apartheid histories of South Africa with Israel-Palestine. Cecil Rhodes's influences in the diamond industry are still being played out more than a century after his death. His imperialist vision in 1877 of British and American 'power so overwhelming as to render all wars simply impossible' remains the determinant of the war business.

The war business pours even more weapons into the Middle East, as if deliberately pouring petrol on to a fire. President Barack Obama – following Prime Ministers Margaret Thatcher and Tony Blair before him – has become the arms industry's best salesman. The Israeli lobby in Washington has become so formidable that no American president or politician dares to confront it.

Israel's armaments industry, funded by South Africa during the 1970s and 1980s, is a menace to the entire international community. After six decades of wars and war profiteering, the Israeli war business deliberately thwarts all efforts at peaceful resolution of conflict. Israel has become 'a promised land for organised crime' where assassinations, money laundering and other criminal activities are justified in the 'national interest'.

In 2009 and 2010 the writer undertook two three-month placements as a peace monitor in Jerusalem and Bethlehem with the World Council of Churches' Ecumenical Accompaniment Programme For Palestine and Israel (EAPPI). He found the parallels with apartheid South Africa glaring, yet he is also hopeful of a peaceful resolution of the conflict.

He concluded that, irrespective of Zionist ideologies, the occupation of the West Bank and Jerusalem by seven hundred thousand Israeli settlers makes a two-state, Bantustan solution a practical impossibility. A one-state solution in Palestine from the Jordan River to the Mediterranean must eventually prevail, albeit a state in which Palestinians are the majority.

He was the secretary of the South African organising committee for the Russell Tribunal on Palestine. After previous sessions in Barcelona and London, the Tribunal met in Cape Town in November 2011 to consider Israeli apartheid as a crime against humanity and, given the complicity of governments, what non-violent remedial actions can be taken by international civil society to avert catastrophe.

1 • LESSONS IN PERFIDY

Put sex, diamonds, oil, war and money together, and the combination is explosive. Organised crime also appreciates that diamonds are unparalleled – and convey far more cachet than drugs – for money laundering opportunities. Diamonds adorn the queens of England and Hollywood movie stars but, as James Bond confirmed, have also become an essential commodity for the war business.

Lord Randolph Churchill, father of Sir Winston, during a visit to the diamond diggings in Kimberley in 1891 commented: 'All this for the vanity of women.' A quick-witted woman bystander replied: 'And the depravity of men.'[1]

How could stones that are strewn around the world in such abundance become a symbol of marital commitment and, in addition, be vital to 'national security'? Indeed, what in the final analysis actually constitutes 'national security', other than the obsessions of generals and politicians to stifle public investigation into financial corruption and military incompetence?

I began to wrestle with these issues during the 1994-1995 Cameron Commission of Inquiry into Armscor when Unita was selling diamonds to

De Beers to fund the civil war in Angola. South Africa was supplying the weapons. I realised use of 'blood diamonds' to finance wars could quickly destroy the glamorous gemstone images so carefully marketed by the diamond cartel.

I was later appointed to represent the Anglican Church during the parliamentary Defence Review. My professional background was international banking having been, until 1986, Nedbank's Regional Treasury Manager in the Western Cape. There was general agreement at the Defence Review that there was no conceivable foreign military threat to South Africa. Eradication of poverty was the national priority, and would require every cent we could muster.

Arguments in favour of the arms deal were absurd. Government spokesmen insisted that South Africa needed to re-equip the Navy and Air Force with highly sophisticated warships and warplanes as if to deter an attack by the United States. Surely only a fool could swallow the defence minister's patter that R30 billion spent on armaments would generate offsets worth R110 billion and that the arms deal was a generous 'Marshall Plan' to stimulate South Africa's economic development and create jobs?

Criticisms of the expenditures were denounced as racist, especially after allegations wafted around parliamentary corridors in mid-1998 that the British arms company BAE was bribing Tony Yengeni and other politicians with a £1 million 'first success fee'. As a former banker, I could smell the stench of corruption, but could not yet prove it. The evidence soon followed.

I learned that the bribes were being laundered, with the connivance of the British government, via a BAE front company incorporated in the British Virgin Islands. The company was styled Red Diamond Trading Company. Those Caribbean islands, although notorious for money laundering operations, produce no diamonds. The curious choice of corporate name was itself worthy of a James Bond movie, and the shenanigans of British diplomats. Why the choice of 'red diamonds' except that the colour red symbolises both the passions of love and the violence of war?

During December 1998 shop stewards at the National Union of Metalworkers (Numsa) were adamant that a further R30 million in bribes was being transferred through two Swedish trade unions. They told me that the kickbacks were described as funding for an industrial training school. A Swedish television journalist obtained confirmation of the payments, but then the 'shutters came down'.

Through Ann Feltham at Campaign Against Arms Trade (CAAT) in London, I asked the British government to investigate. CAAT contacted the Secretary for Trade and Industry Stephen Byers who, in May 1999, appointed the London Metropolitan Police to the task. I learned eventually that it was not illegal under English law to bribe foreigners and, consequently, that there was supposedly no crime for Scotland Yard to scrutinise.

Byers's successor as Secretary for Trade and Industry Patricia Hewitt finally admitted in 2003 that BAE had paid bribes to secure its arms deal contracts with South Africa but they were, she pleaded, 'within reasonable limits'. The mind boggles at what inducements the British government might have considered excessive!

Bheki Jacobs and his colleagues approached me in June 1999 with information as to how some members of the African National Congress (ANC) intended to turn South Africa into a major centre for organised crime. He told me:

> We'll tell you where the real corruption is – around Joe Modise and the leadership of Umkhonto we Sizwe, who see themselves as the new financial elite in post-apartheid South Africa. We saw the consequences in Russia with the collapse of the Soviet Union, when communists suddenly became super-capitalists. Such a gangster society is not why we went into exile to fight for liberation from apartheid.

The whistleblowers said that the new ANC political elite saw the weapons-for-diamonds trade as a fast conduit to huge wealth. Whilst in exile, Modise had personally profited from the easy and quick money opportunities offered by the illegal trade in diamonds. A dysfunctional police force combined with world-class banking services made South Africa an ideal base for money laundering operations.

From the British perspective, unleashing a culture of corruption would enable British financial interests to retain control of the South African economy. Nothing so discredits democratic governance as corruption. Instead of 'victimless crime', as too often it is portrayed, corruption represents nothing less than theft from the poor. Nigeria, Zimbabwe, Sierra Leone, Ghana, Uganda, Kenya ... the independence of former British colonies in Africa had all proved dismal failures.

The blame could conveniently be pinned on venal Africans instead of Englishmen who were the underlying cause, and who used men such as Modise to do their 'dirty work'. The hard-won battle for freedom would be short-lived, and the struggle against apartheid would be betrayed by greedy and unscrupulous ANC politicians.

I was alarmed by this analysis and information and briefed Njongonkulu Ndungane who had succeeded Desmond Tutu as the Anglican Archbishop of Cape Town, and had appointed me to represent the Church at the Defence Review. I introduced Jacobs to Patricia de Lille, the feisty Pan Africanist Congress Member of Parliament. The 'De Lille Dossier' followed. Some months later I also introduced Jacobs to Sam Sole and other investigative journalists at the *Mail & Guardian* newspaper.

So began the 'arms deal' saga. We will, I hope, eventually expose the sanctimonious British and their American cousins, who present themselves as the paragons of honesty and democracy and who have appointed themselves as the world's policemen.

The whistleblowers told me that the 'arms deal' represented just the tip of the iceberg. It extended to oil deals, toll roads, drivers' licences, the proposed Cell C cellphone system, the Coega harbour development, drugs and weapons trafficking, diamond smuggling and money laundering. The common denominator was a ten per cent kickback to the ANC in return for political protection.

No country, including the US and Britain, has yet resolved how to fund political parties. To hedge their bets arms companies lavishly fund all parties. Hypocrisy and venality in London and Washington around the arms trade completely eclipses the corruption in the so-called 'third world'.

Democracy is thus held ransom to donors and bribe money. In South Africa, the ANC refuses to open its books to public scrutiny, and spuriously argues that it is a private entity.

The influence of BAE in high places was well illustrated in December 2006 when Prime Minister Tony Blair blocked investigations by the British Serious Fraud Office (SFO) into bribes of over £1 billion paid by BAE to Saudi Arabian Prince Bandar. Blair claimed the SFO investigation would jeopardise British national security.

My friends at CAAT and the Corner House took the British government to court, and won. On appeal, the law lords of the House of Lords in July 2008 decided that the government holds the prerogative to determine what does and what does not constitute 'national security'. The scandal of government collusion with Britain's rapacious war industry was again brushed under the carpet.

Ironically, however, Blair's action put new focus on the South African arms deal that was also under investigation by the SFO. Suddenly facing exposure of the arms deal corruption, President Thabo Mbeki angrily denounced Blair as a hypocrite. It was, after all, massive pressure from Blair that had pushed South Africa into what the Institute For Democracy in South Africa (Idasa) describes as the 'litmus test of South Africa's commitment to democracy and good governance'.

Foreign politicians – but especially British politicians and even Queen Elizabeth – flocked to South Africa after 1994 to pay tribute to Nelson Mandela and our new democracy with one hand, and to peddle weapons with the other. The royal yacht *Britannia*, when docked in Cape Town harbour for the Queen's visit in March 1995, also doubled as a floating British armaments industry exhibition.

The Queen had been preceded by Prime Minister John Major in September 1994 and, to step up the pressure, the Defence Minister Malcolm Rifkind followed a few days after the Queen's departure. The urgent needs of South Africans for poverty eradication were deemed secondary to armaments proliferation in a region of the world already awash with weaponry.

The United Nations arms embargo against apartheid South Africa had been rescinded just a few months earlier. Armscor greeted that decision with jubilation, and cynically announced that it intended to treble South African weapons exports in the cause of job creation and foreign exchange earnings, and thus to contribute to the post-apartheid Reconstruction and Development Programme (RDP).

The bishops of the Anglican Church denounced Armscor's intentions. Archbishop Desmond Tutu was even more scathing, and declared that 'the ANC has stopped the apartheid gravy train just long enough to climb on board'. The term 'gravy train' entered South Africa's political lexicon. Mandela was furious, declaring Tutu's criticisms to be 'irresponsible', and that he should first have raised the issue with him before going public.

Tutu replied:

> It is very distressing that the President is behaving like an ordinary politician. Instead of answering my criticisms, he is impugning my integrity. It is beneath his stature. What is more distressing is the impression the President gives that I did not speak personally to him. I raised my concerns with him about salaries and about the arms trade some weeks before I expressed them publicly.[2]

Oliver Tambo had once described South Africa's armaments industry as 'a Frankenstein monster that cannot be reformed and must be destroyed'. Mandela, regrettably, insisted that the arms trade was a lucrative business in which issues of morality should play no part. He lobbied vigorously on behalf of the arms industry, even making a special trip to the US in a futile effort to convince President Bill Clinton to drop American criminal charges against Armscor and its offshoot, Denel.

South Africa has come a long, long way since 1994 when the world expected a racial bloodbath. Nonetheless, the ANC government could have done so much better. Three issues define Mbeki's disastrous presidency from 1999 until 2008: Zimbabwe, Aids, and the arms deal scandal. The arms deal eventually became the cause of Mbeki's ignominious dismissal from office. Mbeki had been hailed as 'Mr Delivery' when he came to office.

Mandela had focused on reconciliation but Mbeki, it was expected, would deliver houses, education, and jobs, jobs, jobs. He waxed lyrical about 'the African renaissance', and we all so desperately wanted to believe that he was a massively gifted intellectual. Little did we know then that when Mbeki talked about the 'renaissance', he was not referring to Leonardo da Vinci but, instead, meant Niccolò Machiavelli.

We soon learned that if anyone stepped on Mbeki's toes on Monday, he would be politically dead by Wednesday, and that the funeral would be on Friday![3]

Mbeki has a master's degree in economics from the University of Sussex. He quoted English poets, smoked a pipe, dressed meticulously in expensive English clothes, and drank copious quantities of Johnny Walker Blue Label whisky. Having been in exile for twenty-eight years, many township mamas even long before 1999 dismissively described Mbeki as 'that black Englishman'.

In itself, that was a lesson and pointer. Township mamas may be poor, they may be illiterate, but they are not stupid. The cartoonist Zapiro captured Mbeki's distain for the poor with his arrival in the presidential limo at the gates of parliament in Cape Town. A drunken *bergie*[4] rushes forward to beg for change, to which Mbeki replies: 'Change? Don't you know that change takes time?'

Mbeki's younger brother Moeletsi, who is a political analyst and director of the South African Institute of International Relations, declared in a speech in London:

> When the British decided in 1910 to give up political control of South Africa, they had two choices: to yield control to the small black elite, educated by British missionaries in the Eastern Cape and Natal, or to Afrikaner nationalists. The British chose the Afrikaners and, although the model was clearly defective, it surprised many by lasting eighty-four years before being obliged to hand power to black nationalists.
>
> Unlike Afrikaner landowners, black nationalists owned no wealth. Big Business however, had anticipated this and came up with its solution. It would transfer just a small part of its wealth to individual leaders of the ANC, and thus co-opt them. These leaders found the offer of instant wealth

hard to resist, and were easily co-opted – and thus corrupted.

Anglo American Corporation, which once had accounted for more than fifty per cent of the Johannesburg Stock Exchange was allowed to disinvest from South Africa, except for mining interests deemed vital to British financial and war interests – platinum, diamonds, gold, coal and iron ore.[5]

Like the Afrikaners before them, the new political elite were quickly corrupted by sudden acquisition of unearned wealth. The banks competed to fund them with recklessly leveraged and unsustainable loans. Other than purchases of luxury cars, houses and ostentatious consumption, the new elite have contributed virtually nothing to post-apartheid South Africa's economic or social development. On the contrary, misallocation of resources is reflected in non-delivery riots all over the country.

In this vein, the former ANC Member of Parliament Andrew Feinstein[6] describes the City of London and its financial district as 'the most corrupt square mile on the planet Earth'. The essentials of the apartheid system have remained unchanged. The arms deal represents nothing less than the betrayal by the ANC of the struggle against apartheid.

Moeletsi Mbeki's commentaries would however hold greater validity were it not for his association with his former business partner Ivor Ichikowitz, an arms trader, a wheeler-dealer who makes no apologies for bribing his way into business deals with dubious governments.[7] BAE Land Systems exports of mine-protected armoured vehicles for use by British and American forces in Iraq and Afghanistan are reported to exceed R4 billion, thus making a mockery of South Africa's commitments not to export weapons to war zones.[8]

Huge bribes were paid with deliberate British government connivance to unleash a culture of corruption to subvert a young and immature democracy. Umkhonto we Sizwe (MK) had been infiltrated by the British MI6 as early as the 1980s, perhaps even earlier. Even before Mandela was released from jail in February 1990, MI6 and other covert organisations were already busy weaving webs of intrigue and double-dealing to ensure that British interests received preferential treatment.[9]

The intention was that South Africa would remain a cheap supplier of natural resources and thus continue, in effect, a British economic dependency.

With Chris Hani's assassination by Janusz Walus in April 1993, the conspirators attained a major objective towards achieving Mbeki's ambition to succeed Mandela. Modise and the MK leadership have many times been accused of involvement with Walus in that killing.[10] Amongst still unanswered questions is whether Walus was ultimately employed by John Bredenkamp and BAE.

Modise, who in his youth was a township thug, allegedly became an operative for the United States Central Intelligence Agency (CIA) plus the British MI6, as well as the South African Police. Just before Modise died in November 2001, Mbeki and cabinet ministers rushed to his deathbed to bestow on him the Order of the Star of South Africa Grand Cross in gold.

'Bra Joe' was loathed by many MK soldiers because of his brutality. Winnie Mandela notably refused even to attend his funeral. Displaying her talent for conspicuous absence and/or presence, she deliberately attended the funeral that same afternoon of Marike de Klerk, divorced wife of former President F W de Klerk.

Of course 'Winnie' had her own dabblings in diamond smuggling with Hazel Crane and her husband, the Israeli gangster Shai Avissar.[11] In a mafia-type ambush and a foretaste of the Brett Kebble murder two years later, Crane was gunned down in Johannesburg in November 2003.

Various rival factions within the ANC were trading diamonds from Africa's numerous war zones against weapons. The stones would then be cut and polished in Johannesburg or Kimberley and re-exported, certified as South African. *Noseweek* magazine in June 2010 published its sensational exposé that legendary rugby player, the Springbok Wilf Rosenberg, had been a crucial cog in illegal diamond rackets and a long-time member of the Israeli mafia.[12]

Diamonds symbolise the money laundering, criminality and the get-rich-quick characteristics of South African history.

The British government and its armaments industry got their claws into the ANC government with appalling ease. Despite historic links between the Cape and Indonesia, there was considerable surprise that one of Mandela's first overseas visits after his release from jail in 1990 was to Indonesia to meet its military dictator, Mohamed Suharto.

What, one queried, did Madiba and that wily tyrant have in common? Mandela was universally acclaimed as the liberator of South Africa from apartheid. Suharto was universally despised as a corrupt and cruel despot, responsible for the deaths of millions of people. Mandela was rewarded with Suharto's personal cheque for US$10 million as a contribution to ANC campaign funds. Unashamed or embarrassed, Mandela then demanded US$25 million from the Japanese government but was immediately rebuffed.[13]

Suharto's dictatorship was internationally notorious, but he was included in the ranks of thugs such as Chile's General Augusto Pinochet with whom British Prime Minister Margaret Thatcher kept decidedly shady company. She described Suharto as 'one of our very best and most valuable friends'.[14] He was the archetypal military dictator supported by the British and American governments, and ranked by Transparency International as the world's most corrupt leader.[15]

By the time Suharto's regime collapsed, Indonesia was US$250 billion in debt, of which it owed British taxpayers £705 million. Willingly or unwillingly, they had underwritten the exports of BAE Hawk fighters and Scorpion tanks which were used for the suppression of the people of East Timor.[16]

TIME magazine estimated that Suharto and his family enriched themselves by about US$15 billion during the three decades that they terrorised Indonesia.[17] Other commentators put the figure as high as US$35 billion. The relationship between Mandela and Suharto was cemented by several more visits to Indonesia when Mandela actively promoted exports of South Africa's weapons. The weapons would only be used, he declared naively, 'for external self-defence'.

On one such occasion, Mandela commented that Burma's Aung San Suu Kyi was a very brave lady but that, as a fellow Nobel Peace Laureate, he would do nothing on her behalf. The international community was subsequently aghast when South Africa – during its two-year tenure on the UN Security Council – aligned itself with China and Russia in support of the Burmese military junta.

Other payments flowed from Malaysia, Morocco, Libya and Saudi Arabia. Before long, South Africa's foreign policies in the post-apartheid era were being determined by bribes to the ANC. Expectations that the 'new South Africa' would make promotion of human rights the premise of its foreign and domestic policies were soon discarded and brushed aside.

In turn, Suharto visited South Africa in November 1997, and was awarded the Order of Good Hope in recognition of his support in the struggle against apartheid.[18] Six months later, when Suharto was swept from power, the repercussions shook the international financial system to its foundations. The 'Asian Contagion' caused massive impoverishment of the Indonesian population when the corruption bubble burst. South Africa was quickly caught up in the chaos.

The South African Reserve Bank squandered US$25 billion in foreign exchange speculation. Even worse, the prime beneficiaries of the apartheid system – the mining houses such as Anglo American and De Beers and financial institutions such as Old Mutual Insurance – were permitted to transfer their domiciles from South Africa to London. South Africa was suddenly deemed too small a market for their talents!

What bribes to ANC coffers 'greased' their flight? Old Mutual executives unctuously declared that the townships were too dangerous for investment of shareholders' money. Old Mutual promptly lost tens of billions of dollars gambling on New York markets. Such inexplicable decisions and sheer government incompetence signalled the international investment community that the 'new South Africa' was already on the skids.

Before long, all four of South Africa's main banking groups also became foreign-owned. Even the Reserve Bank, which in apartheid days subordinated banking prudence to a political agenda, is foreign-controlled. This makes a mockery of the much touted but oft-flouted principle of independence. The independence of the Reserve Bank is a myth. Its policies are controlled by powerful banking lobbies headquartered in London, who were the real beneficiaries of South Africa's apartheid era and who, in different guise, continue to 'pull the strings'.

That, too, is a consequence of the arms deal and the corruption it unleashed. Underwritten by British taxpayers, Barclays Bank is funding the acquisition of BAE Hawk and BAE/Saab Gripen fighter aircraft. So, not surprisingly, its purchase of South Africa's largest banking group, ABSA, was speedily approved and then trumpeted as a massive vote of confidence in South Africa. The reality soon proved very different when huge dividend transfers flowed out of the country. ABSA and South Africa were being 'milked'.

Right until the collapse of apartheid Thatcher had rigorously backed P W Botha and F W de Klerk in phoney and futile reform efforts intended to keep control of South Africa in 'safe white hands'. Thatcher had made no secret of her contempt for Mandela, whom she considered to be a communist terrorist.

I had been in Washington lobbying for banking sanctions against the apartheid government when in October 1989 Thatcher announced at the Commonwealth heads of government meeting in Kuala Lumpur that she and the SA Reserve Bank had together defied the world to reschedule South Africa's foreign debt.

In response to an editorial in *The New York Times* calling for support for De Klerk, I had a few days earlier written a letter which was published under the headline 'It's Not Yet Time To Ease Up on South Africa':

As a (white) South African banker visiting New York and committed to a non-racial, democratic and united South Africa, I am astonished by your pleas to give President F W de Klerk a chance (editorial, Oct 13). The apartheid laager has collapsed under the pressure of the mass democratic movement. You are in effect saying apartheid should be given time to regroup and reform.

Under Mr de Klerk we may now have apartheid with a smile, rather than the bellicose P W Botha. Mr de Klerk is nonetheless rooted in and committed to ethnicity and 'group rights' – a euphemism for apartheid. Mr de Klerk is reportedly responsible for Mr Botha's notorious Rubicon speech of August 1985, which led less than two weeks later to the debt standstill. Little wonder such animosity exists between the two when Mr de Klerk has the gall to present himself as the leader to clean up Mr Botha's mess!

Herman Cohen, your Assistant Secretary of State for African Affairs, has now developed an initiative calling for the end of the state of emergency by the beginning of the parliamentary session in February and the repeal of apartheid legislation by the end of that session in June. That coincides also with the expiration of the South African debt accord.

After forty-two years of apartheid, June 1990 must be the deadline for constitutional negotiations. Mr Cohen's initiative needs to be commended. Church leaders after their discussion with Mr de Klerk last Wednesday found no reason to tell the world to put sanctions on hold. It is not helpful for you to suggest an easing up of the pressure.[19]

I had met Mbeki earlier that month in Lusaka, Zambia when the ANC's national executive committee approved a proposal by the Archbishop of Canterbury to use his good offices to mediate between the international banking committee and the ANC, and thus to speed the pending collapse of the apartheid system. As Allan Boesak reveals in his book *Running With Horses*, Mbeki was double-dealing and was actively colluding with Thatcher just two weeks later to derail the banking sanctions initiative.[20]

Boesak's extramarital affairs were an embarrassment, but I do believe his subsequent legal troubles and imprisonment were driven by collusion between Mbeki and right-wing Danish politicians. In other words, Boesak was framed by Mbeki to neutralise him politically, and the court that convicted him was a travesty.

Churches and the New York City Council had joined forces with an ultimatum to key New York banks. The banking sanctions campaign was adopted by church leaders as a last non-violent option to avert a civil war. The banks must choose, we told them, between apartheid South Africa or lose the business of church pension funds as well as the City's payroll accounts. The balance was obvious. South Africa's financial structures would quickly collapse without access to foreign exchange markets and the US dollar payment systems.

It proved to be the decisive strategy that led to De Klerk's speech on February 2, 1990. Mandela was released nine days later and greeted by about seventy thousand people on Cape Town's Grand Parade. My wife Lavinia and I were amongst that crowd. A few hours later she had the honour of welcoming Mandela to Bishopscourt, Archbishop Tutu's official residence, where he spent his first night of freedom.

We had outmanoeuvred the 'Iron Lady' at least for the critical period until the transition to democracy was irreversible. The world had anticipated a racial bloodbath, but the British were still worried about their investments in South Africa and embarked upon strategies to undermine a post-apartheid society.

Throughout her time in office from 1979 until 1990, Thatcher was complicit with the apartheid government in transferring British nuclear weapons, missile and other military technology to South Africa. The Coventry Four case confirmed that British officials, politicians and arms dealers considered themselves to be beyond reach of the law.[21]

Ironically, the massive expenditures on armaments – far from defending apartheid – became the cause of its collapse. Military 'securocrats' bankrupted the country with absurd squandering of South Africa's financial resources on nuclear weapons and other armaments that proved totally useless. The 1985 'debt standstill' was just the opportunity for which church leaders had been waiting.

Dr Beyers Naudé, then the Secretary General of the South African Council of Churches and Tutu, then the Bishop of Johannesburg, met me at the UN in New York. We appealed to international bankers to apply political conditionality in the rescheduling of debts until the apartheid government conceded the necessity of a democratic society representative of all South Africa's people.[22]

We increased that pressure after the US Senate in October 1986 overturned President Ronald Reagan's veto of the Comprehensive Anti-Apartheid Act, and again in 1989 when the first George Bush became president.

Yet – when the banking sanctions campaign proved successful in bringing about the collapse of the apartheid government – Thatcher and the British ambassador Robin Renwick brazenly claimed the credit for South Africa's 'miracle'. Mandela was prevailed upon to understand that the ANC's commitments to the eradication of poverty and implementation of the principles of the Freedom Charter were simply unrealistic, and that they would lead to massive capital flight.

Mandela was a quick learner, and was soon shamelessly pressuring businesses and wealthy individuals to contribute massively to the ANC and to the numerous Mandela foundations. He kept company with dubious characters and thugs from Muammar Gaddafi to Charles Taylor. He was blinkered about the motives of flattering donors, and oblivious to probable consequences.

Corruption in Indonesia and Malaysia instigated by the British and Americans became the models by which post-apartheid South Africa's economy would be restructured to ensure the failure of our hard-won democracy.[23] It was a model that Oppenheimer himself had used in the 1960s to co-opt the apartheid government through his giveaway of General Mining to Sanlam and Afrikaner financial interests.

Instead of reparations for the poor, Black Economic Empowerment (BEE) became simply enrichment of the elite. It was evident from the start that BEE would end in tears with a financial crisis when the beneficiaries would be unable to service their highly geared loans. The manner in which BEE was instituted also reinstated apartheid's racial classifications, and thus the most offensive and divisive racism.

Another of Thatcher's 'best friends' included Saudi Arabian Prince Bandar. Whilst in office and on behalf of BAE, she had negotiated the massive £43 billion Al Yamamah deal to supply Saudis with British armaments against payment in oil. By extraordinary coincidence, one of Mandela's other 'best friends' was also Prince Bandar, the only foreigner invited to witness his secret marriage to Graça Machel. In a foreword to Bandar's biography, Mandela gushingly described him as:

> … an outstanding man – a charming, eloquent, and nonetheless humble figure, who has so often guided the pattern of world events. He has worked relentlessly in the cause of peace, and I unconditionally applaud him as a man of principle, a diplomat of astonishing calibre, and one of the great peacemakers of our time.[24]

Most embarrassingly, soon after the biography was published Bandar was 'outed' as a 'bagman' for both the CIA and BAE. Even the British government buckled when threatened that there would be 'blood in the streets of London' if the SFO pursued its investigations into bribes to Bandar that BAE laundered through the American banking system.

Bandar's private Airbus 340 was a frequent arrival at South African airports during the Mandela era when both Mandela and Mbeki most curiously chose Saudi Arabia as their favoured holiday destination.

By then the new political elite – who to a man had been paupers just a few years earlier – were now millionaires and billionaires and even revelled in the ostentatious description of 'black diamonds'. When he left office in 1999 after only one term of five years, Mandela's various foundations were estimated to be worth R1 billion. That most certainly could not have been earned from his presidential salary or royalties from his autobiography *Long Walk To Freedom*.

Tokyo Sexwale is a key role player in and funder for the ANC whose fortune is repeatedly linked to diamonds from the Democratic Republic of the Congo (DRC).[25] Indeed, the still unresolved murder in 2005 of Kebble, Sexwale's mentor, is suspected to be connected to a blood diamond deal gone wrong.[26] In reports by the United Nations and the Donen Commission, Sexwale was named as one of the prime beneficiaries of the Iraqi oil-for-food scam.[27]

Kebble had embezzled an estimated R2 billion,[28] and his funeral at St George's Cathedral in Cape Town was an extraordinary occasion during which government representatives competed in their lavish praise for the crook.

In turn, Kebble's murder was linked to the Commissioner of the South African Police Services and also President of Interpol, Jackie Selebi.[29] Three presidents took unprecedented measures over a ten-year period to protect Selebi from prosecution. The original charges against Selebi included diamond trafficking. The case against Selebi finally came to court in October 2009, but immediately degenerated into a farce when the government insisted that testimony against Selebi by the former director general of National Intelligence would 'jeopardise national security'. The judge, and subsequently the Appeal Court, gave this argument short shrift.

Mbeki encouraged corruption amongst the ANC hierarchy because his Machiavellian traits appreciated that involvement in organised crime afforded him a measure of protection from political rivalries. He could always threaten to expose corruption, and thus keep his rivals in line. Jacob Zuma may have had sticky fingers in connection with the arms deal, but they were not nearly as sticky as Mbeki's.

Zuma's problem, essentially, was the old honeytrap of too much sex and not enough money. The world is bedazzled by his polygamous marriages, the rape case against him and by the number of children he has fathered. Zuma was consequently an ideal candidate for bribery by the arms industry, albeit he was a very junior role player. Mbeki despised the 'country bumpkin'. He tried to divert attention from his own pivotal role in the arms deal scandal by scapegoating Zuma, but his manipulations backfired spectacularly and disastrously.

Mbeki had overlooked the reality that South Africa's revolution and its transition from apartheid were driven by civil society and the United Democratic Front (UDF), not by the ANC in exile or MK which, with misguided zeal, still believed in 1990 that apartheid would be overcome by military confrontation. The UDF was a coalition of one thousand organisations committed to democracy in a united and non-racial South Africa.[30]

The ANC hierarchy simply could not fathom grassroots democracy or, alternatively, its hierarchy believed that everyone could be bribed to remain silent. When rank and file members of the ANC backed Zuma against Mbeki, they did so in protest against Mbeki's autocratic rule.

There was also the media which, in the 1980s, despite huge difficulties got the apartheid struggle story out to the international community. It was the media that in the years since the arms deal scandal first broke continued to investigate the corruption that permeated the hierarchy of ANC exiles.

My submission during the Cameron Commission of Inquiry included a plea that action should be taken to prevent De Beers from buying diamonds from Unita, the Angolan guerrilla movement headed by Jonas Savimbi. These 'blood diamonds' were annually worth about US$500 million, and the proceeds paid for weapons to devastate that country through civil war.

Regrettably, Mandela himself intervened to assure the Cameron Commission that South Africa would pursue a 'responsible arms trade policy'. The commissioners naively accepted those assurances instead of Anglican

Church arguments for closure of Armscor and Denel and conversion of their assets to peaceful purposes. An opportunity was lost, and South Africa's armaments industry has remained notorious for equipping warlords and the world's dirtiest wars.[31]

The 'Iron Lady' and her successors – but Blair in particular – had well baited their trap to keep the ANC under control. The National Audit Office investigation into the Al Yamamah affair was suppressed in 1992 when its report was apparently deemed too politically sensitive.

The report was withheld even from British parliamentarians. The deal was that BAE would supply one hundred and twenty Tornado fighter aircraft to the Saudis, who transferred oil to Shell and BP. In turn, these companies paid for the oil by crediting an account with the Bank of England, from which the Ministry of Defence paid BAE.[32]

The opportunities for intervening 'commissions' and corruption were huge. Saudi royals and their entourage profited massively from such deals. The bribes for the Al Yamamah deals are estimated at twenty-five per cent of £43 billion, of which Mark Thatcher is reported to have received £12 million. Curiously interlinked with these arrangements was Banque du Credit et Commerce Internationale (BCCI) – widely known amongst bankers as the 'bank for crooks and criminals international'.

BCCI had been established in 1972 in Abu Dhabi by Pakistani bankers with later support from the CIA. Abu Dhabi is the largest and wealthiest member of the United Arab Emirates (UAE), which was formed in 1971 after a British-led coup d'etat a few years earlier had installed Sheikh Zayed as head of the sheikdom.

BCCI founder Agha Hassan Abedi not only managed the Sheikh's personal affairs but also the UAE's billions in oil wealth. The Bank of America, then the world's largest bank, took a thirty per cent shareholding. With these connections, BCCI quickly became a substantial player in international banking. It was registered in Luxembourg, but its operational headquarters were in London where the Bank of England's supervisory standards were lax. At its peak, BCCI had over four hundred branches in seventy-eight countries and, by assets, was the world's seventh largest bank.[33]

It crashed in 1991 in the aftermath of the Cold War when the Americans finally 'pulled the plug'. BCCI had specialised in money laundering operations for drug and weapons trafficking, prostitution, property frauds, plus financing Pakistan's nuclear weapons programme.

One reason that the Bank of England repeatedly refused in the so-called 'national interest' to investigate BCCI was that it was the conduit for the Matrix-Churchill trade in machine tools with Saddam Hussein's Iraq with which Mark Thatcher was allegedly involved.[34]

After Margaret Thatcher suddenly fell from power in late 1990, she was 'head-hunted' for, and was seriously considering, the job of President of BCCI.[35] What a triumph that would have been! Thatcher was only very narrowly saved from such ignominy by a Senate investigation in the US conducted by Senator John Kerry – the Democratic Party's unsuccessful presidential candidate in 2004.

The bank was also the channel through which the CIA in conjunction with the Saudis funded Osama bin Laden's operations against the Russians in Afghanistan, as well as the operations of Latin America's drug cartels. Its client list included not only petty dictators – most notably General Manuel Noriega of Panama – but also Denis Thatcher, and both Presidents George Bush Senior and George Bush Junior who borrowed US$25 million in 1987.[36]

The Bush family has had long business connections with the Bin Laden family, whose construction businesses dominate many Middle Eastern economies. Investigations of the BCCI scandal came to conclusions back in the early 1990s that the Bush family's political ambitions were being funded by Saudi oil money. Wayne Madsen, a former CIA operative and now a Washington analyst noted:

> Though Bush told the *Wall Street Journal* he had no idea BCCI was involved, the network of connections is so intensive that the *Journal* concluded their investigation of the matter in 1991 by stating: 'the number of BCCI connected people who had dealings with Harken Energy Corporation since George W Bush came on board raises the question whether they mask an effort to cosy up to a presidential son.' Or even the President.[37]

There were plenty of other crooked bankers around the world to replace BCCI, as the sub-prime mortgage crisis attests. One bank that was repeatedly involved in laundering money for both the arms trade and dictators was the now-defunct Riggs Bank in Washington DC. Its advertising boasted that its clients for one hundred and fifty years included America's presidents, and that it was 'the most important bank in the world's most important city'.[38] As well as being bankers to the presidents, Riggs Bank specialised in servicing Washington's diplomatic community.

The BAE bribes to Prince Bandar were routed through Riggs Bank, and became the subject of an investigation by the US Department of Justice.[39] In February 2010, after prolonged plea bargaining, BAE agreed to pay a fine of US$400 million to the Americans.[40] A paltry fine of £30 million was applied by the SFO as penalty for BAE bribes paid in Tanzania. In addition, BAE subsequently in May 2011 agreed to pay another US$79 million fine because of more than two thousand, five hundred bribery payments for numerous arms deals, including the BAE/Saab Gripen fighter aircraft contracts with South Africa.[41]

BAE was desperate to avoid blacklisting in the US arms market from which it now obtains more than half of its business. In a blistering article published in *The Guardian* newspaper, Andrew Feinstein and Sue Hawley of the Corner House wrote:

> The Serious Fraud Office's settlement with BAE Systems is a travesty of justice. It is also a slap in the face for the people of countries BAE has allegedly corrupted, the British taxpayer and the British justice system. BAE has always believed itself above the law. [The settlement] proves again that it is.
>
> The prosecution of BAE for bribery in Africa and Eastern Europe was a key test of the UK's ability to restore its credibility after the dropped investigation into corruption allegations relating to the Al Yamamah arms deal. It has failed. The people of Tanzania, South Africa, the Czech Republic, Hungary and Romania deserve to know how much they were ripped off by BAE, and which officials were being paid off.
>
> At the time of the deal, Tanzania was the world's third poorest country,

but it was persuaded by the UK government and BAE to buy a multi-million pound radar system it didn't need. The almost six million South Africans with HIV/Aids were told their government couldn't afford the anti-retroviral medication they needed to stay alive, but could spend billions on unnecessary weapons.[42]

Another preferred client at Riggs Bank was the dictator of Equatorial Guinea, President Teodoro Obiang Nguema, whose deposits were reported to exceed US$750 million. The saga continued. In 2004 the world was astonished by news that Mark Thatcher had been arrested in Cape Town in connection with a coup d'etat to remove Nguema from office.

The plot allegedly had the support of the governments of Spain, Britain and the United States. Thatcher faced fifteen years' imprisonment in South Africa, but was permitted to plea bargain his way out of the fiasco. He was sentenced to a suspended four-year jail term, fined R3 million and deported.[43]

In their last operation before being disbanded in December 2008, the Scorpions – South Africa's counterpart to America's Federal Bureau of Investigation (the FBI) – swooped upon various offices and premises connected to BAE's operations. In due course, I received one hundred and sixty pages of affidavits by South African and British officials.

The documents detailed how, to whom and into which bank accounts BAE had laundered £115 million (R1.5 billion) in bribes to secure its arms deal contracts. These were the payments which the British government minister back in 2003 had deemed to be 'within reasonable limits'. The documents explained the history and purpose of Red Diamond Trading Company incorporated in the British Virgin Islands as a BAE front company for covert operations.

That British colony, with a population of only twenty-three thousand people, has eight hundred and thirteen thousand registered companies, and is notorious as a tax haven for money laundering operations. British company law is excessively lax. A study in 2009 revealed that about four thousand individuals suspected of terrorism, drug trafficking and illicit trading are running British companies.[44]

The affidavits I received confirmed and corroborated the criminal charges of perjury and money laundering that I had filed in August 2008 against Trevor Manuel. Manuel took me to court, and obtained a gagging order in an attempt to prevent that information from becoming public knowledge. I was vindicated just one month later.

Judge Chris Nicholson in September 2008 found that Mbeki had irregularly interfered in the judicial system during his arms deal wrangling with Zuma, and he recommended the need for a judicial investigation into the arms deal. His judgment was subsequently severely criticised by the Supreme Court of Appeal but, in the meantime, Mbeki was unceremoniously booted from the Presidency by the ANC, deliciously the victim of his own skulduggery.

A report headlined 'BAE Money Trail Leads to Thatcher' published by *Executive Intelligence Review* noted:

> The trail begins and ends at the doorstep of British elites, including that of former Prime Minister Margaret Thatcher. Those so far identified as under investigation stand at the centre of British moves to destabilise South Africa. BAE Systems is not only the keystone of the British military industrial complex it is central to British intelligence operations worldwide. The trail points to the BAE/Bandar slush fund. [45]

Endnotes

1. Martin Meredith: *Diamonds, Gold and War*, Simon and Schuster, London, 2007, p 272.
2. John Allen: *Rabble-Rouser For Peace*, Random House, London, 2006, p 345.
3. A description by William Mervin Gumede, author of *Thabo Mbeki And The Battle For The Soul Of The ANC*, Zebra Press, Cape Town, 2005.
4. The colloquial term in Cape Town for a homeless person in Cape Town, meaning a 'mountain man'.
5. Moeletsi Mbeki, address to the Royal Institute of International Affairs at Chatham House, London, September 9, 2009.
6. Andrew Feinstein, who was forced out of office because of his determination to investigate the arms deal bribes, is the author of *After The Party*, Jonathan Ball Publishers, Johannesburg, 2007.
7. 'Ivor The Invincible', *City Press*, October 10, 2010.
8. Michael Schmidt: 'Top Notch Armoured Military Vehicles Are Coming Straight Out Of Benoni', *Cape Argus*, March 3, 2007.
9. 'How Arms Dealer Got Its Hooks Into The ANC', *Mail & Guardian*, January 17, 2007.
10. R W Johnson: *South Africa's Brave New World*, Penguin Books, London, 2009, pp 30-51.
11. David Kray: *Hazel Crane, Queen Of Diamonds*, New Africa Books, Cape Town, 2004.
12. 'Gangster On The Wing', *Noseweek* 128, June 2010.
13. Anthony Sampson: *Mandela*, HarperCollins Publishers, London, 1999, p 419.
14. John Pilger: 'Our Model Dictator: The Death Of Suharto Is A Reminder Of The West's Ignoble Role In Propping Up A Murderous Regime', *The Guardian*, January 28, 2008.
15. Brendan Koerner: 'How Did Suharto Steal $35 billion?' March 26, 2004.
16. 'Cancellation Of Indonesian Arms Debts', *Jubilee Scotland*, September 2007.
17. 'Suharto Inc, The Family Firm,' *TIME* magazine, May 24, 1999.
18. 'Suharto Awarded South Africa's Highest Honour', BBC News, November 22, 1997.
19. Terry Crawford-Browne: Letter to the Editor: *The New York Times*, October 25, 1989.
20. Allan Boesak: *Running With Horses*, Joho Publishers, Cape Town, 2009, pp

188-192.

21. Peter Hounam and Steve McQuillan: *The Mini-Nuke Conspiracy*, Faber and Faber, London, 1995.

22. Letter dated October 28, 1985 to the international banking community. See Appendix B to *Eye On The Money* by Terry Crawford-Browne published by Umuzi, Cape Town, 2007.

23. Naomi Klein: *The Shock Doctrine*, Penguin Books, London, 2008.

24. William Simpson: *The Prince*, Harper, New York, 2007.

25. Mungo Soggot: 'Conflict Diamonds Are Forever', The Center For Public Integrity, Washington DC, November 8, 2002.

26. Chiara Carter: 'Kebble And Dirty Diamonds', *Sunday Independent*, May 14, 2006.

27. Mpumelelo Mkhabela: 'The Report Mbeki And Zuma Hid From You', *Sunday Times*, August 22, 2009.

28. Barry Sergeant: *Brett Kebble: The Inside Story*, Zebra Press, Cape Town, 2006.

29. Stefaans Brummer, Sam Sole, Zukile Majova and Nic Dawes: 'Kebble Arrest: What Now For Selebi?' *Mail & Guardian*, November 17, 2006.

30. Allan Boesak: *Running With Horses*, Joho Publishers, Cape Town, 2009.

31. Edward Malnick: 'SA Arms Trade Mess', *Weekend Argus*, August 16, 2009.

32. David Robertson: 'Margaret Thatcher Ordered Bugging Of The Prince', *The Times*, April 11, 2008.

33. Jeffrey Robinson: *The Laundrymen*, Simon and Schuster, London, 1994.

34. Kenneth R Timmerman: *The Death Lobby: How The West Armed Iraq*, Bantam Books, London, 1992, and William Schmidt: 'British Will Study Iraqi Arms Sales', *The New York Times*, November 11, 1992.

35. Paul Halloran and Mark Hollingsworth: *Thatcher's Gold: The Life and Times of Mark Thatcher*, Simon and Schuster, London, 1995.

36. David Sirota and Jonathan Baskin: 'Follow The Money: How John Kerry Busted The Terrorists' Favorite Bank', Washington Monthly, September 2004.

37. Wayne Madsen: 'Tracking Bin Laden's Money Flow Leads Back to Midland, Texas', *In These Times*, November 12, 2001.

38. US Senate Permanent Sub-Committee On Investigations Report: 'Keeping Foreign Corruption Out Of The United States: Four Case Histories', February 4, 2010, pp 16-107.

39. Tom Hamburger and Josh Meyer: 'Former FBI Director Defends Saudi

Prince From Bribery Allegations', *Chicago Tribune*, April 7, 2009.

40. Hopewell Radebe: 'Arms Deal Details Consigned To Dark', *Business Day*, February 8, 2010.

41. Stephen Foley: 'BAE To Pay "Final" $79m Fine Over US Violations', *The Independent*, May 18, 2011.

42. Andrew Feinstein and Sue Hawley: 'An Affront To Justice', *The Guardian*, February 7, 2010.

43. 'Thatcher Fined Over Coup Plot', BBC News, January 13, 2005.

44. Prem Sikka: 'UK Co Law Is Terrorism's Friend', *The Guardian*, January 20, 2010.

45. Dean Andromidas: 'BAE Money Trail Leads To Thatcher', *EIR*, December 26, 2008.

2 • THE ROCKS ON WHICH APARTHEID WAS BUILT

War is the business upon which the British Empire was founded. Only decades ago the Empire 'owned' one fifth of the world, and one quarter of its population. The British aristocracy and monarchy did not make their wealth by altruistic generosity or even industrial ingenuity. They plundered foreign countries and established their financial institutions on the proceeds first of the slave trade and, subsequently and still, in the arms trade.

The Empire's glamour and power are best symbolised by the crown jewels housed at the Tower of London. Their lavish magnificence annually astonishes millions of tourists. It is a drama reflected in the schoolboy jibes of my Irish republican sympathies that 'the sun never sets on the British Empire because God cannot trust the English in the dark'.

Indeed, with unique British eccentricity, the Tower and its jewels have for centuries been guarded by at least six ravens. Tradition dating back to King Charles II holds that in the absence of the black birds, the monarchy will fall and England will face disaster. The British Empire finally collapsed, but successive British governments are still, with their American 'cousins', the world's self-appointed policemen.

Many of the crown jewels, to it put mildly, have controversial histories. The Koh-i-noor diamond dates back about four thousand years, in due course becoming the most prized possession of Mogul emperors. Then, the Nadir Shah of Persia invaded India in 1739 and gained possession of the Mogul treasures, including the Koh-i-noor. Amongst the myths around the stone is that possession by a man is dangerous – often leading to his death – but that it brings good fortune and power to a woman.

After political upheavals in Persia, the diamond was returned to India, and became part of the Lahore treasury. The British East India Company in 1849, as part of the spoils of the Sikh wars, took the diamond to England for presentation by Dunleep Singh to Queen Victoria. The Governor General of India, Lord Dalhousie, wrote then that his intention in arranging the presentation was that it should represent British conquest of India:

> My motive was it would be more of an honour of the Queen that the Koh-i-noor should be surrendered directly from the hand of the conquered prince into the hands of the sovereign who was his conqueror, than it should be presented to her as a gift and thus a favour.[1]

Oblivious of its long and often bloody history, to increase its brilliance the Koh-i-noor was cut down from seven hundred and eighty-seven carats to one hundred and six carats. Its name reputedly means 'Mountain of Light', and tradition claimed that the stone's owner would rule the world.

The Koh-i-noor was used during the ceremonial proclamation of Victoria as Empress of India in 1877 and, subsequently, in the crowns of Queen Elizabeth, the 'Queen Mum', in 1937 and her daughter Queen Elizabeth II at her coronation in 1953. The 'Imperial Crown' was fashioned out of platinum, and includes about two thousand eight hundred diamonds.

The Pakistani government in 1976 unsuccessfully requested that the Koh-i-noor should be returned to Lahore as a 'convincing demonstration of the spirit that moved Britain voluntarily to shed its imperialist encumbrances and lead the process of decolonization'. The official reaction in London was that Britain had clear title to the diamond since long before Pakistan was even a country.[2]

Still more stunning amongst the crown jewels is the Star of Africa. The five hundred and thirty carat diamond forms the head of the royal sceptre, and a smaller stone of three hundred and twelve carats was mounted into the Imperial Crown. These are the biggest of nine large and ninety-six smaller stones cut from the Cullinan diamond which was found in 1905 at the Premier Mine forty kilometres east of Pretoria and which, before cutting, had weighed in at a massive three thousand, one hundred and seven carats.

For over a century, the Cullinan diamond has remained the largest ever found. It was bought by the government of the Transvaal Colony as a sixty-sixth birthday gift for King Edward VII, a gesture that in the aftermath of the South African War (1899-1902) caused considerable rancour.[3] Like the Koh-i-noor in India before it, the Cullinan diamond became a symbol of British conquest.

Until the discovery of diamonds in 1867, the Cape had been an economic backwater of the British Empire. The Cape's only value to the British was the sea route to India, and with the construction of the Suez Canal even that strategic use became redundant. Diamonds became the foundation stones of the South African economy, and its turbulent politics.

Within four years, about twenty thousand white and over thirty thousand black diggers flocked to Kimberley in search of wealth. They included Cecil Rhodes, a sickly eighteen-year-old son of an English clergyman, who arrived in November 1871. In the early days there were about one thousand, six hundred claims at the diamond diggings, and often chaotic rivalries resulted as diggers jostled to extract stones that might make their fortunes.

Sir Charles Payton, who spent six months of 1871 in Kimberley, wrote:

> Farmers trekked to the fields with ox wagons, family and a retinue of servants. Recent immigrants who accounted for quarter of the white population soon adopted the South African way of life. They too hired blacks to pick, shovel, break, haul and sift ground. Most whites are disinclined to work during the hot summer months. It is quite sufficient for them to sit under an awning to sort the stones from the dirt, leaving the 'kaffirs' to perform all other work.[4]

Although still in his thirties, by 1890 Rhodes was prime minister of the Cape Colony. He was influential in British politics and with Queen Victoria, and had become one of the richest men in the world. He modelled himself after Robert Clive, whose conquests in India in the eighteenth century relied on the parallel use of corruption and military force, and who had also used diamonds and emeralds to transfer his own looted fortune to England. Many biographers have interpreted Rhodes, but with widely varying success. Robert Rotberg is the most proficient of these writers. Rotberg is himself a Rhodes Scholar, and in his definitive work *The Founder* declares:

> Rhodes accomplished far more than most of the empire builders, corporate tycoons and political giants of the nineteenth century. He had made a fortune, carved out countries, and governed an old colony and two new ones. He was not merely an important overseas figure in the heady last decades of Victorian aggrandizement, but a major actor in Europe as well.
>
> It is no accident that his name lives on through the gift of his scholarships. Nor is it surprising that his memory still occasions bitter controversy. Rhodes was great and good, despite his flaws, say his supporters. Rhodes was despicable and exceptionally evil – a true rogue – say his detractors.
>
> Was Rhodes essentially good? Was he a true benefactor who, despite defects of method, not only meant well but also contributed – as he intended – to the betterment of mankind in Africa? Or, as critics have suggested, was he predominantly a devious power-monger who wanted riches and glory for himself, and deliberately destroyed other individuals, other cultures, and more promising initiatives as he cut his wide sway through Africa?[5]

The diamond industry in Kimberley, with racially segregated living quarters and dependent on migrant black labour, set the basis for South Africa's tortured race relationships and, in due course, the apartheid system. Massive fortunes were suddenly amassed by a lucky few, but the contrasting poverty for most diggers was manifest in a huge illicit diamond trade. Labourers developed an active business in stolen stones, and Payton also noted:

> Many wealthy diggers laid the basis of their fortunes by buying stolen gems. They robbed the small man of his diamonds and claims, became big mine

owners and were then loudest in denouncing the practice. The myths include that 'coloured' claimholders are more successful than white ones because they receive stones stolen by relatives and friends. The partially civilized 'kaffir' rapidly develops into a thief. The 'raw kaffir' fresh from the kraal is best and most trustworthy. Above all, mistrust a 'kaffir' who speaks English and wears trousers.[6]

Many stolen stones were paid for in guns. As Donald Morris wrote:

A gun was the only European artefact that would bring a native five hundred miles afoot for a season's work, and it was in firearms that the diamond fields paid their labour. A growing trickle of armed natives fanned out from Griqualand West ... and petty chieftains far and wide found young men of their kraals fondling cheap muskets and breathing a new and hard defiance. The military strength these men contributed to the clans was negligible, for a native armed with a smoothbore flintlock and an uncertain ammunition supply was much less of a threat than the same man armed with an assegai.[7]

It is estimated that the gun trade during the 1870s amounted to seventy-five thousand weapons. White settlers in Natal then numbered about eighteen thousand people. They were incensed about the dangers these weapons posed. Although possession of firearms was not forbidden, an ordinance made it illegal to own unregistered weapons. Zulus soon learned that registration was an invitation to confiscation. This became the cause of the 1873 Langalibalele rebellion.

Langalibalele was a minor chief who was ordered by a magistrate in Natal to enforce the firearms ordinance. The Natal colonial government viewed his refusal to do so as rebellion, and then dispatched troops to arrest him. Langalibalele escaped into Basutoland (now Lesotho), and in fury the government retaliated by burning his kraals and confiscating eight thousand head of cattle. Over two hundred amaHlubi were killed, and more than five hundred prisoners were assigned as farm labourers in conditions of virtual slavery.

Langalibalele was betrayed and captured in December 1873, and tried on charges of murder, treason and rebellion. No legal counsel was willing to defend him. After a travesty of a trial, he was illegally sentenced to life imprisonment on Robben Island. Being outside the colony's jurisdiction, the Natal government had no authority to transport him there. After representations by Bishop John Colenso to the imperial government in London, Langalibalele was in due course released.

In 1877, just ten years after the discoveries, the writer Anthony Trollope described Kimberley and its surroundings 'as nothing pretty'.

> There are no trees within five miles of the town, nor blades of grass within twenty. Everything is brown. Within the town all of the buildings are of a hideous corrugated iron. The meat is bad, the butter uneatable, vegetables a rarity ... milk and potatoes are luxuries. An uglier place, I do not know how to imagine. Yet Kimberley mine is one of the most remarkable spots on the face of the earth. It is the largest and most complete hole ever made by humans.[8]

> Who can doubt that work is the great civiliser of the world – work and the growing desire for those good things that work only will bring? The winning of diamonds from the earth by Africans permits such a civilising influence to be expanded. I have not myself seen the model Christian perfected; but when I have looked down into the Kimberley mine and seen three or four thousand men at work…I have felt that I was looking at three or four thousand growing Christians.[9]

Most inconveniently, the newly discovered diamond fields were just outside the boundaries of the British Cape Colony on land occupied by several thousand mixed-race Griqua people. A border dispute was deliberately fabricated and, after a brief and turbulent existence, Griqualand West was annexed to the Cape Colony in 1880.

The early discoveries had been alluvial diamonds washed down the Orange River from Lesotho, and deposited along the banks of the river. Then diamonds were discovered in several extinct volcanoes in 'pipes' that once had been molten rock and had been thrust up to the surface from deep in the bowels of the earth. The hill of Colesberg Kopje would in just a few years be cut away to form the 'Big Hole', and the world's deepest man-made crater.

As excavation became increasingly difficult and capital-intensive, small-scale operators found themselves obliged to sell out to larger mining companies. Mine owners claimed that between one third and a half of diamonds discovered were stolen and smuggled out of Kimberley. A special court was established to try cases of illicit diamond buying (IDB). The Trade in Diamonds Consolidation Act of 1882 imposed fines of up to £1 000 or fifteen years imprisonment (or both) for unlawful possession of uncut diamonds. Under the law, IDB suspects were assumed guilty until proven innocent, and the police were given powers to search without warrants.[10]

Blacks were searched every day, and stripped naked so that every orifice was examined. Even these measures were inadequate to staunch the trade in IDB, so it was proposed that penalties should be extended to include the lash and life imprisonment. When regulations in 1883 required that everyone except managers should strip naked when they left work, white miners complained that they too were being degraded to 'kaffir levels'. A general strike followed in which six men from the 'French company' were shot dead by company guards.

The Langalibalele rebellion produced war hysteria amongst colonial officials and Natal's administrator Sir Theophilus Shepstone was determined to conquer the Zulus. In dispatches to the British government, he declared that no permanent peace could be hoped for until the Zulu power had been broken.[11] Border disputes were deliberately fabricated, leading to the Zulu war of 1879.

The Congress of Berlin in 1884/85 decided that Africa was there for exploitation by Europeans, albeit lofty commitments were expressed about 'the preservation of the native tribes, and to care for the improvement of their moral and material well-being'.

Profits from diamonds in Kimberley provided much of the capital needed to develop the goldfields discovered in 1886 on the Witwatersrand. Again, foreigners flocked to the Transvaal Republic in huge numbers, and within a decade Johannesburg was a city of one hundred thousand people. The Transvaal government despised what were described as the *uitlanders* (foreigners), but also taxed them heavily. Gold backed the British pound sterling, and soon became both the cause and means for yet more wars to expand the British Empire.

North of the Transvaal in what is now Zimbabwe, King Lobengula of Matabeleland had acquired a fondness for champagne, rifles and other trappings of European 'civilisation'. Accordingly, Rhodes's business partner Charles Rudd tricked him into awarding the British South Africa (BSA) Company the right to prospect for gold and other minerals with a monthly payment of £100, a feather plumed hat, the promise of a gunboat for the Zambezi River plus a supply of one thousand Martini-Henry rifles and one hundred thousand rounds of ammunition.[12]

An arms deal thus became the origin of Zimbabwe's continuing conflicts and tragedy. Through a variety of schemes and manipulations, Rhodes amalgamated numerous companies in 1888 into De Beers Consolidated Mining, and thereby established a world monopoly on diamond sales. He was 'on a roll' and seemed especially blessed by the 'Midas touch'.

NM Rothschild merchant bank in London, as the second largest shareholder in De Beers, was generous not only with financial support but also in introducing Rhodes to influential British politicians. The bank had a long history of funding British imperial ventures, having been founded in 1811 soon after Nathan Rothschild moved from Germany to England.

Just four years later Rothschilds backed the British in the Battle of Waterloo so ending the Napoleonic war, and in 1875 the bank funded Prime Minister Benjamin Disraeli's purchase of the Suez Canal.

The lure of gold in Mashonaland, where deposits were reputed to exceed those around Johannesburg, was more than ample inducement to steal countries from their occupants. In 1889 Queen Victoria approved a royal charter for the BSA Company. Again, Rothschilds provided the funding.

There were no geographic limitations either to the BSA's jurisdiction or business. It was empowered to obtain land anywhere in Africa, which was exactly the plan on which Rhodes embarked to expand the Empire from Cape to Cairo. The map of Africa was 'to be painted British red'.

One consequence of Rhodes's consolidation of the diamond mines in Kimberley in 1888 was massive unemployment. Desperately impoverished white miners were easily recruited by the BSA Company to form the Pioneer Column of one hundred and eighty-six adventurers plus nineteen mining prospectors.

The Pioneer Column in September 1890 hoisted the Union Jack at Fort Salisbury (now Harare), its leader reporting back to Kimberley: 'All well. Natives pleased to see us.'[13] The pioneers were rewarded with fifteen mining claims each – albeit that fifty per cent of profits would revert back in perpetuity to the BSA Company – plus huge acreages of land for development as farms. So began the tragedy that still afflicts not only Zimbabwe but the whole of southern Africa.

That year, Rhodes also became the prime minister of the Cape Colony at the age of thirty-seven, a position he used to further extend the power of the mining industry. He had no qualms about any conflicts of interest, believing the destinies of De Beers and South Africa to be identical. Similarly, Rhodes had no compunctions about the use of bribes, believing that there was no man on earth who could not be 'squared'. It was just a matter of discovering his opponent's vanities or other weaknesses.

The Martini-Henry rifles that the BSA Company supplied to Lobengula were already redundant. Just five Maxim machine guns in 1893 ensured the conquest of Matabeleland, and the colonisation of both Northern Rhodesia and Southern Rhodesia.[14]

In collusion with *uitlanders* in Johannesburg, in 1895 Rhodes instigated a revolution in the Transvaal Republic, in what became known as the Jameson Raid. The intention was to hoist the Union Jack and to establish British rule, but the Raid was a complete fiasco. The leaders of the *uitlanders* were arrested, tried and sentenced to death but later pardoned.

Rhodes resigned in disgrace, but the Raid set the course for the South African War. He died at the age of forty-nine just shortly before that war ended, having breathtakingly decided in one of his numerous wills:

> I have considered the existence of God and decided that there is a fifty-fifty chance that God exists. Therefore, I propose to give him the benefit of the doubt. Now, what would God want for the world? He would want it well run.

I have viewed the peoples of the world, and have come to the conclusion that the English speaking race is the highest ideals of Justice, Liberty and Peace. Therefore, I shall devote the rest of my life to God's purpose and make the world English.

I shall work for the furtherance of the British Empire, the bringing of the whole civilised world under British rule, for the recovery of the United States of America, for the making of the Anglo Saxon world into One Empire. What a dream ...[15]

The Rhodes Scholarships were instituted in 1901 for that very purpose. Although funded on the sweat of illiterate South African diamond miners, they are disproportionately allocated to Americans to educate their elites at Oxford University. President Bill Clinton is their most notable beneficiary.

The war in South Africa, as a rehearsal for the First World War, ushered in the twentieth century as the bloodiest in history. The racism and animosities that it spawned resulted in the apartheid system, the tragic consequences of which have yet to run their course. Rhodes's partner in fomenting that war was the British High Commissioner in South Africa, Lord Alfred Milner. It was yet another lesson in British covert destabilisation policies.

A decade earlier, in 1891, three Englishmen had met in London to establish the foundations of an extraordinary network of influential Britons and Americans. They were Rhodes, a journalist named William Stead and Lord Reginald Brett. Milner became the fourth member, and the leader of the cabal after Rhodes died.[16] It was a network that continued to control the world's destiny throughout the twentieth century, and which only now is being seriously challenged in the political upheavals of the Middle East.

Perchance, 1902 was not just the year when Rhodes died, but it was also the year that Ernest Oppenheimer arrived in South Africa at the age of twenty-two with only £50 to his name. Oppenheimer immediately established himself as an astute and successful diamond buyer, and within three years was challenging the directors of De Beers. They disdainfully regarded him as an upstart.

Oppenheimer rapidly eclipsed even Rhodes's achievements. He was a German-born Jew, a later convert to Christianity, who within twenty years of arriving in South Africa was knighted for his work on behalf of the British war effort.

Diamonds were discovered in the Belgian Congo in 1907 and in the neighbouring German colony of South West Africa in 1908. The diamond fields there were even more abundant than those discovered in Kimberley forty-one years earlier. When South African forces conquered the territory in 1915, *The New York Times* reported:

> Much speculation has been indulged in as to the value as a possession of the immense territory of German Southwest Africa, wrested by the Union of South Africa forces from the Germans, who had occupied it since May 1883.
>
> Before the war the territory supported a white population of fifteen thousand people and two hundred and fifty thousand natives. The diamond fields form a rich treasure house, and immense quantities of the precious 'stones of fire' still lie in the sands of the Namib. From 1908 to the end of 1913, gems to the value of US$35 522 000 had been recovered.
>
> British occupation will surely lead to far more rapid development with an influx of capital, especially to exploit its mining possibilities.[17]

With Oppenheimer's encouragement, Prime Minister Jan Smuts attempted to annex South West Africa as South Africa's fifth province. Most inconveniently, the League of Nations insisted that the country should be administered as a 'sacred trust' on behalf of the indigenous population. So began international legal wrangles over seven decades with first the League and, subsequently, the United Nations (UN).

Vast areas in both South Africa and Namibia for many years were demarcated on maps as 'forbidden land' where trespassing was strictly forbidden. Extraordinary escapades occurred in usually vain efforts to beat the prohibition. The penalty for trespassing in this seemingly empty, desolate land along the Atlantic coastline ranged from one year's imprisonment to a shot in the back by a trigger-happy guard. It was repeatedly alleged that under South African administration the treatment of the population was akin to slavery.

With encouragement from the British war cabinet, Anglo American

Corporation of South Africa Ltd was established in New York in 1917 with capital subscribed by JP Morgan. Yet for many years after the Second World War the company's directors dared not set foot in the US because they faced arrest for violations of anti-trust legislation.

South Africa and South West Africa (now Namibia) until the 1930s were the only places in the world where, without a permit, it was actually illegal to possess an uncut diamond. The irony was that diamonds had been found in such abundance that the myths of priceless rarity could only be sustained by a ruthless cartel and governmental collusion. In defiance of numerous UN resolutions and decisions, Namibia was in effect a colony run primarily for the benefit of the Oppenheimer family and its political cronies.[18]

In the aftermath of the South African War and revulsion about British behaviour, Milner was recalled to Britain in 1905 under a political cloud. Nonetheless, the momentum by then was already far advanced towards Rhodes's dream of the Union of South Africa as a country for white settlement and domination.

Objections and representations lodged by what in 1912 became the African National Congress were ignored. An alliance of the mining industry and white farmers ensured supplies of cheap and impoverished black labour by the passing in 1913 of the notorious Land Act, under which white landowners eventually owned eighty-seven per cent of South Africa.

After leaving South Africa, Milner went into business with Rothschilds as chairman of Rio Tinto. With the outbreak of the First World War, he was co-opted to organise coal and food production for the war effort, and eventually became the Secretary for War.[19]

In that position, Milner worked closely with Basil Zaharoff, a notorious arms trader known as 'the merchant of death'. Given various mergers and acquisitions in the British armaments industry in subsequent years, Zaharoff can be considered as the 'godfather' of what is now BAE.

Zaharoff had been born in the slums of Constantinople in 1849, and in his youth touted for brothels and petty swindlers. He found his vocation at the age of twenty-seven when he began selling armaments for the Anglo-Swedish firm Nordenfelt. He sold the first submarine to Greece, and then two to Turkey, Greece's traditional enemy, followed by a fourth to Turkey's other enemy, Russia.

As chief salesman for Nordenfelt, Zaharoff quickly saw the potential for Maxim machine gun and negotiated a merger between Nordenfelt and Maxim which, in turn, were bought out by the British Vickers Steel Company in 1897. Not surprisingly, the major shareholder in Vickers was NM Rothschild bank. In his book *Men Of Wealth*, John Flynn notes:

> By 1890, England set out upon an ambitious naval programme. Vickers, which had been a builder of guns, now went into naval construction. It became a great department store of lethal weapons and could supply its customers with anything from a rifle to a battleship. Zaharoff was its sales genius. In the South African War, Tommies armed with Vickers rifles were scientifically mowed down with Maxim quick firing cannons supplied to the Boers by Zaharoff of Vickers.
>
> Vickers grew and spread out – plants in Britain, Canada, Italy, Africa, Greece, Turkey, Russia, New Zealand, Ireland, Holland; banks, steelworks, cannon factories, dockyards, plane factories, subsidiaries of all sorts; an arms empire. It had share capital larger than Krupp's and had more extensive connections and possessions than Krupp's. And this growth was chiefly the work of the French citizen of Greek blood who, acting the role of ambassador-salesman, had planted the Vickers standard all over the world, from Ireland to Japan and from the North Sea to the Antipodes.
>
> It was done with the aid of British-government backing and pressure, the immense financial resources of British finance; by means of bribery and chicanery, by the purchase of military and naval authorities and the press wherever newspapers could be bought.
>
> It is a dark, sordid story of ruthless money getting without regard for honour, morals, and either national or humane considerations, while the Europe which they upset with their conspiracies and terrorized with their war scares, and to which they sold hatred as the indispensable condition of marketing guns, slid along with the certainty of doom into the chasm of fire and death in 1914.

A British Labour Party parliamentarian, Philip Snowden told the House of Commons just before the outbreak of the First World War:

We are in the hands of an organisation of crooks. They are politicians, generals, manufacturers of armaments and journalists. All of them are anxious for unlimited expenditure, and go on inventing scares to terrify the public and to terrify the ministers of the Crown.

Flynn noted:

Every business attracts to itself men who have the taste, talent and morals suited to its special requirements. This armaments industry in Europe was a behind-the-scenes world of intrigue, chicanery, hypocrisy and corruption. It involved a weird marriage of burning patriotism and cold, ruthless realism. And the men who rose to leadership in the industry were men who combined the vices of the spy, the bribe-giver, the corruptor.[20]

A long-standing premise of British foreign policy had been support for the Ottoman Empire, which for centuries had controlled the countries of the Middle East, including Palestine. That policy was reversed with the outbreak of the War when Turkey was aligned with Germany. British energies now became focused on taking over the Ottoman Empire and control of the Suez Canal as the route to India.

Zaharoff became a 'bagman' to bribe Turkish politicians. His rewards included a British knighthood even though he was a French citizen. He was reported by *The New York Times* in 1921 to be the richest man in the world. He had by then also gone into the oil business in conjunction with the British government to gain control of the oil fields of Persia (Iran) through what became British Petroleum (BP).

Despite the deaths and devastation of the First World War, Zaharoff and Prime Minister David Lloyd-George continued from 1919 until 1922 to manipulate Greece to resume the war against the collapsing Ottoman Empire. As part of the diplomatic manoeuvring at the Versailles peace conference, Lloyd-George encouraged expansion of Greek territory to include recovery of Constantinople (Istanbul) and other areas of Turkey. Another incendiary ingredient was provocation of the war as a crusade of Christians against Muslims.

The Greco-Turkish War was a disaster. An estimated two million Christians – Armenians, Assyrians and Greeks – died. The remaining Greek residents in the newly established Turkish republic were expelled. Eventually Lloyd-George resigned in disgrace. Zaharoff thereafter restricted himself to reorganising the finances of the principality of Monaco and the profitability of its casino, and lived in Monte Carlo in 'friendless solitude' until his death in 1936.

As the corruption scandals around arms deals with Saudi Arabia, South Africa and numerous other countries with concerted British government collusion attest, the culture amongst the ruling elite in London has not changed one iota in the past century. Foreigners, especially darker-skinned foreigners, are fair game for bribery and corruption. It is part of the myths, as expressed by Rhodes, of British virtues.

Margaret Thatcher in 1981 reorganised and privatised the British armaments industry as British Aerospace, now known as BAE. In the subsequent three decades BAE, in conjunction with America's own covert operations, has become central to joint British and US destabilisation efforts in Asia and Africa, and including post-apartheid South Africa. BAE is organised crime on a scale that, frankly, makes the Italian mafia seem like saints.

Imperialist visions remain the prime motivation of the war business more than a century after Rhodes's death, and diamonds are a critical component in the twenty-first century. Of course, Rhodes and Milner had not reckoned that the British would become decidedly the junior partner when the US took over as the world's only superpower.

Milner's role in imperialist history included a hand in drafting the Balfour Declaration in November 1917 that bears the name of the then British foreign secretary. It was a reward to Zionists for their success in whipping up anti-German hysteria and in bringing the US into the First World War. Addressed to Lord Walter Rothschild, it declared:

His Majesty's Government view with favour the establishment in Palestine of a national home for the Jewish people, and will use their best endeavours to facilitate the achievement of this object, it being clearly understood that nothing shall be done which may prejudice the civil and religious rights of existing non-Jewish communities in Palestine, or the rights and political status enjoyed by Jews in any other country.[21]

The Balfour Declaration became nothing less than a British government licence to steal yet another country on behalf of British imperialism. Many influential Jews were then, and still remain, vigorously opposed to Zionist ideas of a Jewish state in Palestine. The Orthodox, Conservative and Reform branches of Judaism all rejected Zionism as a heresy.[22] Secular Jews believed that Zionism would jeopardise their assimilation in Europe and the US.

Lord Edwin Montagu, who became the British Secretary of State for India, told Lloyd-George: 'All my life I have been trying to get out of the ghetto. You want to force me back there. Zionism is a mischievous political creed, untenable by any patriotic citizen of the United Kingdom.'[23] Similar views were expressed in Germany.

Palestinian representations to the peace conference in Paris in 1919 were ignored, as were warnings by prominent American Jews:

> We raise our voices in warning and protest against the demand of Zionists for the reorganisation of the Jews as a national unit, to whom, now or in the future, territorial sovereignty in Palestine shall be committed. We ask that Palestine be constituted as a free and independent state, to be governed under a democratic form of government recognising no distinctions of creed or race or ethnic descent, and with adequate power to protect the country against oppression of any kind. We do not wish to see Palestine, either now or at any time in the future, organised as a Jewish state.[24]

The League of Nations in 1919 repudiated the Balfour Declaration as incompatible with its Covenant. It specifically pledged that former colonies and territories of the defeated countries, including Turkey, would be governed under a 'sacred trust', and that 'the wishes of these communities must be a principal consideration' whilst they were prepared for self-determination and independence.

The British government remained determined to defy all protests. Milner and Herbert Samuel (who became the High Commissioner in Palestine) promoted a pro-British Zionist state in Palestine as a bulwark to secure British control of the Suez Canal and the sea route to India. Already dominant in Egypt, Britain in 1922 rewarded itself with League of Nations mandates over Palestine and Mesopotamia, and 'gave' Syria and Lebanon to France whose troops conquered Damascus in 1920.

In a speech to the House of Lords, Milner declared:

> You cannot ignore the fact that Palestine is the cradle of three of the greatest religions in the world. It is a sacred land to the Arabs, but it is also a sacred land to the Jew and Christian. The future of Palestine cannot be left to be determined by the temporary impressions and feelings of the Arab majority in the country.[25]

Winston Churchill was also an ardent Zionist, and argued that equitable division of the land and its resources would enable both Arabs and Jews to fulfil their destinies:

> Personally, my heart is full of sympathy for Zionism. The establishment of a Jewish national home will be a blessing to the whole world, including to all the inhabitants of Palestine without distinction of race and religion.[26]

The rising anti-Semitism amongst European Christians, including pogroms in Russia and Poland and the Dreyfus trial in France, had prompted Theodore Herzl in 1896 to write *The Jewish State* to promote the idea of a homeland for Jews. Herzl was a secularist, non-religious man who had even considered converting to Christianity. He proposed that the Jewish homeland should be in Uganda, Madagascar or Argentina rather than Palestine, but this suggestion was shouted down at the Zionist conference in 1899 by delegates who insisted on Palestine.

Indeed, Herzl subsequently wrote to Rhodes expressing admiration of his imperialist visions, and saying that he intended to model the colonisation of Palestine after the activities of the BSA Company in Rhodesia. British colonial laws developed in South Africa and Rhodesia became the basis by which Israel still maintains supremacy over Palestinians.

European Christians as early as the 1840s had been promoting a myth that Palestine was 'a land without people for a people without land'. It was a slogan remarkably akin to insistence in apartheid South Africa that there were no Africans at the Cape when Dutch settlers arrived in 1652. In her definitive study *A History Of Jerusalem*, Karen Armstrong writes:

> Europeans were eying Palestine possessively. They tended to see their bringing of modernity to Jerusalem as a 'peaceful crusade,' a term which laid bare the desire to conquer and dominate. The French looked forward to Jerusalem and the whole orient coming under the rule of the cross in a successful crusade. Their task would be to liberate Jerusalem from the Sultan, and their new weapons would be colonialism. The Protestants who built the German colony called themselves the Templars and urged their government to complete the work of the Crusaders.
>
> The British had a rather different line. They developed a form of gentile Zionism. Their reading of the Bible convinced them that Palestine belonged to the Jews, and already in the 1870s sober British observers looked forward to the establishment of a Jewish homeland in Palestine under the protection of Great Britain. It had become the received idea to many people in Protestant England, where the Bible was read rather literally, that the Jews would one day return to Zion and that the Arabs were temporary usurpers.[27]

The Jewish Agency was established in 1923, with support from some members of the Rothschild family and Milner, to encourage Jewish emigration to Palestine. The agency's function was to buy land, and to serve as a quasi-governmental organisation for the Jewish community. There were few economic attractions to Palestine and, consequently, little enthusiasm amongst European Jews to migrate there.

A census in 1922 estimated there were about seven hundred and fifty thousand residents in Palestine, of whom only eleven per cent were Jewish. Political turmoil in Poland between 1924 and 1931 spurred the emigration to Palestine of about eighty thousand Polish Jews.

These settlers were primarily petty merchants and small-time industrialists who, within a few years, had established the foundations of an urban, industrialised economy. Although established in 1909 by earlier immigrants, the city of Tel Aviv suddenly mushroomed out of the sand dunes along the Mediterranean coast.

Then Adolf Hitler came to power in Germany in 1933. Within three years the Jewish population in Palestine increased dramatically to about four hundred thousand people, or about thirty per cent of the population. This caused riots amongst Arabs who, understandably, demanded an end to the Jewish influx.

A Polish immigrant who arrived in 1908, David Ben-Gurion noted that both Jews and Arabs were fighting dispossession, Jews in Europe and Arabs in Palestine:

> The Arabs' fear of our power is intensifying. They see the Jews fortify themselves economically. They see the best lands passing into our hands. They see England identifying with Zionism. This is a fundamental conflict. We and they want the same thing. We both want Palestine ... By our very presence and progress, we have nurtured the Arab nationalist movement.[28]

From 1918 and throughout the interwar period, Ben-Gurion was at the forefront of the Zionist labour movement, the Histadrut. The 1937 Peel Report recommended that Palestine should be partitioned into separate Arab and Jewish states. Ben-Gurion recognised the Peel Report as being even more important than the Balfour Declaration, saying:

> It is a declaration of a Jewish state in Eretz Israel. After two thousand years of bondage, exile and dependency, a mighty government which has authority over the land, offers us sovereignty in the Homeland, political independence in our country.[29]

The Palestinian writer Ramzy Baroud writes:

> It became evident to Palestinians that the [Peel] commission's recommendations were aimed at legitimizing British official policy. In the eyes of Palestinians, dividing Palestine was an unparalleled injustice. Not only did it undercut the system of the mandate, which was meant to guide Palestinians,

like other Arab nations, to self-government, but it clearly sought full and meaningful independence for Jewish immigrants.

More, the report must have terrified Palestinians, for it effectively sought to grant thirty-three per cent of the total area of Palestine to a Zionist government, whereas at that time total Jewish ownership was less than six per cent of the country. The Jewish state, the report counselled, was to include the most strategic and fertile regions of Palestine, including the fertile Galilee, much of the water access to the Mediterranean, and the cities of Haifa and Acre. The commission went so far as to recommend forcible transfers of those Palestinians who refused to leave the Jewish state.[30]

Contradicting the terms of both the Balfour Declaration and the League of Nations mandate, the British white paper of 1939 declared:

> For in Palestine we do not propose even to go through the form of consulting the wishes of the present inhabitants of the country. The four great powers are committed to Zionism, and Zionism, be it right or wrong, good or bad, is rooted in age-long tradition, in present needs, in future hopes of far profounder import than the desire and prejudices of the seven hundred thousand Arabs who now inhabit that ancient land.[31]

During the Second World War, Ben-Gurion encouraged Palestinian Jews to join the British Army. Some twenty-seven thousand did so, and were thereby trained and prepared for the 1948 war. With the assistance of a British government that was anxious to keep their skills out of the German war effort, Ben-Gurion also orchestrated the escape of thousands of European Jews from the clutches of the Nazis.

These refugees included six thousand Belgian diamond cutters. There were about thirty-five thousand Jews in Antwerp during the late 1930s, who for centuries had dominated the European diamond industry.

The Israel Diamond Exchange had been established in 1930 but during the Depression the diamond industry everywhere faced severe economic difficulties. There were simply no buyers for stones that in themselves had no intrinsic value. So critical was the situation that diamond mines in both South Africa and South West Africa were shut down, and remained closed throughout the Second World War.

Facing financial bankruptcy, De Beers itself was absorbed into the Anglo American group in 1934. Sir Ernest Oppenheimer had finally beaten the old guard, and had taken over Rhodes's mantle. A booming gold price, after South Africa devalued its currency and left the gold standard, also saved the diamond industry from collapse. It was only with the outbreak of war that De Beers regained its economic strength.

The new prosperity flowed not from gemstones but from poorer quality industrial diamonds which were vital to the war effort because of their use in machine tools. Diamonds, in time of war, had become important sources of hard currency used to purchase strategic raw materials. The Nazi Germans were chronically short of foreign currencies, raw materials and industrial diamonds, and to raise funds looted Jewish jewellery for sale on international markets. A few wealthy Jews were able to save their lives by handing over their diamond collections.

Although gemstones had been virtually unsaleable during the 1920s and 1930s, huge windfall profits from industrial diamonds during the Second World War provided De Beers with the financial resources to create and embellish the myths of priceless value. In his definitive book *The Rise and Fall of Diamonds*, Edward Jay Epstein describes how:

> Industrial diamonds were absolutely vital for production of airplane engines, torpedoes, tanks, artillery and other weapons of war. Only diamonds could be used to draw the fine wire needed for radar and the electronics of war. Only diamonds could provide the jewelled bearings necessary for the stabilizers, gyroscopes and guidance systems for submarines and planes. Only diamonds could provide the abrasives necessary for rapidly converting civilian industries into a war machine. Without a continuing supply of diamonds, the war machine would rapidly slow to a halt.[32]

When the US entered the War in 1941 after the Japanese attack on Pearl Harbor, the Americans placed a massive order for six and a half million carats of industrial diamonds. Oppenheimer and De Beers refused to supply the order because they feared they could lose control of their diamond cartel.[33]

Uneasy compromises were eventually arranged after interventions by the British government when the US government threatened to cut off supplies of warplanes to Britain. De Beers was concerned about a risk that the US might later dump diamonds from a strategic stockpile, thus destroying the cartel. After canny manoeuvring and concessions, the required diamonds were stockpiled in Canada, and De Beers emerged from the Second World War with massive cash reserves.

The gemstone business showed some recovery during the War, but dealers in Palestine at the time were De Beers's only customers for rough diamonds. With encouragement of the British government as part of the war effort, the industry in Palestine employed four thousand people. It collapsed yet again after the War, and required preferential treatment to survive after the state of Israel was established in 1948.

The diamond cutting industry became the foundation of Israel's economic development, a reality acknowledged at the Harry Oppenheimer Diamond Museum in Tel Aviv where Oppenheimer is cited as saying: 'We at De Beers feel great affection for Israel both in business and in our heart.'

The diamond industry has been by far the most important in Israel for most of the past sixty years. Only recently has it been overtaken in importance by an even more corrupt and venal business, namely the armaments industry. Less than fifty years after Rhodes's death and only thirty years after the Balfour Declaration, the British Empire was finally financially and politically destroyed by the economic devastation of its wars.

There were lofty hopes that the Second World War would finally usher in the biblical visions of the prophet Isaiah: 'They will beat their swords into ploughshares, and their spears into pruning hooks: nation shall not lift up sword against nation, neither shall they learn war any more.'

The UN was established for that very purpose and, as the bestiality of the Holocaust was revealed, the Universal Declaration of Human Rights was proclaimed and adopted in 1948:

> To affirm faith in fundamental human rights as the foundation of freedom, justice and peace in the world, in the dignity and worth of the human person,

and in the equal rights of men and women determined to promote social progress and better standards of life in larger freedom.

The state of Israel was ostensibly founded upon such values. Alas, 1948 was also the year of the Berlin blockade, and when the National Party was elected in South Africa and formally instituted apartheid.

The war business was already regrouping. Six decades later, like apartheid South Africa, Israel is a military dictatorship masquerading as a democracy. The issue has nothing to do with anti-Semitism or so-called 'Israel-bashing'. The US Ambassador to Israel in May 2009 described Israel as 'a promised land for organised crime', and noted that in recent years there had been a 'sharp increase in the reach and impact of organised crime networks'.[34]

Endnotes

1. Wikipedia, the Koh-i-noor diamond.
2. 'Bhutto Approached UK Over Kohinoor', Agence France Presse, December 29, 2006.
3. 'The History Of The World Famous Cullinan Diamond', Diamond Views Com, 4/1/05.
4. Jack and Ray Simons: *Class And Colour In South Africa 1850-1950*, Penguin Books, London, 1969.
5. Robert I Rotberg: *The Founder: Cecil Rhodes And The Pursuit Of Power*, Oxford University Press, New York, 1988 (Preface, p viii).
6. Jack and Ray Simons: *Class And Colour In South Africa 1850-1950*, Penguin Books, London, 1969.
7. Donald R Morris: *The Washing Of The Spears*, Jonathan Cape, London, 1966, p 234.
8. Robert I Rotberg: *The Founder: Cecil Rhodes And The Pursuit Of Power*, Oxford University Press, New York, 1988, p 110.
9. Ibid, p 121.
10. Martin Meredith: *Diamonds, Gold and War*, Simon and Schuster, London, 2007, p 116.
11. Ibid, p 90.
12. Ibid, p 219.
13. Ibid, p 300.
14. Robert I Rotberg: *The Founder: Cecil Rhodes And The Pursuit Of Power*, Oxford University Press, New York, 1988, pp 437-449.
15. 'A Tribute To Cecil John Rhodes', www.rhodespropertycompany.co.uk
16. Carroll Quigley: *The Anglo-American Establishment: From Rhodes to Clivedon*, Books in Focus, New York, 1981.
17. 'South West Africa Has Great Promise: British See Great Possibilities In Immense Territory Now Wrested From Germany', *The New York Times*, July 11, 1915.
18. Laurie Flynn: *Studded With Diamonds and Paved With Gold*, Bloomsbury, London, 1992, pp 35-70.
19. Carroll Quigley: *The Anglo-American Establishment: From Rhodes to Clivedon*, Books in Focus, New York, 1981.
20. John T Flynn: *Men Of Wealth*, Simon and Shuster, New York, 1941, pp 337-372.

21. Rich Cohen: *Israel Is Real*, Jonathan Cape, London, 2009, pp 186 and 187.
22. Naim Ateek: *A Palestinian Christian Cry For Reconciliation*, Orbis Books, Maryknoll, New York, 2008, p 84.
23. David Lloyd-George: *Memoirs Of The Peace Conference*, Volume II, Yale University Press, New Haven, CN, 1939, p 733.
24. Mazin Qumsiyeh: *Popular Resistance In Palestine: A History Of Hope And Empowerment*, Pluto Press, New York, 2011, p 52.
25. Patrick Tyler: *A World Of Trouble: America In The Middle East*, Portobello Books, London, 2009, p 31.
26. Ibid.
27. Karen Armstrong: *A History Of Jerusalem, One City, Three Faiths*, HarperCollins Publishers, London, 1996, p 360.
28. David Ben-Gurion, brief biography and notes citing 'Expulsion of the Palestinians', p 18, www.palestineremembered.com
29. 'In Memory Of The Man, The Leader And The Prophet Of The Zionist Idea', David Ben-Gurion Centennial, World Zionist Organisation, Jerusalem, 1986.
30. Ramzy Baroud: *My Father Was A Freedom Fighter*, Pluto Press, New York, 2010, p 18.
31. Ibid, p 21.
32. Edward Jay Epstein: *The Rise And Fall Of Diamonds: The Shattering Of A Brilliant Illusion*, Simon & Shuster, New York, 1982, chapter nine.
33. Stefan Kanfer: *The Last Empire: De Beers, Diamonds And The World*, Hodder and Stoughton, London, 1993, p 228.
34. Yuval Mann: 'Promised Land For Organised Crime?' YNet News.com, December 2, 2010.

3 • AFRICA'S FIRST WORLD WAR

Africa is estimated to have eighty-eight per cent of the world's reserves of platinum, seventy-three per cent of its diamonds, sixty per cent both of its manganese and its cobalt, forty per cent of its gold,[1] and thirty per cent of its uranium. Illustrating the vital importance of the continent to the war business, it was Congolese uranium that was the raw material for the atomic bombs that the United States Air Force exploded over Hiroshima and Nagasaki in 1945.

Within the next few years, Africa will have replaced the Middle East as the main source of US oil imports, as it has already for China. The new 'scramble for Africa' is already evident in the rivalries between the US and China to secure strategic minerals, mainly for military use. A report by Stephen Burgess at the US Air War College in Alabama is unapologetic about the urgency or America's pre-emptive rights

> … to secure Southern Africa's uranium, manganese, platinum, chrome, cobalt, and rare earth minerals for America's industrial needs and for its military for its maintenance of weapon systems. To triumph in this scramble, all instruments of US power must be deployed. The challenge is most acute in two southern African countries, South Africa and the Democratic Republic of

Congo, but also growing in Zambia, Zimbabwe and Namibia. A 'worst-case' scenario might see the US having to use coercive diplomacy in order to regain access to vital resources. The new scramble for African mineral resources is most similar to the 19th century European scramble that contributed to interstate conflict, especially the First World War.[2]

Despite enormous natural wealth and potential, Africa remains the 'third world of the third world'. Virtually every country on the continent is today very considerably poorer than sixty years ago. Africa has been cursed by incompetent and corrupt leadership, compounded by wily foreign vultures eager to pick over its carcass. For example, Angola, although devastated by wars and corruption, is expected to be supplying a quarter of American oil imports by 2015.

The Cold War erupted in 1948 with the Berlin Blockade, and for forty-five years the world hovered at the brink of nuclear annihilation. The US alone spent an estimated US$12 trillion on nuclear weapons. In his farewell address when he left office in 1961, President Dwight Eisenhower warned ominously about the dangers of the 'military-industrial complex':

> In the councils of government, we must guard against the acquisition of unwarranted influence, whether sought or unsought, by the military industrial complex. The potential for misplaced power exists and will persist. We must never let the weight of this combination endanger our liberties or democratic processes.[3]

A school of thought that includes film-maker Oliver Stone, who produced 'JFK' in 1991, argues that Eisenhower's successor as president, John Kennedy, was assassinated on behalf of the 'military industrial complex' in 1963. Kennedy disagreed with militarist demands for massively increased taxpayer expenditures on armaments, and this explanation remains much more credible than the official but contested Warren Commission report that Lee Harvey Oswald was the lone killer.

The standing argument that the arms industry is an important creator of jobs and foreign exchange is spurious. It is a capital intensive and highly subsidised industry which diverts public resources away from socio-economic priorities such as education and health. The supposed economic 'spin-off' benefits of the armaments industry have long ago been supplanted by 'spin-on', meaning that the industry adapts civilian technology to wage war.

Yet its political influence and devastating consequences around the world is evident wherever the US and Britain have deemed their strategic interests to be at stake. President Barack Obama was elected in 2008 as the peace candidate who offered 'change'. Instead of using the banking crisis to put an end to America's destructive obsession with 'military security', Obama quickly succumbed to the vested interests and war business that kills people for profit. In contradiction to the principles of the Nobel Peace Prize of which he was the recipient in 2009, Obama very actively has promoted arms exports to Israel, Saudi Arabia, India and other countries. US weapons exports have doubled since he came to office.

The war business is unlike any other, and it is booming. It depends upon taxpayer largesse for research and development and, in the name of job creation, then manipulates politicians and foreign policies to spend even more public funds on weapons.[4] It is a coalition of arms, oil, mining and other associated companies, universities supplying the research and banks the money.

The American-British wars in Iraq and Afghanistan since the 9/11 attack on the World Trade Center were driven by lies, but have been massively 'profitable' for the corporate backers of the Bush administration. The 'blowback' will take generations to heal.

Destabilisation of the countries of Central and South America had long been a feature of US foreign policy, but Africa still fell within the orbits of European colonial rule. The devastating and disastrous wars in Asia, in Vietnam, Iraq and Afghanistan were still to come.

Half a century ago, the Congo was already the world's largest diamond producer in terms of carats, albeit that its stones were mainly alluvial, poor quality industrial diamonds rather than the gem quality found in Angola, South West Africa (Namibia) and South Africa.

The Belgian, British and US governments were already conspiring to sabotage Congolese independence within days of the country's freedom from colonial rule. The CIA in January 1961 orchestrated the assassination of Prime Minister Patrice Lumumba, but employed Belgians to perform the deed. Half a century later a team of Belgian lawyers and historians has formally lodged charges of war crimes against a dozen still-surviving Belgian government officials and army officers.[5]

When the United Nations intervened with a peacekeeping force, Secretary General Dag Hammarskjöld was killed in a plane crash in Northern Rhodesia (Zambia) in September 1961. It was widely alleged at the time that the crash had been instigated by the South African government. Documents finally unearthed in 1998 by the Truth and Reconciliation Commission confirmed South African involvement, but also revealed that the CIA and Britain's MI5 were the prime plotters in destabilising the Congo.[6]

Mercenaries, mainly from South Africa and Rhodesia, led by 'Mad Mike' Hoare, compounded the chaos. Hoare and his mercenaries claimed that they were motivated by anti-communism. The reality was that they were thugs hell-bent on looting a once prosperous economy. The Congo became another victim of the Cold War, from which its inhabitants have never recovered.

The late Jackie Kennedy Onassis's lover Maurice Tempelsman is a wheeler-dealer and political manipulator par excellence. The family firm of diamond dealers was established in Belgium in 1909, just two years after the discoveries in the Congo. Tempelsman was born in Belgium but his family migrated to the US just before the Second World War whilst he was still a child.

Tempelsman has been an active member of the Council on Foreign Relations with long and close associations with both the African-American Institute and the CIA, and a major financial contributor to the Democratic Party. He was the key player in November 1965 when the CIA organised the coup d'etat that for the next thirty-two years foisted the kleptomaniac Mobutu on to the Congo.[7] In turn, Mobutu brilliantly played upon American obsessions about communism and the Cold War.

The author Janine Roberts in April 2001 testified before the US Congress about the extraordinary influence that diamonds have held over successive American administrations and, in particular, the role which Tempelsman played.

Roberts noted that De Beers had been indicted by the US Justice Department for price fixing. The Americans believed that rationing of diamonds by De Beers during the Second World War had severely hampered the war effort. They were determined to avoid recurrence of such a risk during the Cold War and stockpiles of various strategic commodities, including diamonds, were established.

Tempelsman was secretly supplied by De Beers with millions of dollars of diamonds to set up the national stockpile. Most of those diamonds originated in the Congo. Roberts writes:

> One of the first acts by Tempelsman was to facilitate the return of the Oppenheimers to the Congo and, with it, to secure funding for Mobutu. Tempelsman succeeded in persuading the White House to secretly buy a vast number of diamonds for the US strategic reserve – at a time when Administration officials were protesting that the reserve was over full. The reason for this deal given in secret US government memos was to support Mobutu and his partner Adoula. This Tempelsman plan made much profit for him and for De Beers.
>
> A State Department cable of 23 December 1964 warned about the need of secrecy over this Mobutu diamond and South African uranium deal because 'it could outrage the moderate Africans we are trying to calm down.' This covert support for Mobutu gave the US a gross excess in the strategic diamond stockpile that was still being sold off in 1997.[8]

When Mobutu was dying in 1997, Tempelsman was again there to recruit South Africa and President Nelson Mandela to facilitate Mobutu's departure for exile in Morocco. Half a century after unleashing chaos in the Congo, Tempelsman is still highly influential in US political circles, and is a major player behind both Obama and Hillary Clinton.

The investigator and commentator Keith Harmon Snow has specialised in exposing what he describes at the 'Holocaust in Central Africa' which since 1996, he estimates, has killed between six and ten million Congolese. He writes:

The CIA, Mossad, the big mining companies, the offshore accounts and weapons deals are all hidden by the western media. The horrors of the concentration camps at Auschwitz, Birkenau and Buchenwald became public knowledge long before they became public outrage. It is the same story for the Congo.

The entire military-industrial-prisons complex revolves around minerals like cobalt, niobium and cobalt oxide, yet the truth about what happens to African people in lands taken over by these mining companies is hidden by the corporate media.

Over the past fifty years, elite Israeli nationals have perpetrated conflict and injustice in Africa, fuelled by and for minerals. Operations associated with the Israeli military or intelligence services – the Mossad – maintain strategic criminal syndicates.

Like most mining mafias in Africa, the Israeli octopus – organised crime syndicates, offshore subsidiaries, interlocking directorships and affiliated mercenaries – has gripped the very heart of the Congo, just like an octopus grips and stuns its prey. Mining regulates the pulse of the Congo, and foreign mining companies with their black sell-out agents are sucking the blood out of the people and the wealth out of the land.[9]

It all comes back to the defence budget. American military, private military of the US and proxy groups we support. This is the largest source of violence, and largest single most devastating impact on human rights around the world [is] unlimited American power. Individuals and institutions from the US are not being held accountable for the massive human rights violations that they are responsible for all around the world, including within the US.[10]

The British, French and Belgian empires in Africa all collapsed quickly during the 1960s. When the Portuguese empire collapsed in the 1970s, South African troops crossed the border into Angola in August 1975 to prevent a communist takeover. The operation unravelled that October when the Soviet Union airlifted thousands of Cuban troops in response to pleas for help from the Angolans, and South African troops ignominiously withdrew in March 1976.[11]

The tragedy was compounded after 1981 when Ronald Reagan became president, and South Africa once again was encouraged by the Americans to invade Angola. Operation Protea was launched with eleven thousand troops, ostensibly to prevent the South West African People's Organisation (Swapo) from 'inflicting bloodshed and terrorism on innocent and non-combatant inhabitants' of Namibia.[12]

Jonas Savimbi and his movement, the National Union for the Total Independence of Angola (Unita), were then being fêted in Washington and Pretoria as great political liberators to save Angola from the scourge of communism. The US spent an estimated US$250 million on covert operations to provide arms shipments to Unita, whilst the Soviet Union countered with similar support for the Popular Movement for the Liberation of Angola (MPLA).

The UN in 1989 reported that the apartheid government's destabilisation policies in neighbouring countries in fourteen years had caused the deaths of up to one and a half million people and killed about one hundred thousand elephants and rhinos. The economic devastation was estimated at US$60 billion.

The American and South African interventions in Angola produced strange bedfellows. They included communist China, which supplied tens of thousands of AK-47 machine guns. These weapons were distributed to Unita against payment to South African generals and arms dealers in ivory, rhino horn and diamonds.

An estimated fifteen million landmines were recklessly scattered about, and it will take decades to clear Angola of these mines. About seventy thousand amputees are testimony to the mindless violence that was inflicted on civilians, often peasant farmers tilling their fields or gathering wood. An article back in 1994 by the journalist Phillip van Niekerk highlighted the tragic consequences:

> The city of Kuito in Angola's central highlands of one hundred and forty thousand people is a city littered with rubble. There is not a tree without bullet holes. At last count, sixty-eight different kinds of explosives from twenty-three nations have been found in the rubble of Kuito. The biggest threat is to children. A cluster bomb looks like a shiny toy.
>
> One of the pities that this war has gone unreported is that it lets off the hook international players who need their noses rubbed in the fly-ridden

rubble of Kuito. Like the Portuguese, who created the original mess, and the Americans who used Angolan lives as pawns in their global chess game.

Most importantly, South Africa – in particular the militarists of the National Party government – have a lot to answer for. They spent millions of our tax rands to build up and defend Savimbi, providing him with the power to hold his country to ransom and destroy it for the sake of his personal ambition.

Yes, we paid for it. We all had a role in reducing Angola to beggary.[13]

The civil war in Angola continued long after the simultaneous collapse of the Soviet Union and apartheid in South Africa. The MPLA controlled the oil producing areas of Angola; Unita controlled the diamond regions. Savimbi refused to accept the results of the election in 1992. In addition to right-wing Americans associated with the Republican Party, Savimbi's backers included Mobutu and De Beers.

Viktor Bout had been a translator for the Soviet army liaison in Angola when the Soviet Union collapsed in 1991. He grasped the opportunity of that chaotic moment to supply Unita with Russian weapons against payment in diamonds.[14] The purchase of three Antonov freight aircraft put Bout into big-time arms trafficking. His market was not only Africa. He supplied both sides in Afghanistan, the Taliban as well as the warlords of the Northern Alliance.

Bout moved to Johannesburg, ostensibly to export flowers to the Middle East and chickens to Nigeria. South Africa's new ANC government closed its eyes to Bout's operations from Lanseria airport. The chairman of the National Conventional Arms Control Committee Kader Asmal unctuously declared that the government could not be blamed for the activities of corrupt policemen and customs officials.

Post-apartheid South Africa became notorious for its complete lack of concern for the consequences of arms exports, and the tiny West African country of Togo became a transit point in the guns-for-diamonds trade. Bout's cargoes included mortar bombs, anti-tank rockets, AK-47 machine guns, rocket launchers and fifteen million rounds of ammunition.[15]

When Mobutu lost office in 1997, Togo's dictator Gnassingbé Eyadéma quickly filled the gap to 'wash Savimbi's diamonds'. The UN's Fowler Report in March 2000 identified Rwanda, Burkina Faso, Togo, South Africa and Belgium as complicit in the trade of weapons and diamonds with Unita.[16] The chaos ended only in 2002 after Savimbi was killed in battle.

Eyadéma profited hugely, supported by contingents of French troops, and when he died in 2005, held the distinction as Africa's longest-serving dictator. His son Faure took over. I spent two months in Togo in 2001 on a fellowship with the UN Centre For Disarmament. The whole West African region was destabilised by the arms trade. One particular recollection of that experience is an encounter at Lomé airport on the evening I left.

The only other white man in the departure lounge was a Hasidic Jew, with beard, hat and tzitzit fringes. He stood out, and I wondered what a Hasidic Jew was doing in Togo. Some minutes later he came over and greeted me in a distinctively South African accent: 'Oh someone who speaks English in this fucking awful country!' Airport officials had evidently taken him to the cleaners for bribes.

My Congolese colleague had saved me from such a fate, intervening to say, 'We Africans don't pay tips!' When they looked at me with my white skin, she added: 'He's African too, we Africans don't pay tips.'

The Hasidic Jew related that when he arrived in Lomé, he had been met by a presidential limousine and driven to meet Eyadéma. There was no presidential limo provided when he left, and he now claimed to be in fear for his life and was very anxious to get out of the country. His intended deal with Eyadéma had obviously gone very sour!

Bout left South Africa suddenly in 1998 for Dubai after an attack at his home in Johannesburg, which was attributed then to rivals within the Russian gangster community. He and his family were held at gunpoint by masked men, who took US$6 million in cash but left other valuables.

After Afghanistan, Bout supplied weapons to Liberia's Charles Taylor, and laundered cash against diamonds for Al Qaeda. The Sierra Leone diamond market had long been controlled by that country's Lebanese community, and was a source of finance for Hezbollah to fund suicide bombers in Israel.

In an extraordinary espionage tale of double-dealing, Israeli operatives in 1998 convinced Osama bin Laden in partnership with Bout to oust the Lebanese, and to develop Dubai as both a lucrative diamond processing hub and a money laundering centre. One-time CIA operative Wayne Madsen reported:

> If one wanted to find the source for most of Al Qaeda's funding, you need not look any further than West Africa's diamond trade and the six biggest banks in New York. Dubai soon rivalled Antwerp and Tel Aviv as a major diamond centre, a business in which Bin Laden is now heavily invested. [17]

Then, quite astonishingly, in mid-2003 Bout made his by-now large fleet of aircraft available to assist the US war against Iraq, thus earning temporary impunity from international efforts to bring him to justice.[18] Parallel with gun running and war profiteering, Bout also supplied his aircraft to the UN for humanitarian relief efforts, such as the tsunami disaster of December 2004.

Bout fell out of favour with the Americans in 2006. The US government seized some of his aircraft and froze many of his assets. In March 2008 he was arrested in Thailand where he had been negotiating the sale to FARC (the Revolutionary Armed Forces of Colombia) of surface-to-air missiles and armour-piercing rocket launchers.[19]

After lengthy court battles in Thailand, Bout was eventually extradited to the US to stand trial in November 2011. The jury took only eight hours to find him guilty, and he now faces the rest of his life in an American jail. Unfortunately, the complicity of the CIA and other US government agencies was carefully excluded from the trial proceedings.

Tragically, the Congo's devastations only worsened after Mobutu's departure when seven neighbouring countries attempted to pick over the carcass. Belgian colonial rule in Ruanda and Urundi (Rwanda and Burundi), which elevated the Tutsi aristocracy over the Hutu population compounded the chaos.

The divisions between Hutu and Tutsi had been deliberately exaggerated and accentuated as a classic colonial example of divide and rule. With Rwandan independence and the tables turned, the Hutus subjugated the Tutsis who, in hate-driven propaganda, they described as 'cockroaches'.

Paul Kagame, born in Ruanda in 1957 into an aristocratic family closely associated with the ousted Tutsi king, grew up in exile and was schooled in neighbouring Uganda. He was recruited in 1979 by Yoweri Museveni into the National Resistance Army, which seven years later ousted Ugandan President Milton Obote in a military coup. Museveni, Uganda's dictator since 1986, dispatched Kagame to the US for military training. It was a pattern similar to the infamous School of the Americas in Panama and Fort Benning in Georgia where Latin Americans such Panama's Manuel Noriega were trained to become thugs, or Sandhurst where the British indoctrinated young men from the colonies to be future military dictators.

In 1990 Kagame abandoned his education with the American army to take charge of the Rwandan Patriotic Front (RPF) which at the time, under the guise of liberating the Tutsi minority, was attempting to overthrow the Rwandan government. UN peacekeepers were sent into Rwanda to maintain a tenuous ceasefire and to apply a power-sharing agreement between Hutus and Tutsis.

Despite repeated and urgent reports back to UN headquarters in New York, the blue-bereted soldiers were prohibited from any interventions that could have averted the impending catastrophe. The US blocked meaningful involvement by the wider international community, insisting that the number of troops involved should be scaled back from the proposed four thousand, five hundred soldiers to a token one hundred men.[20]

The UN soldiers were therefore unable to prevent a surface-to-air missile attack that shot down the plane carrying both Rwandan President Juvenal Habyarimana and Burundian President Cyprien Ntaryamira as it came in to land at Kigali airport. Former UN Secretary General Boutros Boutros-Ghali declared 'the genocide in Rwanda was one hundred per cent the responsibility of the Americans'.[21]

The Clinton administration then orchestrated Boutros-Ghali's dismissal as Secretary General, but his seemingly far-fetched and bizarre accusation is gaining increasing credibility. Former US Congresswoman Cynthia McKinney has twice been driven out of office because of her efforts to expose how both Clinton and Bush administrations were hugely complicit in the plundering of the DRC through Ugandan and Rwandan proxies.[22]

The American ambassador in neighbouring Burundi during 1994 wrote:

I could not fathom how US military leaders had become so enamoured of Kagame. He was one of the US military's own people: he had been trained at Fort Leavenworth, Kansas. I was appalled that his skills had so successfully overshadowed his obvious preference for dictatorship over democracy, and his tolerance, or perhaps appetite for vengeful ethnic slaughter. In time, I was sure that the truth about the RPA [Rwandan Patriotic Army] would come out. But how many lives would be lost, how much suffering endured, how much fear and despair would be borne in the interim?[23]

The planned and orchestrated mass killings by Hutu extremists began the very night that the presidential plane was shot down. A French investigation headed by Judge Jean-Louis Bruguière in November 2006 accused Kagame of having personally ordered the attack.[24] A former member of the RPF command unit testified at the inquiry that Kagame had ordered the shooting down of Habyarimana's plane fully aware that it would unleash the genocide of Tutsi civilians.

> Kagame's ambition caused the extermination of all of our families, Tutsis, Hutus and Twas. Can Kagame explain to the Rwandan people why he stopped the UN intervention which was supposed to be sent to protect the Rwandan people from the genocide? The reason was to allow the RPF leadership to take over the Kigali government, and then to show the world that they had stopped the genocide.[25]

The Rwandan government protested vociferously and broke off diplomatic relations with France, but under French law the judge could not indict Kagame for war crimes because he was a head of state. Then in 2008 a Spanish judge came to a similar conclusion, and issued an indictment against Rwandan army officers involved in raping and murdering Spanish nuns. Despite the slaughter of the Tutsi population, it was Kagame's Tutsi-led and Ugandan-supported RPF that in only three months emerged triumphant.[26]

More than a million Hutus, fearing retribution from the Tutsis, fled across the border to Goma in Mobutu's Zaire. Conditions there were appalling and, within days, tens of thousands of Hutu refugees died of cholera. They had taken with them huge quantities of weapons supplied to Habyarimana's regime by the French, South African and Egyptian governments.

The new Tutsi government in Rwanda cleverly milked the world's sympathy. It pleaded that it was defenceless against an attack by the Hutu Interahamwe militias in Goma. Museveni and Kagame were fêted around the world – but most especially in Washington – as the new generation of African leaders who would transform the continent. Parallels are frequently drawn between Rwanda and the Nazi Holocaust in Europe in the 1940s, albeit the 'speed' of the death rates in Rwanda exceeded even Nazi efficiencies.

The reality was that the US army poured military aid and training into the Rwandan Patriotic Army (RPA) in preparation for intervention in the Congo. At stake were the raw materials deemed essential to the American armaments industry, the 'military-industrial complex'.

Within three weeks, the supposedly defenceless Rwandan government forces, backed by the Ugandan army, attacked both the Interahamwe and genuine refugees in Goma. Tens of thousands more people were massacred. As Rwandan and Ugandan forces plundered Congolese economic resources, an even greater tragedy was unfolding. Museveni and Kagame employed Laurent Kabila to launch a war against Mobutu's tottering regime.

Kabila's misrule was even more barbaric than Mobutu's. Within a year Kabila fell out with his corporate backers, and even with Museveni and Kagame. Their prime interest was to loot the Congo's timber, gold, tin, cobalt, copper and other natural resources, including diamonds. Desperate for support against marauding Ugandans and Rwandans, Kabila signed away the Congo's wealth to Angolans, Namibians and, most especially, to Zimbabweans.

The Zimbabwe Defence Industry (ZDI) provided an estimated US$150 million's worth of ammunition and other military supplies to Kabila's forces against a licence to pillage the country. A diamond concession at Mbuji Mayi valued at US$1 billion was allocated to Zimbabwean beneficiaries in gratitude for the loan and use of the Zimbabwean army. The chief executive of ZDI, Tshinga Dube, was in business with the Ukrainian-Israeli diamond and arms dealer Leonid Minin who, in turn, was working closely with the Italian mafia.[27]

Over thirteen thousand Zimbabwean troops were assigned to the Congo to prop up Kabila's regime. The arrangement was that the costs of support estimated at US$27 million per month would be recouped not from Zimbabwean taxpayers, but from exploitation of gold, cobalt and diamond operations. The intention was to develop the Mbuji Mayi concession. Investigative journalists learned that diamonds from Mbuji Mayi were being smuggled through Johannesburg airport. They were being cut and polished, and then fraudulently exported from South Africa, and certified in terms of the Kimberley Process as 'conflict free'.[28]

Zimbabwean influence in the Congo waned after Laurent Kabila was assassinated in 2001. He was replaced by his son Joseph who remains firmly under the control of American and Israeli protectors. With the Zimbabwean military having proved incapable of the tasks expected, Israelis took charge of security.

Israeli businessman Dan Gertler's companies were awarded a monopoly over the Congo's diamonds exports against agreement to organise Israeli training of the rag-tag Congolese army, and so replace the ineffective Zimbabweans. The agreement was in due course revoked, but not before prompting a political scandal in Israel that continues to reverberate within the highest levels of the military and political establishment.[29]

Gertler's move displaced both De Beers and Tempelsman. Thanks to his support for Kabila junior, he has since extended his influence into a web of Congolese commodities that also includes copper and cobalt.[30] The state-owned Gécamines[31] is the successor company to the Union Minière du Haut Katanga, which in 1906 became the foundation for immensely profitable and exploitative Belgian colonial rule of the Congo.

Because of the kleptocracy of the Mobutu and Kabila presidencies, the company repeatedly teeters on bankruptcy and, under pressure from the World Bank and the International Monetary Fund, is now scheduled for privatisation. In addition to huge copper deposits, it is the holder of the world's biggest cobalt reserves. Yet Gécamines is indebted to the World Bank and others for up to US$1.5 billion, and suffers financial losses of US$20 million per month.

Gertler secretly purchased of some of Gécamines company's assets.[32] His influence in Israel's cut-throat politics stems from alignment with and funding of the right-wing foreign minister, Avigdor Lieberman. Both Gertler and Lieberman are under investigation in Israel for corruption, but the political will to prosecute them was still lacking at the beginning of 2012.

It is estimated that as many as eight hundred thousand Congolese work alluvial diamond pits in circumstances worse than slavery. Young boys displaced by the war are the preferred labour. They are lowered down into thirty-metre deep holes to dig around in the mud for stones, and many drown. A report by Partnership Africa Canada and Global Witness in 2004 found:

> Diamond diggers are amongst the poorest people in Africa – even though they produce great wealth for others. This is a human security issue; it is about development at its most basic; and it is about justice. Smuggling continues, and diggers face appalling working conditions. Residents of mining areas complain of environmental degradation, water pollution, and the influx of migrant labour, with high rates of prostitution and HIV/Aids. Family and societal violence follow.
>
> Most diamond diggers lead hard, insecure, dangerous and unhealthy lives. With average earnings of less than a dollar a day they fall squarely into the broad category of 'absolute poverty'. Until these problems are fixed, diamonds will continue to be a source of insecurity; conversely, change could produce significantly better lives for diggers and their communities.[33]

The UN Security Council in 2001 accused Kagame and Museveni of being 'the godfathers of illegal exploitation of natural resources and continuation of the conflict'. Yet no action was taken against them thanks to highly placed connections in the British and American governments. Former British Prime Minister Tony Blair proudly describes himself as one of Kagame's advisers, and 'friend'. Huge amounts of British financial aid have been poured into Rwanda which, most curiously, has also been accepted as a member country of the Commonwealth.[34]

Blair's reputation has been shredded on many issues, to the extent that he is now widely nicknamed 'Bliar', and described as a war criminal who should be in jail. Within the first six years of his tenure he involved Britain in five wars, including the disastrous and illegal war against Iraq. His promotion of the British war industry included a cover-up of massive bribes paid to members of the Saudi royal family plus his involvement as 'number one salesman' for BAE in the South African arms deal scandal.

There were also a myriad of allegations at the UN and around the world about John Bredenkamp, a British intelligence agent and bagman for BAE. He had been a tobacco and arms sanctions-buster during the Rhodesian UDI days, but both he and multimillionaire Zimbabwean businessman Billy Rautenbach became untouchable in Zimbabwe once they became Mugabe's major financial patrons. The US Treasury in November 2008 finally froze Bredenkamp's assets in America, describing him as:

> A well-known Mugabe insider involved in various business activities, including tobacco trading, gray-market arms trading and trafficking, equity investments, oil distribution, tourism, sports management and diamond extraction. Through a sophisticated web of companies, Bredenkamp has financially propped up the regime and provided other support to a number of high ranking officials. He also has financed and provided logistical support to a number of Zimbabwean parastatal entities.[35]

Only in May 2010 did South Africa's Supreme Court of Appeal finally uphold Standard Bank's decision to blacklist Bredenkamp, and to close his accounts.[36] Barry Sergeant, author of *Brett Kebble: The Inside Story*, has investigated who bankrolled Mugabe, and writes:

> Why have the names of those bankrolling Zimbabwe's deranged president, Robert Mugabe, been kept so well under wraps? For one thing, the deals behind the bankrolling are not simple, and for another, the robber barons are pretty smart and can also be pretty darn dangerous. Depending on how you count, there are four or five individuals bankrolling Mugabe and they are all palefaces. This may be surprising given Mugabe's year 2000 'land reform' package where he booted an estimated four thousand palefaces off Zimbabwe's commercial farms.
>
> Mugabe relies on patronage from his chosen palefaces, and the robber barons have become increasingly bold. Rautenbach did not come by his

DRC assets by accident. He was described by a UN panel as a major player in the elite network of twisted politicians, military commanders and shady businessmen that organised the transfer of billions of dollars of state assets to private companies with no compensation or direct revenue benefit accruing to the state treasuries of either the DRC or Zimbabwe.[37]

Gertler and other Israeli diamond interests not only had ousted De Beers in the Congo, but the long-running and sensational Angolagate scandal in France revealed extraordinary tales of French, Israeli and Russian involvements to take control of Angolan diamonds. The son of former French President François Mitterand, a former government minister plus several senior French government officials were implicated.

Russian-born Arcadi Gaydamak is one of numerous gangsters who flocked to Israel from the Soviet Union during the 1970s, albeit he soon re-emigrated to France to make his fortune. His colleague in the Angolagate affair was an Algerian *pied-noir*, Pierre Falcone, whom Angolan President Eduardo dos Santos had appointed as economic adviser. Both Gaydamak and Falcone were issued with Angolan diplomatic passports, and claimed diplomatic immunity when the legal noose began to tighten.

The Angolagate arms deal was estimated to have been worth US$791 million. Gaydamak and his cronies in the French government between 1993 and 1998 sold huge quantities of Soviet armaments to the Angolan government for use against Unita. The French wanted access to Angolan oil irrespective of the devastation and human miseries resulting from yet more weapons in a country already awash with arms. Gaydamak managed to escape back to Russia to avoid a six-year jail sentence for gunrunning.[38]

Extraordinarily, the Paris Court of Appeals in April 2011 overturned the judgment. It ruled that irrespective of the UN arms embargo, it was not illegal to import weapons into Angola, and therefore dismissed the charge of arms trafficking. Israeli newspapers in July 2011 reported that Gaydamak is back in business in Angola.

Having looted Angola's oil and diamond wealth and squirrelled it away in Brazil and elsewhere, President Dos Santos is said to be both the richest man in Angola and the second richest man in Brazil. His daughter Isabel maintains a close relationship with Lev Leviev, who is now fast replacing De Beers and the Oppenheimer family in the battle to control the diamond industry.

Over the past thirty years De Beers has found it increasingly difficult to control the huge new sources of diamonds being found all over the world. Diamonds have been discovered in over twenty countries – notably not Israel – but most especially in Russia, Canada and Australia. The new Marange field in Zimbabwe is allegedly the largest. The whole mystique and value of diamonds would immediately collapse but for the unique monopoly that De Beers created and ruthlessly defended during the days of colonial and apartheid South Africa.

Back in 1975 the Israeli diamond industry accounted for almost forty per cent of Israel's non-agricultural exports. It employed more than twenty thousand workers. Even then, the Israelis were increasingly rebellious about operating under rules determined in Johannesburg and London. They challenged De Beers by amassing a stockpile that was funded by Israeli banks. The cartel retaliated and by ruthless dumping and pricing policies between 1978 and 1980 almost destroyed both the Israeli banking and diamond industries. About three hundred and fifty diamond firms went bankrupt.[39]

De Beers won that round, but many Israelis who were severely burned neither forgot nor forgave. Amongst them was Leviev, who migrated to Israel in 1971 at the age of fifteen from Tashkent in what is now Uzbekistan. He had apprenticed himself as a diamond cutter, and he was both street-smart and industrious. Having been born in the Soviet Union, he also spoke Russian.

The New York Times reported in 2007:

Leviev saw an opportunity in 1989. De Beers had encountered anti-trust problems in the US. In South Africa, the apartheid government was losing political power. At the same time, the Soviet Union, whose leaders had long had a mutually profitable partnership with De Beers, was nearing collapse.

One of Leviev's first moves in Russia was to set up a high-tech cutting and polishing plant. It provided jobs and, more important, showed the Russians how they could gain control of their own industry. In turn, the Russian government helped him gain a foothold in Africa.

Leviev bought into the Catoca diamond mine in Angola, and soon established warm ties with the Angolan president, José Eduardo Dos Santos. Dos Santos was fighting a civil war against Unita rebels, who were financed by the sale of smuggled 'blood diamonds.' Leviev had a suggestion: Why not create a company to centralize control of all diamonds? The company that grew out of that idea was the Angola Selling Corporation, or Ascorp, jointly owned by the Angolan government, Omega Diamonds and Leviev.

Unita surrendered in 2002, after the death of its leader, Jonas Savimbi. By then, the Angolan government had pushed De Beers out of the country, and Ascorp had generated great sums for the Dos Santos government and, it is rumoured, the Dos Santos family.[40]

Other reports were not so flattering. Leviev's dealings in Russia and Angola produced a vast fortune, variously estimated in 2007 as being from US$4.1 billion to US$8 billion. Angolan human rights activists, in particular Raphael Marques, documented atrocities by Leviev's companies,[41] and the European Union in 2008 also warned him against selling 'blood rubies' that finance the Burmese military dictatorship.

In addition, Belgian police learned in 2009 that Leviev's partner in Ascorp, Omega Diamonds, was involved in a multibillion euro laundering scheme. Yes, multibillions, not multimillions! Omega Diamonds, established only in 1994, had suddenly become the second largest diamond cutting and polishing firm in Antwerp. Investigations revealed that Omega had been buying diamonds in Angola and the Congo at dumping prices dictated by Dos Santos's daughter Isabel, and traded through Dubai, Tel Aviv and Geneva.[42]

Leviev's success in Russia and Angola was such that in 1997 for US$400 million he purchased a seventy-five per cent shareholding in Africa-Israel Investment Company, Israel's leading property development and financial institution. The company, perchance, was established back in 1934 by South African Zionist Jews to purchase land in Palestine. The Jewish community in South Africa was then the most affluent anywhere in the world in terms of per capita income, and was hugely supportive of the Zionist initiative.

Africa-Israel offered Leviev a unique opportunity to launder the proceeds of 'blood diamonds' through property development in the illegal construction of settlements in the West Bank. Africa-Israel became a multi-faceted organisation operating in numerous countries in addition to Israel and including Russia, Britain and the US.

For the following ten years it was trumpeted as hugely successful, and rapidly expanded into the US and Russia. The reality was that its subsidiaries, including Danya Cebus, were leading building contractors in illegal construction of settlements in the West Bank, including Zufim near Jayyous, Har Homa near Bethlehem and Ma'ale Adumin between Jerusalem and Jericho.

Leviev epitomises the unscrupulous behaviour and corruption of war profiteering, and the collapse that often follows. The financial opportunities offered by Israel's occupation of the Palestinian territories provided unique opportunities to launder such ill-gotten gains.[43]

Leviev was conspicuous in funding philanthropic causes. He relished acclaim as the world's leading diamond polisher and the man who cracked the De Beers diamond cartel. Leviev Diamonds is Israel's largest diamond company, and its stores now grace the prime shopping districts of Dubai, New York, London and Moscow.

His troubles began in 2008 when the people of Jayyous appealed to Unicef to stop accepting donations from Leviev or his companies.[44] Norwegian pension funds then divested from Africa-Israel, and Americans regularly demonstrated outside the Leviev Diamond store on Madison Avenue.[45] Even the British government backtracked from its intention to rent office accommodation from Africa-Israel to house its embassy in Tel Aviv.

When Africa-Israel crashed during the 2008/2009 financial crisis, it was deemed too big to fail because Israeli pension funds were now so entangled in its web. The diamond industry buckled, with Israeli exports to the crucial US market collapsing by forty per cent to US$5.6 billion.[46]

Africa-Israel had also made massive investments in both the Russian and American property markets just before the property bubble burst. The company's share price on the Tel Aviv Stock Market fell by more than ninety per cent, and the company was US$5.5 billion in debt.

All Israeli banks were deeply involved,[47] and a restructuring agreement was approved by the Tel Aviv District Court in December 2009.[48] The Israeli banking and financial system looked extremely vulnerable to collapse, as reflected in a sober analysis published by *Haaretz* entitled 'Judge's creativity on Africa-Israel may cost us dearly'.[49]

One year later, however, the company had already repaid most of that debt. It also announced in November 2010 that for business rather than political reasons it was withdrawing from housing construction in the settlements.

De Beers also, albeit not so quickly, recovered from the 2008/2009 crash. It reported a ninety-seven per cent drop in profits during the first six months of 2009 to only US$3 million, and a loss for that year of US$220 million. For 2010 the company reported a fifty-three per cent increase in sales to US$5.08 billion, and a return to profitability of US$546 million.

After a fourteen-year investigation, in April 2008 the company finally agreed to pay a fine of US$295 million to American diamond traders and consumers. Court papers declared: 'De Beers violated anti-trust and unfair competition and consumer protection laws by monopolising diamond supplies, conspiring to fix, raise and control diamond prices and in disseminating false and misleading advertising.'

De Beers denied the allegations, and claimed it had done nothing wrong. Its press statement declared that it chose to settle the suit to preserve its reputation, and did not want 'the burden and distraction of litigation'.[50]

In November 2007 De Beers sold the Premier (Cullinan) Mine for R1 billion in cash to a black economic empowerment consortium comprising Petra Diamonds and Saudi Arabia investors. This was followed in January 2011 by the sale of Finsch's mine for R1.4 billion, also to Petra.[51]

As it did in Namibia during the 1970s and 1980s, De Beers has 'cherry-picked' its diamond properties in South Africa, and is now yielding to even more ruthless gangsters in the war business. The Oppenheimer family has shrewdly seen the end of an era. In its heyday De Beers controlled up to ninety-five per cent of the diamond market. That dominance has already been reduced to only forty per cent.

The announcement was made in November 2011 that the Oppenheimers had sold their forty per cent stake in De Beers for US$5.1 million.[52]

Endnotes

1. Cynthia Carroll: 'Africa's Century Must Be Grounded in Partnership', *Business Report*, February 6, 2008.
2. Stephen Burgess: 'Sustainability Of Strategic Minerals In Southern Africa And Potential Conflicts And Partnerships', US Air War College, Maxwell Air Force Base, Alabama, May 2011.
3. President Dwight Eisenhower, January 17, 1961.
4. Mina Kimes: 'America's Hottest Export: Weapons', *Fortune Magazine*, February 11, 2011.
5. Slobodan Lekic: 'Charges Sought In Death Of Congo Leader Lumumba', *The Seattle Times*, June 21, 2010.
6. Marlene Burger: 'CIA and MI5 linked to Hammarskjöld's death', *Mail & Guardian*, August 28, 1998.
7. Larry Devlin: *Chief Of Station, Congo: Fighting The Cold War In A Hot Zone*, Public Affairs, New York, 2007.
8. Janine Farrell Roberts: 'How US Foreign Policy Over Decades Was Influenced By The Diamond Cartel', statement to US Congressional committee, Washington DC, April 23, 2001.
9. Keith Harmon Snow: 'Gertler's Bling Band Torah Gang', *Dissident Voice*, Santa Rosa, California, February 9, 2008.
10. Keith Harmon Snow: 'The Political Economy of Genocide – Conflicts in Contemporary Africa and the New Humanitarian Order', New York, January 26, 2009.
11. William Minter, *King Solomon's Mines*, Basic Books, New York, 1986, pp 268 and 269.
12. Ibid, p 315.
13. *Weekly Mail*, November 5, 1994.
14. The character Orlov in the film 'Lord Of War' is said to have been modelled after Bout.
15. Douglas Farah and Stephen Braun: 'The Merchant Of Death', *Foreign Policy* magazine, November/December 2006.
16. Final Report of the UN Panel of Experts on Violations of Security Council Sanctions Against Unita, 'The Fowler Report', S/2000/203, United Nations, New York, March 2000.
17. 'Diamonds, Dubai, the Russian-Israeli Mafia and Bin Laden', Wayne Madsen

Report, March 3, 2006.

18. John C K Daly: 'Viktor Bout: From International Outlaw to Valued Partner', Global Policy Forum, New York, October 21, 2004.

19. Chiara Carter: '"Merchant of Death's" secret SA connections', *Sunday Argus*, March 9, 2008.

20. Robert and Kathleen Krueger: *From Bloodshed To Hope In Burundi*, University of Texas Press, Austin, 2007, p 108.

21. Robin Philpot: 'Rwanda 1994: Colonialism Dies Hard', The Taylor Report, University of Toronto, 2004.

22. Cynthia McKinney radio interview, KPFK radio station, Los Angeles, December 4, 2008.

23. Ibid, pp 110-111.

24. Holly Manges Jones: 'French judge recommends Rwanda president face war crimes trial', Paper Chase Jurist, University of Pittsburgh School of Law, November 21, 2006.

25. Michael Chossudovsky: 'The Geopolitics behind the Rwandan Genocide: Paul Kagame accused of War Crimes', Global Research, Montreal, November 23, 2006.

26. Chris McGreal: 'France's Shame', *The Guardian*, January 11, 2007.

27. 'Diamonds Seized from ZDI Boss's Home', *Zimbabwe Independent*, March 2, 2007.

28. Rick Hines and Keith Harmon Snow: 'Blood Diamond: Doublethink and Deception Over Those Worthless Rocks', Global Research, Montreal, July 29, 2007.

29. Gidi Weitz, Uri Blau and Yotam Feldman: 'Ace of Diamonds', *Haaretz*, July 19, 2009.

30. Barry Sergeant: 'Playing Poker With Africa', Moneyweb, Johannesburg, June 3, 2007.

31. Gécamines – Le Générale des Carrières des Mines.

32. Michael J Kavanagh and Franz Wild: 'Sale of Top DRC Mine May Stymie Share Offer', *Sunday Independent*, July 3, 2011.

33. Partnership Africa Canada and Global Witness: 'Rich Man, Poor Man – Development Diamonds and Poverty Diamonds: The potential for change in the artisanal alluvial diamond fields of Africa', 2004.

34. Chris McGreal: 'Tony Blair defends support for Rwandan leader Paul Kagame', *The Guardian*, December 31, 2010.

35. 'John Bredenkamp, Billy Rautenbach added to US sanctions list', Statement by US Treasury, November 25, 2008.
36. 'Court upholds right of bank to close Zimbabwean tycoon's accounts', Politicsweb, May 30, 2010, citing case 599/09 and judgment delivered on May 27, 2010.
37. Barry Sergeant: 'Zimbabwe's Pale Barons', Moneyweb, June 28, 2008.
38. Yossi Melman: 'French court sentences Gaydamak to six years' jail time for gunrunning', *Haaretz*, October 25, 2009.
39. Stefan Kanfer: *The Last Empire; De Beers, Diamonds and the World*, Hodder and Stoughton, London, 1993, pp 331-335.
40. Zev Chafets: 'The Missionary Mogul', *The New York Times*, September 16, 2007.
41. Raphael Marques: 'Rinsing The Blood From Angola's Diamonds', Oxford University Africa Society, January 27, 2007.
42. Avi Krawitz: 'Omega Diamonds Suspected of Multibillion-Euro Fraud', Diamonds.Net, February 16, 2009.
43. Michael Rochvarger: 'Leviev's Diamonds in the Rough', *Haaretz*, January 5, 2010.
44. 'Settlement-builder Lev Leviev's Company Africa-Israel in Dire Straits', http://adalahny.org
45. 'At Leviev Store, Protesters Tell Business Leaders "No Business As Usual With Apartheid Israel"', Adalay-NY, http://www.adalahny.org, December 5, 2009.
46. 'US diamond imports and exports by country', International Trade Commodities, March 7, 2010.
47. Michael Rochvarger: 'Can Lev Leviev Repay NIS 23 billion?' *Haaretz*, November 26, 2009.
48. Calev Ben-David and Jonathan Ferziger: 'Court approves Africa-Israel deal', *Jerusalem Post*, December 22, 2009.
49. Meirav Ariosoroff: 'Bottom Shekel: Judge's creativity on Africa-Israel may cost us dearly', *Haaretz*, December 25, 2009.
50. Bheki Mpofu: 'De Beers to pay R2.3 bn to settle lawsuit in US', *Business Day*, April 17, 2008.
51. Allan Seccombe: 'Petra to buy Finsch mine for R1.4 bn', *Business Day*, January 24, 2011.
52. Sharda Naidoo: 'De Beers No Longer Need The Jewel In Crown', *Mail & Guardian*, November 11, 2011.

4 • WHEN VICTIMS BECOME PERPETRATORS

It was already evident by November 1983 that the apartheid state was teetering and on the verge of collapse. The tricameral constitution imposed by P W Botha – endorsed by Anglo American Corporation/De Beers as 'a step in the right direction' and approved overwhelmingly by the white electorate in a referendum – was intended to strip three quarters of South Africans of their citizenship. Apartheid would thus be entrenched in perpetuity. In theory, there would be no 'black' South Africans.

'Blacks' would supposedly become citizens of impoverished and economically unviable 'homelands' known as Bantustans. There, puppet dictators bedecked themselves in gold braid and looted the public till. With the notable exception of Israel, no country gave the Bantustans diplomatic recognition as independent states. As fraudulent and pariah entities, they were ostracised by the international community, but the Bantustan model and mentality became the formula for the equally monstrous so-called 'two-state solution' in Israel-Palestine.

Riots erupted throughout the country and South Africa's currency crashed on foreign exchange markets. The wars 'on the border' in Angola and Namibia were now compounded by insurrection in the townships. The rand in 1979 had been worth US$1.50 when, in the aftermath of the Iranian revolution that toppled the Shah, the gold price rocketed to over US$800 per ounce.

Criminals and bankers poured into the country to offer their sanctions-busting services. Just four years later, during the referendum campaign, the value of the rand plummeted below parity with the American dollar and capital haemorrhaged out of the country. Television coverage of the riots and heavy-handed brutality by the security forces only compounded global revulsion. Even international bankers now decided that apartheid was simply 'too much hassle'!

Botha and his advisers were convinced that all criticisms of apartheid originated with communists to serve the objectives of the Soviet Union. Thus, a 'total strategy' was devised to counter the 'total onslaught'. Military responses to political conflicts permeated the economy and every aspect of society. Botha, nicknamed 'the big crocodile', believed he could rely on British Prime Minister Margaret Thatcher and United States President Ronald Reagan to save him and apartheid from the consequences of his arrogance.

In the 'national interest' and 'security', censorship, secret police, detentions without trial, torture, assassinations and corruption were rife in a paranoid dictatorship desperate to hold on to power. In his 'Rubicon speech' during August 1985, Botha told the world to go to hell, and within days the rand was trading at less than thirty-three American cents.

I was then Nedbank's Regional Treasury Manager in Cape Town, and the senior manager involved in international banking transactions. Nedbank was the apartheid government's preferred bank for sanctions-busting operations. Personally, I was sickened by the corruption and collusion, phoney documentation and the fraudulent transactions in which, in the 'national interest', I had become complicit.

Nedbank, like all banks and financial institutions, had 'prostituted' itself for the sake of short-term profit and political gain. Only a few months later in June 1986, Nedbank actually went bankrupt. Quietly, albeit in violation of existing legislation that prohibited shareholdings exceeding fifty per cent in banks, it had to be re-capitalised by Old Mutual insurance company. Old Mutual and its industrial subsidiary Barlow-Rand were also deeply involved in financing and developing Armscor, the state-owned armaments company.

Ken Owen, the editor of *Business Day* newspaper, subsequently described the militarised and dictatorial mentality that Botha instituted:

> The evils of apartheid belonged to the civilian leaders: its insanities were entirely the property of the military officer class. It is an irony of our liberation that Afrikaner hegemony might have lasted another half century had the military theorists not diverted the national treasure into strategic undertakings like Mossgas and Sasol, and Armscor and Nufcor that, in the end, achieved nothing for us but bankruptcy and shame.[1]

The arms embargo against apartheid South Africa approved by the UN Security Council in November 1977 had been the international response to the deteriorating situation. It followed the June 1976 Soweto uprising, the war in Angola and domestic political suppression in September 1977 after the murder of Steve Biko by security police.

Abuses of human rights in South Africa were now deemed to pose a threat to international peace and security. The decision by the Security Council was hailed at the time by the Carnegie Institute as the 'most significant development in twentieth century diplomacy'. National sovereignty and domestic jurisdiction could no longer be cited to cloak political repression. In due course, apartheid would be defined in international law as a 'crime against humanity'.

Israel and apartheid South Africa were both pariah states, and the arms embargo coincided with the election that year of Israel's right-wing government. When Menachem Begin's Likud Party came to office, the National Party and right-wing revisionist Zionism in Israel became political soulmates. Begin's government emphasised military might, national survival, and the denial of political rights to the enemy.[2] Hatred and anti-Arab racism expressed by Likud supporters eclipsed even the vehemence of anti-black racism of the apartheid government.

Botha's predecessor, Prime Minister John Vorster, had been fêted when he visited Israel in 1976. That state visit was a gesture of thanks for South Africa's rapid assistance with spare parts and fighter pilots during the 1973 Yom Kippur war. By contrast, the US dithered for a week after the outbreak of war over the political implications of dispatching military supplies until Israel threatened to drop a nuclear weapon on Damascus.[3] That Vorster had been a Nazi sympathiser who was interned during the Second World War was brushed aside when he was conducted around the Yad Vashem holocaust museum in Jerusalem.

Israel was then economically in dire straits, and desperate. The country was spending twenty-three per cent of its gross national product on defence,[4] and inflation was out of control. By contrast, South Africa's mineral resources still sustained delusions that it was a wealthy and impregnable country that could defy the rest of the world.

A secret defence agreement between Israel and South Africa had been signed in April 1975. As one of the world's major producers of uranium, South Africa had been interested in the nuclear industry from its beginnings. Prime Minister Jan Smuts as early as 1946 had appointed a uranium research committee, and three years later the Atomic Energy Board was established.

Similarly, in Israel the Weizmann Institute established a department of isotope research in 1949, and young Israelis were sent abroad to study nuclear energy and nuclear chemistry. Researchers at the Institute as early as 1953 had pioneered a new process to create heavy water required to modulate a nuclear chain reaction. They had also devised more efficient methods of extracting uranium from phosphate fields.[5]

As early as the 1950s, South Africa exported uranium to Israel and (after lapses during the 1960s) the traditionally close relationship between the two countries culminated in 1979 in joint testing of a nuclear device over the Atlantic Ocean. That close relationship had long preceded Israeli independence in 1948.

Smuts developed a personal friendship with Chaim Weizmann during his days in British Prime Minister David Lloyd-George's cabinet during the First World War. Weizmann succeeded Theodore Herzl as president of the World Zionist Organisation, and later became Israel's first president.

Before that war, Weizmann was a chemistry professor at the University of Manchester where he developed acetone for use in the manufacture of cordite explosive propellants. Weizmann declined either payment or a knighthood for his vital contributions to the British war effort. He pleaded, instead, for Palestine as a homeland for Jews, and the Balfour Declaration was the culmination of his lobbying efforts.

Smuts was also a keen Zionist and argued that Jewish emigration to Palestine was the best option to advance British interests in the Middle East. The Zionist revisionist leader Ze'ev Jabotinsky visited South Africa several times during the 1930s. The memorabilia and artefacts on display in David Ben-Gurion's museum home in the kibbutz of Sde Boker also confirm the exceptionally close relationship between South Africa and Israel during the early days of Israel's existence.

During the 1970s and 1980s but in contravention of the UN arms embargo, South Africa's armed forces were equipped with Israeli-built missiles and navy strikecraft. By 1983 exports of weapons to South Africa constituted ten per cent of Israel's exports.[6] In addition to collaboration on nuclear weapons, Israel and South Africa also jointly developed a range of unmanned aerial vehicles (UAVs) – drones – for surveillance purposes.

Sasha Polakow-Suransky's heavily documented book *The Unspoken Alliance*[7] published in 2010, prompted furious denials by Israeli President Shimon Peres. There were outraged criticisms that Israel was unfairly singled out for its nuclear collaboration with apartheid South Africa. True enough, the British and Americans also flouted the UN arms embargo.

If anything, Polakow-Suransky understates the relationship between Israel and South Africa. His thesis implies that the Israelis were the senior partner in a regrettable aberration born out of strategic necessity. In reality, it was South African money that funded what is now one of the world's major and most reckless armaments industries.

The study confirms what had long been known and revealed in detail by Peter Hounam and Steve McQuillan in their book *The Mini-Nuke Conspiracy*,[8] published in 1995. They recorded that Armscor's 'Hento' glide bomb was developed with European and American technology, and Israeli assistance.

A range of drones or pilotless aircraft was developed for search-and-destroy missions against enemy radar. There was another application. With little modification, the drones could be turned into a simple form of cruise missile and carry a nuclear device.

A model called the Lark, or sometimes the Skylark, had a range of four hundred kilometres. The system came with nine drones per truck and three trucks per system. Each drone was launched with a booster rocket, and then a propeller would take over. Once a target is identified, the drone attacks it by diving at a near-vertical angle. A twenty-two kilo barrel-shaped warhead is mounted in the nose just behind the seeker head.

There was also a faster six metre model called the Skua, with a range of eight hundred kilometres, and a payload of one hundred kilos – big enough for a compact nuclear device. It could fly at a height of forty thousand feet and, like the Lark, be launched from a transportable field station.

The US finally became alarmed in 1989, and intervened in 1995 to close down South Africa's nuclear weapons capacity. By then, South Africa was on the verge of producing intercontinental ballistic missiles capable of dropping nuclear weapons anywhere on earth. As Polakow-Suransky confirmed in a television interview:

> It was George H W Bush who started to crack down and eventually put an end to it. What happened in 1989 is that Soviet and US satellites picked up images of missiles being launched off the coast of South Africa from the Overberg testing range. The plume, the exhaust trail from these missiles, matched the Israeli Jericho exactly. Everyone in the US intelligence community immediately saw this as a signature of an Israeli system or a technology that had been transferred to South Africa, or that there had been such close cooperation that the technology was essentially identical.
>
> So, at this point, Bush reprimanded Israeli Prime Minister Yitzhak Shamir, because this was two years after Israel had imposed its own sanctions against South Africa. Israel had vowed to sign no new arms contracts in 1987 after the US government passed sanctions against South Africa and threatened to cut off military aid to any other country in the world that continued to sell arms to South Africa.[9]

I was in Washington at that time, during the banking sanctions campaign, and well remember the sanctimonious uproar amongst certain American officials and politicians that Israeli-South African collaboration violated the UN arms embargo.

The subsequent protracted court case in Philadelphia over Armscor's theft of state-of-the-art missile technology from International Signal Corporation (ISC) was eventually papered over in 1997 with plea bargains and a US$10 million fine. Reminiscent of the Matrix-Churchill case in England, ISC's chief executive James Guerin ineffectively pleaded that he had only acted with encouragement from his government. He was jailed for fifteen years.[10]

Hounam and McQuillan wrote:

> Guerin had to answer charges of conspiracy, mail fraud, securities fraud, violations of the Arms Export Act and the Comprehensive Anti-Apartheid Act, and laundering US$958 million through a network of Swiss and US bank accounts, using thirty-eight Panamanian and other front companies.
>
> Court evidence showed ISC was a front for sending advanced US computers and computer parts to South Africa, some of which ended up in Iraq and Iran whilst the two countries were at war. Federal investigators said South Africa was supplied with small sophisticated computers destined for the guidance systems of Israeli-built nuclear-capable inter-continental ballistic missiles and other weapons-related components.[11]

President F W de Klerk announced in 1993 that South Africa was abandoning its nuclear weapons capabilities, and that six crude bombs had been dismantled. As Hounam and McQuillan confirm, South Africa's nuclear weapons research and other programmes were far more advanced than officially admitted.

Collaboration with Israel continued until at least 1997 when Israeli Aircraft Industries refurbished and upgraded thirty-eight Kfir fighter aircraft, which the South African Air Force renamed as Cheetahs.[12] The Kfir aircraft were derivatives of French Mirage aircraft, and the programme was negotiated in 1988 in violation of the UN arms embargo.

Although thirty-eight aircraft were taken into operation, spare airframes and engines were included for an additional sixteen aircraft. The fifty-four aircraft were designed for an operational lifespan of a minimum of fifteen years. The Cheetah programme cost an estimated R2 billion in the mid-1990s, but perhaps as much as R20 billion at 2011 values was actually squandered.

South Africa thus had perfectly adequate, virtually new fighter aircraft in 1997 when the late Joe Modise and then Deputy President Thabo Mbeki embarked on the arms deal. Citing potentially embarrassing diplomatic repercussions, the ANC government decided that South Africa should not be dependent on Israeli military technology.

The department of defence was instructed to cease all military dealings with Israel. Amongst the projects then still ongoing were the maintenance contracts for the Cheetahs. The Israeli-supplied Cheetahs, many of them still in their original crates, were hawked around for sale to countries of South America. Eventually in 2010 Ecuador agreed to buy twelve of the aircraft for US$78.4 million, including spares and training.[13]

To replace the Cheetahs, Modise and Mbeki bought twenty-four BAE Hawk and twenty-eight BAE/Saab fighter aircraft purportedly for R17 billion, and overruled the air force generals who objected that these were both too expensive and unsuited to South Africa's needs. The BAE contracts accounted for more than half of the arms deal contracts.

Wild expenditure on armaments, rather than on protecting the apartheid state, had led instead to its bankruptcy. It is now also forgotten that the Israeli economy was on the verge of collapse during the 1980s, and that it was propped up by South African taxpayers, corporations and Jewish donations.

Squandering financial resources on madcap strategic projects such as nuclear weapons finally bankrupted South Africa. That bankruptcy, ironically, made possible the relatively peaceful transition from apartheid to democracy, of which the banking sanctions campaign proved to be the deciding factor. Diamonds were the ideal instrument for money laundering.

The annual value of South African diamond exports to Israel rose from US$400 million in 1974 to over US$3.2 billion by 1994,[14] and became the preferred means of payment. Polakow-Suransky confirms that exports of diamonds from South Africa to Israel were discounted by forty-five per cent and more via the financial rand system applied by the South African Reserve Bank's exchange control structures:

> This turned South Africa into 'a rough diamond nirvana' in the late 1980s because Israeli companies were able to buy rough diamonds at the massively discounted financial rand rate, and then earn windfall profits by selling the finished product abroad. Military elites, the South African Jewish community, and leading businessmen were all determined to maintain the alliance – sanctions be damned.[15]

In his exposé of Israel's nuclear weapons industry, *The Samson Option*, Seymour Hersch revealed:

> By the mid-1980s, the technicians at Dimona had manufactured hundreds of low-yield neutron warheads capable of destroying large numbers of enemy troops with minimal property damage. The size and sophistication of Israel's arsenal allows men such as Ariel Sharon to dream of redrawing the map of the Middle East aided by the implicit threat of nuclear force.
>
> In September 1988, Israel launched its first satellite into orbit, bringing it a huge step closer to intercontinental missiles and a satellite capability. Scientists at Dimona concluded that the rocket booster that launched the Israel satellite produced enough thrust to deliver a nuclear warhead to a target more than six thousand miles away.
>
> Israel has also been an exporter of nuclear technology, and has collaborated on nuclear weapons research with other nations, including South Africa. Israeli physicists are still at the cutting edge in weapons technology, and involved in intensive research into nuclear bomb-pumped x-ray lasers, hydrodynamics and radiation transport – the next generation of weaponry.[16]

Crucial factors in heavy Israeli militarisation are not solely due to hostility in neighbouring Arab states, and the consequent need for defence. The war business has become hugely profitable, financially as well as politically. It includes the propaganda emanating from Yad Vashem. I have visited the Holocaust Centre in Cape Town many times so the narrative is familiar, but the message conveyed is diametrically different.

The Holocaust during the Second World War undoubtedly ranks as the worst depravity in human history. That Germans, arguably then the world's most culturally advanced nation, could embark upon the obscenities of the Holocaust, illustrates how easily the war business brainwashes people and deliberately fans fear and paranoia.

As an exposition of war psychology, Yad Vashem is uniquely grotesque. Its emphasis on war and militarism is an essential contributor to the anxiety that pervades Israeli society. Schoolchildren are regularly brought for indoctrination in preparation for conscription into the military. For Goebbels and Hitler, one could substitute many of Israel's recent political leaders including Ariel Sharon, Avigdor Lieberman and Benjamin Netanyahu.

In contrast to the Cape Town Holocaust Centre, the message at Yad Vashem is not that of the Universal Declaration of Human Rights. That declaration flowed from universal revulsion of the bestiality of the Holocaust, and coincided in 1948 with the establishment of the state of Israel. Indeed, the very purpose of the United Nations itself is declared in the preamble of its Charter:

We the people of the United Nations determined

- To save succeeding generations from the scourge of war, which twice in our lifetime has brought untold sorrow to mankind, and
- To regain faith in fundamental human rights, in the dignity and worth of the human person, in the equal rights of men and women and of nations large and small, and
- To establish conditions under which justice and respect for the obligations arising from treaties and other sources of international law can be maintained, and
- To promote social progress and better standards of life in larger freedom, and for these ends
- To practice tolerance and live together in peace and with one another as good neighbours, and
- To unite our strength to maintain international peace and security, and
- To ensure, by acceptance of principles and the institution of methods, that armed force shall not be used, save in the common interest, and

- To employ international machinery for the promotion of the economic and social advancement of all people.

Instead of commitment to peace, Jews are portrayed at Yad Vashem as repeated victims of history whose survival can only be ensured in a Zionist state. One wants to scream that one understands the pain and the trauma of the Holocaust but that, given their history, Israelis should know better than to inflict brutal treatment upon Palestinians. The ghetto walls in Warsaw are today repeated in the 'apartheid wall', and the deliberate starvation of people in Lodz is eclipsed by the starvation of people in Gaza.

One leaves the museum mentally battered and angry, but one has gained insights into how Germans were brainwashed to support the Nazis, how white South Africans were brainwashed to support apartheid and, indeed, why Americans blunder from one war to the next.

Yad Vashem is an extraordinary perversion where the treatment of Palestinians is justified according to the treatment of Jews by Nazi Germany. It arrogates the bestiality of the Holocaust as a Jewish experience that entitles Israel to plead 'self-defence' and to scream about anti-Semitism whenever its army and soldiers flout international law.

Mark Braverman, a Jewish-American clinical psychologist, in his book *Fatal Embrace* describes his reaction:[17]

> It is a brilliant exhibition. One walks down, into it. It is subterranean – no windows, no light, no escape. You are led through corridors and tunnels, with no control and no way out but through. One traverses the whole, familiar story: from the laws enacted in the 1930s, the walls of isolation, privation and the degradation closing in, to the Final Solution: the ovens, the stacked bodies, the faces of the children. Darkness closes your heart – you feel you will never escape from this horror, this black hole of evil and despair. Then, turning the corner into the final gallery, on display are the blown-up photos of ships bringing the refugees to the shores of Israel, faces shining with hope and gratitude.
>
> There is David Ben-Gurion reading from the Declaration of Independence. And then, suddenly, you emerge. Ascending a wide flight of stairs, you are outside, in the light and the open air, standing on a wide patio that looks

out on the Jerusalem Hills. It is the final exhibit ... and the lesson that the Holocaust must not be compared with any other disaster, crime or genocide. Here is the most terrible irony – that Yad Vashem is built on top of these hills of West Jerusalem, hills littered with the remains of Palestinian villages. Some have been turned into parks. Most are ruins, stones bleaching in the sun, standing guard over uncultivated terraces of olives and grapes, witnesses to shattered lives and a murdered civilisation.

Just hours later that very evening, still mentally bruised and pondering the implications of Yad Vashem, I attended the launch in December 2009 in Bethlehem of the Kairos Palestine document. As a signatory to the South African Kairos document in 1985, I had been invited to represent the South African Council of Churches. In a taped video message to open the event, Archbishop Desmond Tutu declared:

> My dear Palestinian brothers and sisters, and gathered friends. We are reminded by Holy Scripture that when one part of the body suffers, we all suffer. Solidarity with you in your suffering is therefore not a theoretical matter for those of us in the Church, but is a concrete expression of the deep unity we have in Christ Jesus, in his body.
>
> During our struggle in South Africa, we were assured of your solidarity, and we now stand with you not only in your hour of pain and suffering but also in this moment of victory. Your faith, hope and love compel you in the knowledge that the God of the Bible is on your side and will bring you the freedom and justice you long for.
>
> You are in my prayers as you launch this very special document. It is filled with grace, where it could be filled with anger. It is filled with profound and prophetic words that our God will hear your cry.

Both Israelis and Palestinians look expectantly to the South African experience in somehow, almost miraculously, finding non-violent alternatives to the violent oppression of the apartheid era. The parallels between Zionism and apartheid are glaring, including the misuse of religion.

South Africa now observes Reconciliation Day, a holiday known during the apartheid era as Day of the Covenant. It commemorated the Battle of Blood River in 1837 when, purportedly, God gave victory to the Boers over the Zulus and instituted a 'covenant' whereby Boers (Afrikaners) were God's chosen people to bring Christianity and civilisation to Africa. Jews are not the only people who believe themselves to have been specially chosen.

The Boers were later defeated in the Anglo-Boer War when twenty-six thousand Boer women and children died in British concentration camps.[18] The resultant hatred and animosity between Boer and Brit festered, were not addressed and became the rationale for the subsequent obscenity of apartheid. The hearings of the Truth and Reconciliation Commission highlighted how victims of human rights abuses in one generation so easily became the perpetrators in the next generation.

The Lutheran Christmas Church as the venue for the launch of the Kairos Palestine document was itself highly significant. It was heavily damaged during the Israeli army's siege of Bethlehem in April 2002, but has since been repaired and refurbished. The pastor of the Church, the Reverend Mitri Raheb and his family were awakened in the early hours one morning, and learned that the Israeli military had invaded Bethlehem. Raheb writes:

> We'd expected the invasion. Israel had already invaded most of the Palestinian towns and villages. For the last two days, Israeli tanks had been gathering at the checkpoint leading to Bethlehem. But we hadn't expected such a massive operation. There was no reason to invade our little town with hundreds of military tanks and armoured vehicles, accompanied by Apache helicopters.
>
> The excuse Israel used for invading Bethlehem was a suicide bombing a few days earlier in Jerusalem by a young Palestinian woman from Deheishe refugee camp near Bethlehem. The blast killed Ayat al-Akhras and two Israeli people, and injured two dozen more.
>
> The decision to invade, however, had been made weeks before. Before the suicide bombing, Prime Minister Ariel Sharon had already launched his military offensive called Operation Defensive Shield, and Israeli forces were already rolling into Ramallah and had besieged President Yasir Arafat in his headquarters.[19]

Operation Defensive Shield illustrates intentional and long-standing (but illegal in terms of international rules of war) Israeli policies of disproportionate retaliation to any provocation. In vain efforts to defend their city, Bethlehem, some men shot back with rifles against the helicopters and tanks. The fighting that first day lasted for thirteen hours.

Overpowered, about two hundred men retreated to Manger Square and, with other terrified residents, sought sanctuary in the nearby Church of the Nativity. Those seeking refuge, and the sixty monks who welcomed them, assumed that Israeli forces would respect the sanctity of the Church and its historical significance as the birthplace of Jesus.

Instead, it marked the beginning of the thirty-nine day siege of the Church of the Nativity. Israeli troops surrounded the Church and took over the International Peace Centre in Manger Square as their command post. Television viewers were, however, assured that the Israeli army was taking unprecedented measures to avoid bloodshed and damage to buildings.

In fact, laser beams and motion-sensitive automatic guns were attached to cranes, and monitored all movements inside the Church. As bullet-scarred masonry still attests, there were many gun battles. Sound bombs were also used to scare people.

The propaganda war in the world's media was intense.[20] Sharon declared: 'Palestinian murderers have commandeered the Church, and are holding the clergymen hostage.' Palestinians argued that the purpose of invading Bethlehem was to 'destroy the Palestinian Authority and to reassert Israeli control over Palestinian territories'.[21]

No one was allowed access to food, water or medicines. The occupants were eventually starved out, reduced to soup made from the leaves of lemon trees and grass. Eight young men were killed inside the Church over the period of the mayhem, including a mentally retarded bell-ringer, and twenty-two others were wounded. Israeli officials claimed that all the dead men except the bell-ringer were terrorists.[22]

International negotiations to end the siege were protracted, and involved the Vatican and the CIA. Palestinian fighters were exiled to Europe and Cyprus, or banished to Gaza, but strict curfews in Bethlehem continued for nearly ten more weeks.

Thus, the Kairos Palestine document states:

We Palestinian Christians declare that the military occupation of our land is a sin against God and humanity, and that any theology that legitimises the occupation is far from Christian teachings because the true Christian theology is a theology of love and solidarity with the oppressed, a call to justice and equality among peoples.[23]

The document continues:

Our word to the international community is to stop the principle of 'double standards', and to insist on the international resolutions regarding the Palestinian problem with regard to all parties. We call for ... a system of economic sanctions and boycott to be applied against Israel. We repeat again that this is not revenge but rather a serious action to reach a just and definitive peace that will put an end to Israeli occupation of Palestinian and other Arab territories, and will guarantee security and peace for all.

It concludes:

In the absence of all hope, we cry out our cry of hope. We believe in God, good and just. We believe that God's goodness will finally triumph over the evil of hate and death that still persist in our land. We will see here 'a new land' and 'a new human being', capable of rising up in the spirit to love each other of his or her brothers or sisters.

The Kairos Palestine document has garnered support from all over the world. The document also challenges those Christian theologians who provide theological and biblical legitimacy to infringements of Palestinian rights, and notes that the West has sought to make amends for what Jews endured in Europe but, in trying to correct an injustice, the result was a new injustice.

Just days later, an arrest warrant was issued in Britain against Tzipi Livni for war crimes. She was Israel's foreign minister during Operation Cast Lead, and is now leader of the Kadima opposition party. There was apoplexy amongst Israeli government spokespersons that someone of Livni's status could be subjected to such outrageous indignities because of 'absurd' and 'peculiar' British commitments to act against perpetrators of war crimes.

By contrast, a former MP from the liberal Meretz party, Zahava Galon, said the arrest warrant should be a warning to Israeli decision makers: 'Before they embark on military adventures, Israeli cabinet ministers should know what the consequences may be at the international level.' As the controversy raged, and suggesting that the international community is increasingly tired of excusing Israeli transgressions of human rights, Sir Geoffrey Bindman, the chairman of the British Institute of Human Rights, noted:

> War crimes and crimes against humanity are international crimes transcending national boundaries. Universal jurisdiction to put those accused of them on trial is a logical development of that recognition. Such crimes are unlikely to be redressed in the country where the perpetrators hold political power. If they are not, they can only be adjudicated in courts of another state, or in an international court or tribunal.
>
> Since the Second World War there has been a steady expansion of legal mechanisms designed to ensure that there is no hiding place for the perpetrators of international crimes. In complying with UN treaties such as the Geneva Conventions, many countries, including the UK, give their courts the jurisdiction to try specific crimes committed outside their own territory.[24]

Political commentators believe the siege and bombardment of Gaza to have been the Israeli government's worst diplomatic, humanitarian and military blunder. Television broadcasts around the world documented the ferocity of the three-week onslaught, but Operation Cast Lead also exposed the complicity of the US government. Just as the Bush administration in 2006 had actively supported Israel's bombardment of Lebanon so, in its waning days, it colluded in the bombardment of Gaza.

Operation Cast Lead killed about one thousand and four hundred Gazans, destroyed about three thousand, three hundred and fifty homes, hospitals, ambulances, mosques, schools, a flour factory and sewage treatment facilities. A UN warehouse was gutted by fire set off by a white phosphorus bomb. Despite blatant violations of the so-called 'rules of war', the operation actually failed dismally in its primary aim of regime change in Gaza, to remove Hamas from power although it had won a free and fair election in January 2006.

In an essay entitled 'Exterminate All The Brutes: Gaza 2009', Noam Chomsky wrote:

> On Saturday, December 28, 2008, the latest US-Israeli attack on helpless Palestinians was launched. The attack had been meticulously planned for over six months, according to the Israeli press. The planning had two components; military and propaganda. It was based on the lessons of Israel's 2006 invasion of Lebanon, which was considered to have been poorly planned and badly advertised. We may, therefore, be fairly confident that most of what has been done and said was pre-planned and intended.
>
> That surely includes the timing of the assault: shortly before noon, when children were returning from school and crowds were milling in the streets of densely populated Gaza City. It took only a few minutes to kill over two hundred people and wound seven hundred, an auspicious opening to the mass slaughter of defenceless civilians trapped in a tiny cage with nowhere to flee.[25]

The Goldstone Report recommended to the UN Security Council that Israel and Hamas must both launch appropriate investigations, and the Prosecutor of the International Criminal Court (ICC) declared 'that accountability for victims and in the interests of peace and justice in the region require a legal determination that should be made as expeditiously as possible'.[26]

Judge Richard Goldstone, a Jew with admitted Zionist sympathies and a patron of the Cape Town Holocaust Centre, declared himself to have been appalled and embarrassed by the behaviour of the Israeli army. The UN-sponsored report accuses both Israelis and Palestinians of having resorted to war crimes, but concludes that Israel's actions were totally 'disproportionate'.

That Israel survives international censure at the UN and elsewhere is due to lavish financial assistance most especially from the US. Its 'defence' budget for 2010 was NIS 60 billion (US$16 billion), which included a NIS 10 billion contribution from American taxpayers.

Illustrative of the vehemence of the American Israeli lobby to any criticisms of Israeli military excesses, Professor Alan Dershowitz of Harvard University lambasted the Goldstone Report as 'a defamation written by an evil, evil man, who was a traitor to the Jewish people'. Similarly, the US

House of Representatives had apoplexy and in November 2009 condemned the Report as 'anti-Semitic'. It declared that accusations of Israeli war crimes were 'irredeemably biased and unworthy of further consideration or legitimacy'.[27]

In 2006 two American academics, John Mearsheimer and Stephen Walt, caused uproar when they published a critical essay entitled 'The Israel Lobby'. They declared:

> For the past several decades, and especially since the Six-Day War in 1967, the centrepiece of US Middle Eastern policy has been its relationship with Israel. The combination of unwavering support for Israel and the related effort to spread 'democracy' throughout the region has inflamed Arab and Islamic opinion and jeopardised not only US security but that of much of the rest of the world.
>
> Since the October War in 1973, Washington has provided Israel with a level of support dwarfing that given to any other state. It has been the largest annual recipient of direct economic and military assistance since 1976, and is the largest recipient in total since World War Two, to the tune of well over $140 billion (in 2004 dollars). Israel receives about $3 billion in direct assistance each year, roughly one-fifth of the foreign aid budget, and worth about $500 a year for every Israeli. This largesse is especially striking since Israel is now a wealthy industrial state with a per capita income roughly equal to that of South Korea or Spain.
>
> Most recipients of aid given for military purposes are required to spend all of it in the US, but Israel is allowed to use roughly one quarter of its allocation to subsidise its own defence industry. It is the only recipient that does not have to account for how the aid is spent, which makes it virtually impossible to prevent the money from being used for purposes the US opposes, such as building settlements on the West Bank. Moreover, the US has provided Israel with nearly $3 billion to develop weapons systems, and given it access to such top-drawer weaponry as Blackhawk helicopters and F-16 jets. Finally, the US gives Israel access to intelligence it denies to its NATO allies and has turned a blind eye to Israel's acquisition of nuclear weapons.[28]

Just months after that essay was published, Vice President Dick Cheney met Israeli officials in June 2006 to assure them of full backing by the United

States for invasions of Lebanon and Gaza as preliminary to an attack against Iran.[29] The thirty-four day war in Lebanon killed about one thousand, two hundred people, and caused massive structural damage.

An organisation of courageous Israeli soldiers called Breaking The Silence has confirmed the repeated barbarities of Israeli army operations in Hebron, Gaza and elsewhere. The organisation's purpose is to promote awareness amongst Israelis about the moral consequences of the Occupation.

To the embarrassment and increasing anger of the government, it argues that the Israeli army is neither trained nor operationally equipped for the Occupation. In Gaza, houses and mosques were destroyed for no military purpose, and phosphorus gas was fired into populated districts. Most appallingly, officers had deliberately encouraged their troops during Operation Cast Lead to act without moral restrictions.

Only two and a half kilometres from Gaza, huge amounts of money have been poured into the small town of Sderot to build bomb shelters at every corner and in every household. Rockets fired from Gaza at Sderot were the ostensible justification for Operation Cast Lead. I met Nomika Zion[30] in December 2009. She told our group:

> We conduct life in Israel from war to war, and pollute our hearts and mind. It needs a lot of courage in Sderot and Israel to express opposition to war. We have lost the ability to empathise with the other side. We have lost our humanity, and have become a dangerous and violent society. We were traumatised by the rockets, but it was nothing compared to what the people in Gaza are suffering.
>
> The rockets were so inaccurate that only about a dozen people in Sderot were in fact killed in all the years. Some days there were three rockets; other days there were fifty or sixty. The main effect was the trauma, but the rockets themselves did not cause major damage.
>
> We petitioned the government in November 2008 to resolve the problem through non-violence. We emphasised the importance of the June 2008 ceasefire negotiated with Hamas, and begged the government to talk to the Arabs. A meeting was scheduled with the Defence Minister, but he cancelled it. The war started four days later.
>
> I believe that violence begets violence. Hamas is an extremist organisation,

but it is also a practical organisation. I believe that you must make agreements with your enemies. Splits amongst Palestinians make negotiations difficult, but then the Israeli government has deliberately split the Palestinian leadership.

Nomika and a small group of Sderot residents have established an organisation they call The Other Voice, and she regularly briefs international visitors on the traumatic realities of living in a war zone.

I was in Israel and Palestine during October 2009 until January 2010 as a member of the World Council of Churches' Ecumenical Accompaniment Programme for Palestine and Israel (EAPPI). We were team of twenty-five people from ten countries, three of us being from South Africa.

EAPPI was established in 2002 following Operation Defensive Shield and the Bethlehem siege. Its mission is to accompany Palestinians and Israelis in non-violent actions to end the Occupation of Palestine, and to monitor human rights abuses. The guiding principle is 'principled impartiality', meaning that whilst EAPPI does not take sides in the conflict, it is not neutral in standing faithfully with the oppressed and marginalised.

EAPPI maintains six placements in Palestine, in East Jerusalem, Bethlehem, Hebron, Tulkarm, Jayyous and Yanoun. I was assigned to East Jerusalem and, with team mates from England, Brazil, France and Sweden, stayed at the Augusta-Victoria Hospital on the Mount of Olives overlooking the city.

We were issued distinctive flak-jackets as identification, emblazoned with EAPPI and World Council of Churches, and learned that EAs are referred to by Palestinians and Israelis as 'the vests'.

On Fridays we stood with the feisty, but now elderly, Women In Black who, since 1987, have held weekly vigils in West Jerusalem. They hold black-painted posters shaped like stop signs that read in Hebrew, Arabic and English: 'Stop The Occupation'. Some Israelis nod approval and cheer, others heckle. A taxi driver spat at me during the first vigil in which I participated and yelled: 'What occupation?'

Our duties during the three-month assignment included monitoring the Qalandiya checkpoint between Jerusalem and Ramallah. Three mornings a week, we watched and counted how many people passed through the cages and turnstiles. The statistics were collated into weekly reports for the UN, but our function primarily was to be a calming influence and to assure Palestinians that the world was watching.

Perhaps, also, we hoped even the gun-toting soldiers would moderate their behaviour in the knowledge that foreigners were watching. Female Israeli soldiers, we noted, were often far more arrogant and abusive than their male companions.

Pushing and shoving at the checkpoint is often such that tempers boil over. Should they be late for work, the men may lose their pay, or even their jobs – hence the tensions. We would sometimes intervene with Israeli soldiers and private security guards to speed up the process, or to plead with them that the 'humanitarian gate' should be opened to allow women, schoolchildren, old men and wheelchair cases to pass through a side gate rather than through the cages.

The soldiers and guards are visibly bored, but also terrified. They have been inculcated by propaganda that Palestinians are just itching for an opportunity to slit their throats, or else to carry a bomb on to a bus to kill Jewish civilians in Jerusalem. The reality is that components for bombs are far more readily available within Israel itself than in the West Bank.

About twenty people at a time are, typically, allowed through the cages before the supervising soldier, at the press of a button on a console inside his or her bullet-proof glass guard box, suddenly locks the turnstile. The immediate impression is that these unfortunate people are being herded and treated like animals.

The next stage is the metal detector screening. Belts, wallets, cellphones, keys have to be removed, as at airports. Green IDs or Blue IDs determine the lives of Palestinians. Blue IDs indicate permanent residency and the right to work in Jerusalem, but not Israeli citizenship. The blue IDs are also frequently and capriciously revoked. Green IDs denote Palestinians from the West Bank, who have no right to be in Jerusalem unless they can produce work permits.

The checkpoints operate from five o'clock in the morning until seven o'clock at night. Soldiers and guards are separated from the Palestinians either by heavy fences or bullet-proof glass. Instructions are barked over an intercom system. There is no sensitivity to the conservative culture or behavioural norms of Palestinian men and women.

Biometric handprints are compared with those recorded on the ID, and confirm when and at which checkpoint the person last left Israel. Manual labourers often have cement or dirt on their hands, which frequently distorts the images.

A man who is refused passage through the checkpoint must then push his way back against the jostling crowd in one of the cages. It means no pay that day, or even for three weeks until his handprints have been retaken, and by then he may have lost his job. There are thousands more equally desperate for work, and black market scams exploit such miseries.

Qalandiya is a dirty place with litter strewn everywhere, and in winter before dawn it is often bitterly cold. As the main entry point into Jerusalem from Ramallah, the traffic of trucks and buses is chaotic. The ugly, concrete walls are nine metres high and daubed with graffiti about 'Free Palestine'. They are topped by three-metre watch towers that further accentuate the sense of gulag.

Instead of security, Qalandiya is plainly intended to humiliate Palestinians and, equally important, its purpose is to engender a sense of militarised fear amongst Israelis. The clearly intended message: Palestinians are a people under Israeli military subjugation and occupation.

Endnotes

1. Ken Owen: *Sunday Times*, June 25, 1995.
2. Sasha Polakow-Suransky: *The Unspoken Alliance: Israel's Secret Relationship With Apartheid South Africa*, Jacana, Johannesburg, 2010, p 105.
3. Israel Shahak: *Open Secrets: Israeli Nuclear And Foreign Policies*, Pluto Press, London, 1997, pp 48-51.
4. Ethan Bonner: 'Israel Gauges A Conflicted Partner', *The New York Times*, January 30, 2011.
5. Seymour M Hersch: *The Samson Option: Israel's Nuclear Arsenal and American Foreign Policy*, Random House, New York, 1991, p 12.
6. Na'eem Jeenah: 'Israeli infiltration in South Africa', Afro-Middle East Centre, Johannesburg, January 2010.
7. Sasha Polakow-Suransky: *The Unspoken Alliance: Israel's Secret Relationship With Apartheid South Africa*, Jacana, Johannesburg, 2010.
8. Peter Hounam and Steve McQuillan: *The Mini-Nuke Conspiracy*, Faber and Faber, London, 1995, Ch 20.
9. Amy Goodman interview with Sasha Polakow-Suransky, New Democracy television channel, May 25, 2010.
10. Kenneth R Timmerman: *The Death Lobby: How The West Armed Iraq*, Bantam Books, New York, 1992, pp 224-230.
11. Peter Hounam and Steve McQuillan: *The Mini-Nuke Conspiracy*, Faber and Faber, London, 1995, pp 219 and 220.
12. Leon Engelbrecht: 'Denel Hopes Ecuador Cheetah Buy Will Be Complete By Year-End', DefenceWeb, October 8, 2009.
13. Defence Web: 'Denel to help phase out Cheetah', January 31, 2011.
14. Na'eem Jeenah: 'Israeli Infiltration in South Africa', Afro-Middle East Centre, Johannesburg, January 2010.
15. Sasha Polakow-Suransky: *The Unspoken Alliance: Israel's Secret Relationship With Apartheid South Africa*, Jacana, Johannesburg, 2010, p 205.
16. Seymour M Hersh: *The Samson Option: Israel's Nuclear Arsenal and American Foreign Policy*, Random House, New York, 1991, p 319.
17. Mark Braverman: *Fatal Embrace, Christians, Jews And The Search For Peace In The Holy Land*, Synergy Books, Austin, Texas, 2010, pp 38 and 39.
18. The number of Africans who also died in the War has recently been estimated to have exceeded 26 000 people.

19. Mitri Raheb: *Bethlehem Besieged*, Fortress Press, Minneapolis, 2004, pp 3-4.
20. Frontline television: 'The Siege of Bethlehem', PBS, New York.
21. Cameron W Barr: 'Two sides, two stories, one church', *Christian Science Monitor*, April 9, 2002.
22. 'Inside the siege of Bethlehem', *Newsweek*, May 20, 2002.
23. 'Kairos Palestine 2009 – A Moment of Truth, a word of faith, hope and love from the heart of the Palestinian suffering', Bethlehem, December 2009.
24. Ben Lynfield: 'Israel furious at Livni arrest warrant', *The Independent*, December 16, 2009.
25. Noam Chomsky: 'Exterminate All The Brutes: Gaza 2009', www.chomsky. info, January 19, 2009.
26. Paragraph 1767 of the Goldstone Report.
27. Natasha Mozgovaya and Barak Ravid: 'US House backs resolution to condemn Goldstone Gaza report', *Haaretz*, November 11, 2009.
28. John Mearsheimer and Stephen Walt: 'The Israel Lobby', *London Review Of Books*, Vol 28, no 6, March 23, 2006, pp 3-12.
29. Seymour M Hersch: 'US involved in planning Israel's operations in Lebanon', *The New Yorker*, August 13, 2006.
30. Nomika Zion was the author of the award-winning blog 'Diary From Sderot,' published by Huffington Post, January 15, 2009.

5 • ALL DIAMONDS ARE 'BLOOD DIAMONDS'

The late Queen Elizabeth, the 'Queen Mum', had a voracious passion for diamonds that bordered on theft. Discreet suggestions would be conveyed to unfortunate owners that the Queen had admired a particular item which she would be graciously pleased to receive as a gift.

Dame Margaret Greville in 1942 most generously bequeathed most of her magnificent collection of diamonds and emeralds to her. With Dame Margaret having been the heiress to a British brewery fortune, King George VI apparently objected ineffectually that it was inappropriate for royalty to accept such a gift from a commoner. The Greville Collection was then valued at over £1 million. When the Queen Mum died in 2002, at the age of one hundred and one, her private jewellery collection was estimated to be worth about £50 million.[1] Many of the Greville jewels have since been passed on to Camilla, Prince Charles's long-time mistress who is now the Duchess of Cornwall.

So when the then Princess Elizabeth was invited with the British royal family to celebrate her twenty-first birthday in South Africa in 1947, Prime Minister Jan Smuts and Sir Ernest Oppenheimer made sure that she was presented with a 'notable' stone for the occasion. When she and Prince Philip were married in November that year she, of course, was suitably bejewelled in diamonds.

De Beers unashamedly employed both Queen Elizabeths and Marilyn Monroe as the cartel's best salesladies to promote perceptions in England and America that diamonds are an essential part of every girl's love life. Monroe's song 'Diamonds Are A Girl's Best Friend' has been ranked as the twelfth most influential song from a movie.

The royal family's passion for diamonds continues in the younger generations. Princess Diana's eighteen carat sapphire and diamond engagement ring, bought from Garrard Jewellers in London in 1981 for £28 000, on the former Kate Middleton's finger is now described as 'priceless'. And Middleton, meanwhile, has been 'elevated' to Her Royal Highness the Duchess of Cambridge!

What girl would want a 'cheap' diamond? The myth that diamonds are valuable investments is exploded by experiences of anyone who has tried to sell a diamond. The De Beers marketing strategies have been brilliant. The cartel cultivated an image that diamonds encompassed timeless, stellar scarcity. An advertising agency in New York in 1947 came up with what has been described as the greatest advertising slogan of the twentieth century: 'a diamond is forever'.[2]

Instead of romance, the strategic importance of industrial diamonds to thwart evil intentions to hold the world to ransom by nuclear war was the theme of the 1971 James Bond film 'Diamonds Are Forever'. The conspiracy of the 'bad guys' involved a massive quantity of diamonds stolen in South Africa and smuggled to Nevada to be used in laser technology.

Looting has always formed part of the history of diamonds. No one will ever know the full extent of the jewellery that was looted during the Second World War in territories occupied by Nazi Germany. Sales in Switzerland of confiscated gem diamonds alleviated Nazi Germany's chronic shortages of foreign exchange, and supplies of industrial diamonds were essential for the war industries.

A confiscation order in Germany in February 1939 required all Jews within two weeks 'to deliver all objects in their possession made of gold, silver, platinum, precious stones and pearls'. A special collection agency, the Zentralstelle, was established, its task being to convert these into foreign currency and gold reserves critical to the war economy.[3]

Armaments production that needed industrial diamonds included artillery shells, wire and thousands of metal working applications. Yet diamond mines in South Africa were closed for the duration of the war.

Edward Jay Epstein writes:

> Without a continuing supply of diamonds, the war machine would rapidly slow to a halt. Yet nearly all the diamond mines remained closed, and De Beers controlled the world supply. Obtaining these industrial diamonds became a paramount objective for both the United States and Hitler's Germany.
>
> President Franklin Roosevelt ordered the War Production Board, which had the responsibility for mobilising the American economy for war, to buy the necessary six and a half million carats from De Beers.
>
> De Beers had other interests to consider. Its entire system of monopolising diamonds depended on controlling the available stockpile. Oppenheimer argued that if the US had its own stockpile and the war suddenly ended, it might release the diamonds and thus undercut the entire world order that he had so laboriously constructed.[4]

The British government backed De Beers, and a compromise was eventually reached to stockpile the diamonds in Canada. Even decades later, American officials still remain bitter about the cartel's behaviour. Without industrial diamonds the German war effort, including production of V2 rockets which were directed at London, would have collapsed. Germany annually required up to two million carats of industrial diamonds, and somehow maintained sufficient stocks to last the war.

Epstein also records that the US Department of Justice alleged that the diamonds that reached Germany through Belgium originated in the Congo, and were supplied with the complicity of De Beers. Selling to and trading with both sides during wartime is one of the features of the war business.

Those allegations also imply that the Holocaust and the deaths of millions of European Jews and others might have been averted but for sales of industrial diamonds by De Beers to Germany which thereby prolonged the war. After 1945, however, there was no political will in Washington to investigate the matter and thus risk antagonising the British government. The US investigation into De Beers only resumed in the 1990s in terms of anti-trust laws.

South Africa and South West Africa (now Namibia), were the only places in the world where, without a permit, it was actually illegal to possess an uncut diamond. Penalties for illicit diamond buying (IDB) were severe, sometimes even resulting in death. Until the collapse of apartheid and South Africa's transition to democracy, the economies of both countries were controlled by Anglo American Corporation of South Africa Limited, and run primarily for the benefit of the Oppenheimer family and its political cronies.[5]

The 'diamond coast' is a six-hour drive north from Cape Town, but for eighty years was off-limits to both South Africans and foreigners. Mine dumps at Kleinzee reach hundreds of metres into the air, and the desolation is such that the area looks as if a nuclear bomb had been dropped.[6] Diamonds theoretically worth trillions of dollars are scattered along the beaches and offshore under the cold currents of the Atlantic Ocean.

The source of these diamonds is almost three thousand kilometres away in the mountains of Lesotho. The tumbling of diamonds along the course of the Orange River means that the stones recovered along the West Coast are usually (but not always) considerably smaller, but also less flawed than the big stones from either the Premier Mine or Lesotho. They are however, also considerably more abundant, and over ninety per cent are gem quality.[7]

It is recorded that when the geologist Hans Merensky discovered diamonds at Alexander Bay in 1926, he found four hundred and eighty-seven diamonds under just one stone. He sold his prospector's claim for over £1 million to Oppenheimer[8] and, to prevent the diamond market from collapsing because of overproduction, Merensky recommended government intervention.

Just sixty years after discoveries in Kimberley, diamonds were suddenly no longer a rarity associated with royalty and the ultra-wealthy, but had been found in super-abundance. Prospecting was prohibited, and the state took complete control of the area. A state-owned company was established to withhold the stones from the market, to prevent them from compounding the existing glut of diamonds.

The area known as the Richtersveld is perhaps the harshest and most inhospitable part of South Africa. It was annexed to the Cape Colony in 1847, but for eighty years was regarded by successive governments as 'waste and vacant'. It is exceedingly dry, and exceedingly mountainous. Despite its spectacular scenery on the banks of the Orange River, until the discovery of diamonds the area was of no economic interest to either white settlers or the government. Then in 1928 the 'state alluvial diggings' were proclaimed as a state-run public works programme for 'poor whites' in Namaqualand. That situation continued until 1989 when subsidies were withdrawn.

Corruption, theft and economic mismanagement characterised the diamond industry around Alexander Bay right from inception. Given the wealth upon which it is based, the mine quite extraordinarily operated at massive losses throughout its history. Alexkor became a case study example of the apartheid era's managerial incompetence and greed.[9]

Meanwhile, back in the 1960s, a Texan oilman named Sam Collins used barges equipped with giant vacuum cleaners and airlift pumping systems to recover diamonds from the shallow depths at the mouth of the Orange River. His research revealed that ten billion carats of diamonds had been released by soil erosion over a one hundred million year period from the numerous kimberlite pipes in southern Africa.

An estimated three billion carats survived riverine transportation to the coast, of which only one hundred and fifty million carats have been mined in Namibia and the Northern Cape over the past century.[10] De Beers bought out Collins's operations in 1970, and subsequently expanded them into De Beers Marine Diamond Corporation (Debmar). Enormous mining and processing plants disguised as ships are built to recover the diamonds.

Special drill bits seven metres wide drill into the ocean floor to release a mixture of diamonds and ore. This mixture is then sucked up one hundred to one hundred and fifty metres to the surface, where machines separate the diamonds from the waste materials and store the diamonds in sealed aluminium containers.

For security reasons, no human comes into contact with the diamonds during the entire process. Working non-stop every day of the year, the ships annually cover two square kilometres of the ocean bed. No patch is left untouched by this giant vacuuming operation.[11] These offshore deposits remain potentially the world's major source of diamonds in the twenty-first century as the difficulties and expense of recovering them are resolved. It is thus an ideal operation for De Beers to transfer wealth out of Africa to Europe or America.

This massive abundance north of Cape Town totally destroys the carefully crafted myth that diamonds are a rare and precious commodity. South Africa has dominated world gold and diamond mining for more than a century, yet has almost no jewellery manufacturing industry.

In the one hundred and fifty years since they were discovered at Kimberley, diamonds have brought minimal economic benefits, or job creation opportunities, to indigenous populations in South Africa, Namibia or Botswana.[12] About ninety-seven per cent of production has been exported 'in the rough' for cutting and polishing in Belgium, Israel or India.

The value-added and job benefits in the diamond trade are in the cutting and polishing processes. As the world's major diamond producer, it is logical that South Africa should also be a major cutting and polishing centre. De Beers blocked that prospect whenever questions were raised, and offered various limp excuses, from the lack of skilled artisans to the increased risk of thefts and, perennially, that labour costs in South Africa are too high.

The reality has been that with the apartheid government's complicity, De Beers was able to mine and to export almost all its production as it saw fit and, through its London office, to transfer the profits overseas. Israel, by contrast, has not a single diamond mine, but its diamond industry is the foundation of the country's economy.

The diamond industry, stripped of its glamorous image and pseudo-sophistication, has been the ultimate con-deal and a financial vehicle for legitimated, organised crime. The myths that the apartheid government and its corporate allies were relatively free from corruption were exploded by Hennie van Vuuren's report 'Apartheid Grand Corruption' published in 2006 by the Institute for Security Studies.

That report also revealed the corruption and human rights abuses that prevailed in Namibia just across the Orange River. Oranjemund, the De Beers company town on the Namibian side of the border and home to eleven thousand residents, is still closed to strangers. The town was established in 1936, and the nearby beaches were literally stripped of diamonds in massive earth-moving operations by reputedly the world's second largest fleet of bulldozers. Ovambo mineworkers, contracted under the migrant labour system, were brought from the far north of the country and housed in degrading conditions in single-sex compounds.

Security arrangements, adapted from Kimberley back in the 1880s, included stripping naked the workers for communal inspection of their anuses and other orifices for secreted diamonds. Ignoring the terms of the League of Nations mandate and the subsequent transfer of jurisdiction to the United Nations (UN) after the Second World War, the government simply treated Namibia as a fifth province of South Africa. The General Assembly in 1966 declared the League mandate to have been terminated, and in 1971 the International Court of Justice ruled that South Africa's continuing presence in the territory was illegal. UN Resolution 435 in 1978 set the framework for independence, which Namibia finally achieved in 1990.

More than two decades of war in Namibia and Angola had devastating consequences in which an estimated one and a half million people died. The Kumleben Report in 1996 exposed the environmental plunder by the South African Defence Force (SADF) during the 'war on the border'.

One key allegation was that the SADF from the mid-1970s covertly slaughtered and destroyed elephant herds and rhinos, and was involved in the sale and export of both ivory and rhino horn. Compounding the scandal, these operations were authorised and encouraged by government ministers. Jonas Savimbi acknowledged that the SADF provided aid to Unita in Angola, but declared: 'We pay for aid with our diamonds, timber and ivory.' The report continued:

> Savimbi claimed an annual income of US$60 million from diamonds, but SADF sources said that the quantity of diamonds was considerably higher.

No estimate of the quantities of hardwoods is available, but the south of Angola is now severely deforested. Unita still smuggles these commodities out of Angola, but diamonds predominate and go directly to Johannesburg.

It is estimated that between 1975 and 1993 about one hundred thousand elephants were killed for their tusks, and the inquiry established that one hundred and ninety two tons of ivory was smuggled into South Africa and then legally exported.[13]

A decade earlier, in 1985, the Thirion Commission issued a scathing three hundred and fifty-page report about De Beers's subsidiary in Namibia, Consolidated Diamond Mines (CDM). Judge Pieter Thirion found that CDM had been involved in tax evasion but, even more devastatingly, that the company had deliberately 'cherry-picked' the diamond reserves. The intention was to strip Namibia of as much as possible of its diamond wealth ahead of independence.[14]

The lawyer and activist Anton Lubowski was determined to expose and regularise the diamond industry, but he was assassinated just months before independence in 1990. Despite several investigations, including one by the Truth and Reconciliation Commission, there is still no finality as to who actually killed Lubowski.

De Beers, Chevron, Rio Tinto and Texaco were amongst the international corporations to hire Executive Outcomes (EO), which became the first of the world's privatised armies in the post-Cold War era. The Angolan and Sierra Leonean governments followed. EO's connections to the British government through Sandline International and Aegis Defence remain contentious.

The links include highly placed individuals amongst the British elite such as Tony Buckingham, Tony Spicer, Simon Mann and Mark Thatcher. Mann and Thatcher, both living in Cape Town, most notoriously were the drivers of the attempted coup d'etat in Equatorial Guinea in March 2004. Their plan was to topple the long-time dictator, President Teodoro Obiang Nguema, and then to take control of that unfortunate country's massive and recently discovered oilfields.

Mann's erstwhile assistant turned state witness and revealed in 2007 at the 'Wonga trial' in Pretoria that the United States, British, Spanish, South

African and Zimbabwean governments had all been part of the conspiracy to overthrow Nguema. South African government spokesmen angrily rejected Mann's claims on British television that he had official encouragement.[15]

The plot came ludicrously unglued when Zimbabwe's generals and arms industry executives blew the whistle. The weapons for the adventure were being bought in Zimbabwe, where Mann himself confessed to a Harare court that he had planned to dupe Zimbabwe Defence Industries through a side plot to seize diamond mines in the Congo. The story given to his mercenary force was that they were being employed by Sandline as guards for those mines.

After operating in Namibia and Angola, Buckingham and Spicer turned their attention to Sierra Leonean diamond concessions as payment for mercenary services. Diamonds had been discovered in Sierra Leone in 1930, and five years later British colonial authorities granted De Beers exclusive mining and prospecting rights over the entire country for a period of ninety-nine years.

By the mid-1950s there were an estimated seventy-five thousand illicit miners in the Kono area alone, scavenging for stones that local people regarded as worthless. De Beers employed the recently retired head of the British MI5, Sir Percy Sillitoe to counter smuggling. That appointment implied that the diamond industry was somehow inextricably linked to British national security, thus justifying an obsession for secrecy.

Given the tighter security, Lebanese traders began smuggling diamonds to Monrovia in neighbouring Liberia. By 1970 Sierra Leone was mining over two million carats of high quality stones when the newly independent government nationalised the industry. De Beers took revenge. 'Legal' diamond exports dropped to under six hundred thousand carats by 1980, to under fifty thousand carats by 1984 and to only eight thousand, five hundred carats by 1998.[16]

There are about a quarter of a million people of Lebanese origin in West Africa, who have lived there for generations. They dominate commerce, and as the Lebanese civil war of the 1980s gathered momentum, the diamond trade funded the parties in the conflict. That, in turn, prompted Israeli intervention.

In the 1980s Israel and South Africa were collaborating to develop nuclear weapons and were using Sierra Leonean diamonds to circumvent the UN arms embargo. The Israeli-based Liat Construction and Finance Company was controlled by a Russian-born Israeli, Shabtai Kalmanovich who, in partnership with Marc Rich, also brought in American money launderers, drug traffickers and arms dealers.

Having become a prominent millionaire and philanthropist – plus being the 'ambassador' to Israel from the apartheid bantustan of Bophuthatswana – Kalmanovich was eventually arrested in London in 1987. He was exposed as a Soviet KGB agent and jailed for six years. On release, he returned to Russia but was gunned down in Moscow in 2009 in a gangster killing.

Rich was the infamous oil sanctions-buster during the apartheid era and fugitive from US authorities, based in Zug, Switzerland. He became one of De Beers's largest shareholders.[17] Despite his notoriety, Rich was controversially pardoned by President Bill Clinton in 2001 after a financial donation of US$500 000 to the Democratic Party.

Until 1994, like most people, I had been bedazzled by the mystique and glamour around diamonds promoted by De Beers and its marketing strategists. Then Archbishop Desmond Tutu appointed me to represent the Anglican Church at the Cameron Commission Inquiry into Armscor.

The Cameron Commission Inquiry, just months after the UN lifted the arms embargo, was prompted by international revelations that a shipment from South Africa of AK-47 machine guns and other weapons had been seized in Yemen. When I met him, Armscor's general manager Andre Buys initially insisted that the shipment was destined for the Lebanese army which, unusually, had standardised its equipment on AK-47s.

The Lebanese Consul in South Africa angrily and publicly denied that his office had authorised the shipment. Armscor then insisted that the shipment had the full support of the Israeli government, with which South Africa was cooperating in the war against international terrorism. Even more extraordinarily, Buys declared that South Africa, as a Christian country, had a Christian obligation to help in the defence of other Christian countries such as Lebanon.

The fact that most Lebanese were Muslims, and not Christians, had evidently not dawned at Armscor. So how, I asked, could weapons sold to Christian militias in Lebanon end up in a Muslim country such as Yemen? Buys's explanation was that Armscor could not be blamed for criminal actions of third parties.

Given the new political dispensation in South Africa, Armscor was trying to get rid of its remaining stocks of thirty-five thousand Chinese supplied AK-47s. The weapons had originally been imported as part of the apartheid government's destabilisation programme in Angola.

Armscor was prepared to sell to any crooks or terrorists. The shipment was impounded in Yemen en route to Croatia, which was then engaged in a secessionist war from Yugoslavia and itself the subject of another UN arms embargo. The revelations became a major embarrassment for South Africa's newly established democratic government.

Our Anglican stance at the Cameron Commission was to call for a total prohibition of arms exports, and for the armaments industry to be converted to peaceful purposes. Purchases of diamonds by De Beers to finance Unita's war effort facilitated the apartheid government's destabilisation policies in Angola. We also urged the Commission to take measures to block South Africa's further involvement in the weapons-for-diamonds trade which we then estimated amounted to about US$500 million annually.

Unita had developed a diamond smuggling organisation, and in the years between 1993 and 1997 these operations earned about US$3.7 billion.[18] De Beers sanctimoniously pleaded that its purchases were solely intended to prevent Unita from dumping diamonds on the market, and were not intended to finance a war. The proceeds paid for weapons supplied from South Africa, Bulgaria and other countries by the Russian arms trafficker, Viktor Bout.

Government ministers insisted that they could not be blamed when corrupt policemen and customs officials 'closed their eyes' at South Africa's porous airports. Armscor's top secret document on arms export authorisations termed 'Log 17' confirmed that Armscor was prepared to sell weapons to almost anyone, including the world's most unsavoury dictators. Armscor even tried to have the document suppressed at the Cameron Commission on the bizarre rationale that disclosure of its incompetence threatened South Africa's foreign policy relationships.

The Cameron Commission established that Armscor's corporate culture was both corrupt and incompetent, but the two commissioners, Edwin Cameron and Laurie Nathan, rejected our submission that both Armscor and Denel should be disbanded, and that their assets could be converted to peaceful purposes. Although they expressed sympathy with our stance, Cameron and Nathan, unfortunately but naively, accepted assurances from the new government that South Africa would in future pursue a responsible arms trade policy.

That failure subsequently cost South African taxpayers tens of billions of rand in further subsidies poured into both Armscor and Denel on fallacious assumptions that the armaments industry is both economically lucrative and an important creator of employment. Armscor and Denel have proceeded from one corruption scandal to the next, not least being the arms deal.

The wars in Angola and Sierra Leone shattered the glamorous image that De Beers had so carefully cultivated over decades. Perceptions are all-important in the diamond trade. Carefully constructed marketing myths were fast unravelling. De Beers stopped buying Angolan diamonds in October 1999, and in May 2000 made an unctuous, written submission to the US congressional committee on Africa that:

> De Beers knows all too well the deleterious effects that conflict and political instability often have on potential large scale investors. Having spent hundreds of millions of dollars on advertising its product, De Beers is deeply concerned about anything that could damage the image of diamonds as a symbol of love, beauty and rarity.[19]

Japan and, suddenly, China are increasingly important retail markets for diamonds, and their combined demand is expected to double to about forty per cent by 2015. Although down sharply in recent years, the US market still accounts for almost forty per cent. The New York diamond district churns over tens of billions of dollars, and is an extraordinary place where more than two thousand firms haggle for business. The signs on the buildings are a messy clutter of Hebrew and English, and the men on the street are intense hustlers. This is a place where impoverished refugees and immigrants have aspired to rise from rags to riches in affirmation of the American dream.

Forty-seventh Street used to house the 'rag trade' but during the Second World War, when Jews fleeing Europe flocked to America, they brought with them their expertise in cutting and polishing diamonds. About ninety-five per cent of the businessmen on the street are Jewish, over a third of them Hasidic – identifiable by their black suits, tzitzit fringes and full beards.

Greg Campbell, who subsequently wrote the book *Blood Diamonds*, graphically described how diamonds are used by terrorist organisations to fund their operations:

> The RUF [Revolutionary United Front] began its jewellery heist in 1991, using the support of neighbouring Liberia to capture Sierra Leone's vast wealth of diamond mines. Since then, the rebels have carried out one of the most brutal military campaigns in recent history, to enrich themselves as well as the genteel captains of the diamond industry living far removed from the killing fields.
>
> The RUF's signature tactic was amputation of civilians: over the course of the decade-long war, the rebels mutilated some twenty thousand people, hacking off their arms, legs, lips and ears with machetes and axes. The RUF's goal was to terrorise the population, and enjoy uncontested dominion over the diamond fields.
>
> The international diamond industry's trading centres in Europe funded this horror by buying up to US$125 million worth of diamonds a year from the RUF, according to UN estimates. Few cared where the gems originated, or calculated the cost in lives lost rather than carats gained.
>
> The RUF used its profits to open foreign bank accounts for rebel leaders and to finance a complicated network of gunrunners who kept the rebels well-equipped with the modern military hardware they used to control Sierra Leone's diamonds. The weapons – and the gems the rebels sold unimpeded to terrorist and corporate trader alike – allowed the RUF to fight off government soldiers, hired mercenaries, peacekeepers from a regional West African reaction force, British paratroopers, and the most expensive peacekeeping mission the UN ever deployed.[20]

The Sierra Leonean military government headed by General Joseph Momah was overthrown in 1992 in a coup d'etat led by twenty-seven-year-old Captain Valentine Strasser. His troops were mining diamonds to exchange for weapons flown in from Belgium and Rumania. For eleven years the opposing RUF was aided and abetted by the French, Libyan and Liberian governments and the West African francophone states.

The collapse of the Soviet Union in 1991 meant that huge quantities of weapons were looted from armouries by Bout and others and traded for diamonds. Airports in West Africa, especially Lomé in Togo, became transit points for the weapons-for-diamond trade. Togo's long-time dictator Gnassingbé Eyadéma supplied the phoney documentation that kept Savimbi equipped with armaments when South Africa ostensibly withdrew from Angola and Namibia.

Strasser hired EO to expel the RUF from the areas around Freetown and the diamond mines, and, by transferring troops from Angola, within a week EO achieved these initial objectives. By 1996 the RUF was seemingly destroyed, and signed a peace agreement that included a provision for EO's departure from Sierra Leone.

Only three months later, however, another military junta staged a coup against President Ahmed Kabbah and aligned itself with the RUF. The war resumed, and became even more barbaric. From exile in Guinea and with support from the British government, Kabbah then hired Sandline International in 1998. A peace agreement was negotiated in Lomé, Togo in July 1999 and, with six thousand UN troops, at last brought some measure of political stability to Sierra Leone.[21]

The trial of Charles Taylor for war crimes by the International Criminal Court (ICC) in The Hague gave renewed focus to the devastation inflicted by the trade of weapons-for-diamonds.

Although elected as president of Liberia in 1997, Taylor was removed from office in 2003 when rebel soldiers threatened to take over Monrovia, and he was exiled to Nigeria. The Special Court for Sierra Leone in 2004 ruled that he should be prosecuted for war crimes by an international tribunal, and in 2006 he was extradited to Holland to stand trial in The Hague.

The charges against Taylor were five counts of crimes against humanity – murder, rape, sexual slavery, other inhumane acts and enslavement, and five counts of war crimes – acts of terrorism, murder, outrage upon personal dignity, cruel treatment and pillage. In addition, there was another charge in terms of international humanitarian law of enlisting children under the age of fifteen into the armed forces.[22] The ICC had also wanted to indict Libya's Muammar Gaddafi for his role in funding and training the RUF, but the British and American governments objected vehemently. The reason: 'oil politics', because by then Gaddafi had supposedly been 'rehabilitated'.[23]

Taylor's trial started in 2008, and the prosecution called ninety-one witnesses. Most sensationally, the model Naomi Campbell confirmed that in 1997 she had received a gift of three 'dirty looking pebbles' from Taylor whilst both were Nelson Mandela's house guests in Cape Town.

After warnings that mere possession of uncut diamonds is illegal in South Africa, Campbell gave them to the Mandela Children's Fund saying that they should be used to do some good. Still unexplained is whether Taylor was on a weapons buying spree or why Mandela deemed it necessary to host such a notoriously unsavoury character at his home.

Former CIA operative and political commentator Wayne Madsen refutes official US explanations for Bout's extradition from Thailand to New York in 2010 as his dealings with FARC rebels in Colombia. Instead, Madsen offers extraordinary insights into how Al Qaeda and the Israeli Mossad forged an alliance to break Lebanese controls over the West African diamond trade. In fact, Madsen uses the term 'rendition' rather than the word extradition to illustrate how desperate the US government had become to get its hands on Bout.

Given the political leverage that the war business has held in Washington during both the Bush and Obama administrations, seemingly far-fetched conspiratorial theories begin to gain credence. Madsen writes:

> There is a reason why President Barack Obama, in carrying out the wishes
> of the CIA and Israel, wants to put Bout in prison for the rest of his life. If
> Bout were to speak and write from Moscow, he could blow the lid off the

crime of the century – 9/11, and those who planned and executed it, namely the Saudis, Osama bin Laden, Israel and the highest echelons of the Bush administration.

The Bout story is directly linked to relationships between former Soviet Jews and Sephardic Jews in Israel, who, working with partners in Saudi Arabia decided to finance the Taliban as protectors of the Afghan highway project. Benazir Bhutto supported this strategy, and hence in December 2007 was assassinated by pro-CIA forces within the Pakistani army and intelligence services.

The Bush administration believed that war and oil profits mix. The links between Saudi Arabian businessmen with Al Qaeda and the Russian-Israeli mafia need investigation, and one of the most overlooked aspects of the 9/11 attacks was the role of Russian-Israeli organised crime. Afghan-born Jews are highly prized by the Mossad, which used them to infiltrate the Taliban.[24]

Madsen's investigations dovetail with research by the Israeli Committee Against House Demolitions (ICAHD), which is the leading organisation in the Israeli peace movement and with which EAPPI has a close relationship. Director Jeff Halper and his staff are the bane of the Israeli military as well as the international corporations that profit from the occupation of Palestine and the war business.

A briefing by ICAHD's Jimmy Johnson revealed Israeli involvement with the West African weapons-for-diamonds and money laundering rackets:

> The story begins with Al Qaeda diamonds. Shortly after the bombing of the US embassies in Kenya and Tanzania, the US began aggressively searching for ways to disrupt Al Qaeda's financing. In 1998 the Clinton administration succeeded in freezing some US$240 million in assets belonging to either Al Qaeda or the Taliban. This led Al Qaeda to restructure its finances.
>
> Civil war-torn Sierra Leone and the endemic corruption in Liberia provided perfect conditions for Al Qaeda operatives. Long before his trial in The Hague for war crimes, former Liberian President Taylor underwent training in Libya. Upon his return to Liberia in 1989, Taylor led a rebellion which eventually led to his 1997 election and ensuing dictatorship.
>
> The violence generated by Taylor in both Liberia and Sierra Leone led the UN to establish an arms embargo on Liberia in 1992 and in 1997 against

Sierra Leone, followed by an embargo on West African blood diamonds that financed the violence.

From 1996 until 1999, retired Israeli Defence Force Colonel Yair Klein provided material and training to Liberia's anti-terrorism unit and also to the RUF as part of a diamonds-for-arms operation. Klein's anti-terrorism unit, a group widely criticised for gross abuses of human rights, was headed by 'Chuckie' Taylor, the president's son.[25]

When Leonid Minin, a Ukrainian-born Israeli member of the 'Odessa Mafia,' was arrested in Italy, his briefcase included US$500 000 worth of diamonds and a wealth of correspondence detailing his sale to the Liberian government of millions of dollars worth of arms in exchange for diamonds and timber concessions. Yet perhaps the most interesting item in that briefcase was an End User Certificate for one hundred and thirteen tons of ammunition and arms from the Ukraine to the Ivory Coast.

It exactly matched the certificate found when a Hezbollah operative was arrested in Belgium. Hezbollah has a long history of diamond trading, including in the Democratic Republic of Congo (DRC) where Israel also has long associations, including training and equipping the presidential guard.

The picture that emerges from these relationships is not only one of war crimes, profiteering and massive environmental destruction, corruption and greed, but one of Israelis, Hezbollah and Al Qaeda all working together in mutually profitable enterprises regardless of principle or ideology.[26]

Media exposés of atrocities in Sierra Leone by civil society organisations such as Global Witness and Partnership Africa Canada[27] eventually obliged the diamond industry to take action to clean up its image. After all, what girl would want to be reminded of death and blood every time she looked at her engagement ring as symbol of undying love?

The World Diamond Council (WDC) was established during 2000 under the auspices of the UN by representatives of diamond manufacturing and trading companies. In turn, the UN defined blood diamonds as 'diamonds that originate from areas controlled by forces or factions opposed to legitimate and internationally-recognised governments, and used to fund military action in opposition to those governments or in contravention of the decisions of the Security Council'.[28]

The Kimberley Process was then instituted by the diamond industry requiring all shipments of rough diamonds be made in tamper-proof containers and accompanied by a certificate identifying the country of origin, the size and value of each shipment, and the identity of the exporting authority. However, the Kimberley Process also adopted a much narrower definition of blood diamonds than did the UN, and excluded cut and polished stones. In so doing, it made a mockery of UN intentions.

The WDC launched massive public relations campaigns that the era of 'blood diamonds' was past, claiming that only one per cent of diamonds sold as jewellery meets the description. Movie stars were hired and lavishly bedecked at the Oscar award ceremonies in Hollywood to bolster the images of glamour and beauty.

A report by Human Rights Watch in 2009 exposing that fraud unleashed a furore, and called

> ... on the Kimberley Process Certification Scheme (KPCS) to press Zimbabwe to end the smuggling of diamonds, and to ensure that all diamonds from Marange are lawfully mined, documented and exported in compliance with KPCS standards. South Africa was urged to press for speedy reforms and policy changes to stop the export of smuggled diamonds from Marange into South Africa and, in addition, to ban Marange diamonds to protect Zimbabweans from abuse but also help South Africa protect its own diamond industry. [29]

Predictably, nothing of substance followed, but one of the founders of the Kimberley Process system, Ian Smillie, eventually resigned in disgust declaring:

> [I can] no longer contribute to the pretence that failure was success. The UN spends billions on peacekeeping, but the Kimberley Process cannot get even close to proper diamond tracking in Angola and the DRC. Some of its reviews are completely bogus.
>
> Angola has obvious human rights problems. Hundreds of thousands of illicit Congolese diamond diggers have been expelled over the past three or four years to the accompaniment of serious human rights abuses. Miners are

beaten, robbed, raped and force marched hundreds of miles. The Kimberley Process has had nothing to say about this because 'it is not a human rights organisation'.

Zimbabwe, rife with smuggling and gross diamond-related human rights abuses, consumed months of ineffective internal debates throughout 2009. Between eighty and two hundred illicit diamond miners were killed by Zimbabwean armed forces late in 2008. This was widely reported in the media and by Zimbabwean human rights organizations, and the Kimberley Process was finally shamed into sending a review mission.

Its report recommended suspension of Zimbabwe, but that recommendation was denounced ... because it might damage the interests of an Australian company with connections in Zimbabwe. For these governments and others ... business and politics trump human rights and the very purpose of the Kimberley Process. They trump good management, they trump common sense and decency and they trump the long-term interest of the entire diamond industry.[30]

The lure of gold and diamonds fictionalised in Rider Haggard's *King Solomon's Mines* in 1885, motivated Cecil Rhodes and his imperial obsessions back in 1890 to take over Africa from the Cape to Cairo. Yet as if disproving and contradicting Haggard's tales, Rhodesia throughout its colonial history seemed poorly endowed with mineral wealth. Its economy was developed on agriculture, albeit supplemented by relatively small deposits of gold, nickel and chrome.

Ironically, for twenty years De Beers held exclusive rights for diamond prospecting in the Marange area of Zimbabwe. In line, however, with its fundamental strategy of blocking new discoveries and of preventing supplies from glutting the jewellery market, De Beers deliberately did not develop what may prove to be the largest diamond field in the world. Its licence lapsed in 2006 and was taken up by African Consolidated Resources (ACR), whose chief executive is a fourth generation white Zimbabwean, Andrew Cranswick.

The 'blowback' consequences of President Robert Mugabe's misadventures in the Congo in August 1998 to support Laurent Kabila quickly devastated Zimbabwe. In his book *Mugabe*, Martin Meredith notes:

The folly of intervening in a distant foreign war in which Zimbabwe had no interest, at a time when the country's finances were in a ruinous state and the government was heavily over-borrowed, was evident to all. Both at home and abroad, the Congo intervention was seen as a sign of Mugabe's growing megalomania. Opinion polls showed it to be deeply unpopular. Western governments queried the need for providing Mugabe with financial assistance if he was prepared to squander money on foreign adventures.

For a select group of defence officials and businessmen however, the Congo offered rich pickings. In return for military support, Kabila was prepared to hand out mining and timber concessions and offer preferential trade in diamonds, cobalt and other minerals.

The intention was said to be to allow Zimbabwe to recoup some of the cost of the war, but the beneficiaries tended to be members of the ruling elite. At the centre of the Congo network was Emmerson Mnangagwa, Zanu-PF's business controller. Another key figure was John Bredenkamp, a former Rhodesian sanctions-buster and millionaire arms dealer.

There were military setbacks in the Congo. Rebel forces inflicted humiliating defeats on Kabila and his allies in October 1998, killing and capturing Zimbabwean soldiers. Casualty figures were kept secret, but rumours circulated in Harare about serious disarray within the military. Senior officers were said to have refused to obey orders. There was talk of mutinies and desertions.[31]

The economy collapsed and to keep his political and military cronies in line, Mugabe seized white-owned commercial farms and parcelled them out to his friends. Literally facing starvation, millions of Zimbabwean refugees fled to South Africa, Britain and Botswana. Cholera killed tens of thousands of people when the public water system failed.

Compounding the poverty in urban areas, shacks and houses were bulldozed in 2005 in an operation referred to as *murambatsvina*, meaning 'drive out the rubbish'. The pretext was that shanty towns in the cities harboured criminals. Mugabe refused to accept defeat in the 2008 elections and then, with support from President Thabo Mbeki, continued to cling to power. Zimbabwe's assets were mortgaged to Libya, China and South Africa.

Mugabe's crony Gideon Gono, the governor of the Reserve Bank, made an immense fortune from his control of the printing machines. So did a handful of Zimbabweans, both black and white, who had access to foreign currencies. However, soldiers, policemen and others employed by the state had to be paid in Zimbabwe dollars and kept loyal to the regime.

By July 2008 the official annual inflation rate was two hundred and thirty-one million per cent. Even computers could not keep up with the destruction of the currency, and the country. A Zim$100 billion note might buy three eggs, but only one hour later the price might rise to Zim$150 billion. Gono's printing presses could not cope.

Shops were empty and the most basic commodities were unavailable, unless illicitly paid for in US dollars or South African rand. In April 2009 the Zim dollar was finally abandoned in favour of dollarisation of the economy. The unemployed had no dollar income, but Mugabe had found a new source of foreign currency income in the diamond fields at Marange, which are said to cover more than five hundred and sixty-six square kilometres of the Zimbabwean bushveld in the Chiadzwa district.

ACR's licence was revoked and despite several successful legal challenges upheld by Zimbabwe's Supreme Court, its mining rights were reallocated to the police and army. Thousands of illegal miners invaded the site. The military responded in October 2008 by shooting hundreds of miners after Gono realised that he and Mugabe were losing up to US$50 million per week because of gold and diamond smuggling, mainly into South Africa.

Reports appeared in the world's media estimating that the Marange field was worth £800 billion and that it contained one quarter of the world's diamond reserves. *Leadership* Magazine declared:

> The construction of the airstrip and active participation of China in working the diamond fields at Marange forms part of an alleged arms-for-diamonds deal between Zimbabwe and China. According to witnesses, Chinese soldiers are not only participating in bolstering the security at Marange, but they also help to supervise the large number of Zimbabweans who are forced to work under slave conditions.[32]

As Cranswick comments:

The mind boggles why the Chinese need a military style airstrip on our concession. It must be for dubious purposes. After all, the world's entire production of diamonds in a single day can be carried away in one helicopter.[33]

Early in 2010 I was asked by human rights activists to verify whether Israeli 'diamond king' Lev Leviev was financing the extraction of the Marange diamonds. They were ninety-eight per cent certain, but definitive confirmation eluded them. The state-owned Zimbabwe Mining and Development Corporation (ZMDC) had licensed two small South African companies to develop the mines, neither of which had the expertise to undertake such a venture.

The online news service 'Zimonline' reported:

> The two companies' operations are shrouded in controversy, amid revelations that some members of their boards were once illegal drug and diamond dealers in the Congo and Sierra Leone. Some of the directors are also known to have close ties to Zimbabwe's military establishment.[34]

One of the companies, Core Mining and Minerals, had advised ZMDC that its principal was domiciled in Israel and that he would be responsible for financing the entire project. Benny Steinmetz denied his involvement, saying he had no intention of investing in diamond projects in Zimbabwe unless human rights and legal issues were fully resolved.

US intelligence operatives let it be known that Leviev was developing relationships with the 88 Queensway Group in Hong Kong, an organisation which the Americans believe is nothing less than a cover for covert Chinese operations in Africa and other resource-rich regions of the world.[35]

Quite extraordinarily, Air Zimbabwe in August 2011 was able to buy two new Airbus A340-200 passenger planes courtesy of Mbada Diamonds in a scheme designed to keep income from the Marange fields in the hands of Mugabe's cronies.[36]

Coinciding with this development, Human Rights Watch and Partnership Africa Canada identified three Zimbabwean banks – Banc ABC, Commercial Bank of Zimbabwe and Premier Banking Group – as complicit in the sale of the Marange 'blood diamonds'. The three banks all have long money laundering histories, yet internationally are connected with Standard and Barclays Banks, Absa and other foreign shareholders.[37]

The International Monetary Fund in September 2011 announced that Zimbabwe had been placed on its alert list as a safe haven for syndicates engaged in money laundering and the financing of terrorism. It noted that due to its weak law enforcement and lax banking controls, Zimbabwe is seen as a playground for money launderers, some of whom have links to international terrorist cells.[38]

Endnotes

1. Andrew Pierce: 'Ring Owned by Queen Mother a onetime "foe".' *The Times*, February 12, 2005.
2. Linda Davies: *Wilderness of Mirrors*, Orion Publishers, London, 1996.
3. Michael MacQueen: 'The Conversion of Looted Jewish Assets to Run the German War Machine', *Holocaust and Genocide Studies*, Oxford University Press, 2004, pp 27-45.
4. Edward Jay Epstein: *The Rise And Fall of Diamonds, 'Diamonds For Hitler'*, Simon & Schuster, New York, 1992.
5. Laurie Flynn: *Studded With Diamonds, And Paved With Gold*, Chapter three, 'How To Steal A Country', Bloomsbury Publishing, London, 1992.
6. Fran Blandy: 'De Beers to Spend R463 m on restoring mined-out Diamond Coast landscape', *Cape Times*, August 24, 2009.
7. Alfred Levinson, John Gurney and Melissa Kirkley, 'Diamond Sources and Production: Past, Present and Future', *Gems and Gemology* Magazine, Winter 1992.
8. Bruce Caincross and Peter Tarassoff: 'Who's Who in Mineral Names: Two South Africans Hans Merensky (1872-1952) and Cecil John Rhodes (1853-1902)', *Rocks and Minerals*, 77: 48-53, 2001.
9. COSATU/National Union of Mineworkers submission to the Parliamentary Public Enterprises Portfolio Committee on the Alexkor Amendment Bill, 5 September 2001.
10. 'Sam Collins: Texan in Namibia', Bryon Burke Diamond Corporation, 2001-2003.
11. Nicholas Stein: 'The De Beers Story: A new cut on an old monopoly', *Fortune* Magazine, February 19, 2001.
12. Ann Crotty: 'De Beers slammed on Botswana mines,' *Business Report*, September 25, 2008.
13. Chris Gordon: 'SADF Poaching Industry Exposed', *African Business*, No 209, April 1, 1996.
14. Laurie Flynn: *Studded With Diamonds, And Paved With Gold*, Chapter three, How To Steal A Country, Bloomsbury Publishing, London, 1992.
15. 'Mann's coup plot claim outrageous says SA', *Cape Times*, March 13, 2008.
16. Ian Smillie, Lansana Gberie and Ralph Hazelton: 'The Heart Of The Matter: Sierra Leone, Diamonds and Human Security', report by

Partnership Africa Canada, January 12, 2000.

17. R Hengeveld and J Rodenburg: *Embargo: Apartheid's Oil Secrets*, Shipping Research Bureau, Amsterdam University Press, 1995.

18. Lauren Thompson: 'Angola: Opportunity Missed', *Professional Jeweller Magazine*, October 2000.

19. 'De Beers sees threat of blood diamonds', CNN, January 18, 2001.

20. Greg Campbell: '*Blood Diamonds: Tracing The Deadly Path Of the World's Most Precious Stones*, Westview Press, Boulder, Colorado, 2002.

21. Leslie Hough: 'A Study Of Peacekeeping, Peace-Enforcement And Private Military Companies In Sierra Leone', Institute For Security Studies, Pretoria, 2003.

22. The Hague Justice Portal –Taylor, Charles.

23. Noam Chomsky: BBC News, April 15, 2011.

24. Wayne Madsen: 'Viktor Bout Knows Too Much About 9-11', RT Television interview, January 25, 2011.

25. Chuckie Taylor in 2009 was sentenced in Florida to a jail term of ninety-seven years.

26. Jimmy Johnson: 'Israelis and Hezbollah Haven't Always Been Enemies', ICAHD, September 6, 2006.

27. Ian Smillie: 'Diamonds and Human Security', Occasional Paper #6, Partnership Africa Canada, 2002.

28. 'Conflict Diamonds; Sanctions and War', UN Security Council, UN Department of Public Information, New York, March 21, 2001.

29. 'Diamonds In The Rough', Human Rights Watch, June 26, 2009.

30. Ian Smillie: 'Ian Smillie Addresses Human Rights, Diamonds and the Kimberley Process', Rapnet, September 10, 2009.

31. Martin Meredith: *Mugabe*, Jonathan Ball Publishers, Cape Town, 2008, pp 148 and 149.

32. 'Zimbabwe horror continues unchecked', *Leadership* Magazine, Johannesburg, October 11, 2010.

33. Jon Swain: 'Robert Mugabe's Dirty Diamonds', *Sunday Times* (London), April 4, 2010.

34. Ndodana Sixholo: 'Israeli funding Zimbabwe Diamond Mine', Zimonline, April 20, 2010.

35. Yossi Melman: 'US ties Israeli billionaire with Chinese Intelligence', *Haaretz*, January 28, 2010.

36. Ray Ndlovu: 'Strike-Ridden Air Zimbabwe Ready To Soar with New Aircraft', *Mail & Guardian*, August 19, 2011.
37. Erin Conway-Smith: 'Zimbabwe Selling Blood Diamonds: Banks Launder Payments For Mugabe Regime's Illegal Diamond Sales', *Global Post*, August 30, 2011.
38. Vusimusi Bhebhe: 'Zim: Money Laundering Playground', *The Zimbabwean*, September 9, 2011.

6 • 'WHY IS "OUR" OIL UNDER THEIR SAND?'

My first job as a fifteen-year-old teenager back in 1958 was as a radio operator in Libya for British Petroleum (BP) at its local head office in Tripoli. A year later I was promoted to administrative clerk at a seismic camp in the Sahara Desert. BP and dozens of American oil companies were then pouring into Libya to begin the search for oil. Esso made the first strike in 1960 with a well that produced five thousand barrels of oil per day.

Libya had been an Italian colony before the Second World War. Benito Mussolini had dreamed of resurrecting the glories of the Roman Empire that are still evident in the ruins at Leptis Magna and Sabratha. It is estimated that in the eastern province of Cyrenaica perhaps half of the population was exterminated during resistance to Italian colonisation. The resistance leader Omar Mukhtar was hanged in 1931. Others were thrown out, alive, from airplanes.

Although the Second World War had nothing to do with Libyans, their country became a major battleground between the Germans and British. The Battle of El Alamein in 1943 was the turning point. For many years the desert was littered with landmines and other war debris. The harbour at Tripoli was blocked by ship wrecks, and the cities of Benghazi and Tobruk were virtually demolished. The economy was devastated. Libya's only exports were esparto grass used for making high quality paper and scrap metal.

My father was the British commissioner for trade and supplies in the province of Tripolitania, his job being to attempt to restore the economy. Given the war destruction, Libya was then considered the poorest country in the world. In 1951 the United Nations decided on independence. Even the British did not want it as a colony. A report to the Italian government in 1938 had noted that there was no prospect of finding oil in Libya.

As a toddler I spoke Arabic and Italian as much as English, but later was sent to boarding school on the nearby island of Malta. St Edward's College was a colonial institution that attempted to mould the sons of the Maltese aristocracy into pseudo-English gentlemen and we were taught to speak the 'Queen's English' as spoken by the BBC. My parents remained in Libya until 1960 when they returned to Ireland and I, at the age of seventeen, went to the United States to go to university.

BP had been established during the First World War by none other than Winston Churchill. As had 'the merchant of death' himself, Basil Zaharoff, Churchill realised that in the twentieth century oil would replace gold and diamonds as the determinant and lubricator of the war business. BP has had a very chequered history in Libya given turbulent relationships with Muammar Gaddafi. Libyan oil reserves of forty-four billion barrels plus fifty-four trillion cubic feet of natural gas now make it Africa's most important oil producing country.[1]

The British imperialist mindset continues even into the twenty-first century. Prime Minister Tony Blair's disastrous misadventures in Iraq and Afghanistan highlight how some British leaders still hanker for past military glory. Under the guise of a 'special relationship' with the US, the war business in England bankrolls politicians and determines British foreign policies to play 'second fiddle' in the American band.

Blair's testimony at the Chilcot inquiry confirmed that he had no regrets about Britain's role in the Iraq war in 2003. The inquiry also confirmed that he had been repeatedly informed that the war would be illegal in terms of international law.[2] Intelligence information was deliberately 'sexed-up' to justify a war that killed more than one million Iraqis.

Iran (Persia) was the first experience of unprincipled collusion between the CIA and the British MI6 when they conspired to prevent nationalisation of BP assets in 1953. Extraction of Iranian oil was Britain largest single foreign investment and dated back to discoveries in 1908. The Shah was put back on his 'peacock throne', and his dictatorship until 1979 relied heavily on American supplies of weapons.[3]

A new enemy, communism, was created in both America and Britain as the bogey to strike fear into politicians and the taxpayers.

The Suez Crisis was next. Repeated nationalist and anti-British riots culminated in an army coup in 1952 in which the corrupt King Farouk and his entourage were deposed. Gamal Abdel Nasser emerged as the new leader. The very purpose of British occupation of Egypt had dissolved with the independence of India and Pakistan in 1947. Control of the Suez Canal remained the symbolic expression of British power and grandeur, except that the waterway had become the vital passage for European oil imports from the Persian Gulf.

When Nasser announced that Egypt would nationalise the Suez Canal, the British reaction was close to apoplexy. The British, French and Israeli governments conspired to attack Egypt in November 1956, and within a matter of days had won the war militarily.

On that occasion, even President Dwight Eisenhower was hugely offended by their duplicity. To British disbelief and humiliation, the Americans 'pulled the plug' by threatening to destroy the pound sterling on foreign exchange markets. Facing banking sanctions and diplomatic disaster, the British and French government quickly backed down and withdrew their troops.

The reckless attack on Egypt also prompted me, as a teenager, to begin questioning the myths of my childhood that Britain was the home of fair play, decency and honesty.

The repercussions of the Suez invasion in neighbouring Arab countries were immense. My parents were amongst the handful of expatriates who did not flee and remained in Libya. In the months before the war anti-French, anti-British and anti-Israeli rioters almost daily passed our home in Tripoli en route to the king's palace.

Our immediate neighbours were Jewish. They had six daughters and, with good reason, were terrified by mobs in the street outside. In the 1940s, the Jewish community numbered almost forty thousand people. It was relatively prosperous and dominated commerce, but had also suffered grievously from the late 1930s when Italian colonial officials enforced Nazi anti-Semitic laws. About six hundred Jewish Libyans died in Nazi concentration camps.

The history of Arab Jews in Libya dated back over three thousand years. Simon of Cyrene, who carried Jesus' cross along the Via Dolorosa to the crucifixion, is the best known. Cyrene had been a sophisticated city of one hundred thousand people, mostly Jews, when Libya was the breadbasket of the Roman Empire. Yet by the late 1960s the community was extinct after Gaddafi, as a twenty-seven-year-old colonel, seized power and abolished the monarchy. The few remaining Jews were expelled.

What was not known or understood in the 1950s was how Israeli provocateurs deliberately inflamed anti-Jewish hysteria throughout the Middle East. Dozens of synagogues in Tripoli were destroyed. Bombs were set off across the Arab world, but usually the Muslim Brotherhood and/or communists were blamed.

The reason was that the Israeli army wanted more soldiers as cannon-fodder in war zones and, secondly, believed that Arab Jewish immigrants could also be exploited as cheap labour. Deals were struck between Israeli agents and government officials to confiscate Jewish assets and to expel their owners. Arab Jews were expected to be eternally grateful to the state of Israel that they had escaped with their lives, even if at the loss of their property.

By the end of the Second World War, Jews across the Middle East had numbered about eight hundred thousand people. One third of the population of Baghdad was Jewish. Naeim Giladi, an Iraqi Jew, recounts in his memoirs entitled *Ben-Gurion's Scandals*:

> To terrorise the Jews, Zionists planted bombs in synagogues. Soon leaflets began to appear urging Jews to flee to Israel. Although evidence showed the

bombings to be the work of an underground Zionist organisation, Hashura, most of the world believed reports that Arab terrorism had motivated the flight of Iraqi Jews whom Zionists had 'rescued', really just to increase Israel's Jewish population.

Uneducated Jews were told of a messianic Israel where the blind see, the lame walk and onions grow as big as melons. Educated Jews had bombs thrown at them.

Iraqi Zionists were tried and executed for the bombings. By the time of the executions in January 1952, all but six thousand of an estimated one hundred and twenty-five thousand Iraqi Jews had fled to Israel.

An ancient, cultured and prosperous community had been uprooted and its people transplanted to a land dominated by East European Jews whose culture was not only foreign, but entirely hateful to them.[4]

Giladi was himself a member of the Zionist underground. At the age of seventeen, he was caught smuggling Jews out of Iraq and sentenced to death. He managed to escape from jail, and made his way to the new state of Israel. He arrived in May 1950 but after a few years he was disillusioned. He wrote:

Ben-Gurion needed 'oriental' Jews to farm the land left by Palestinians who were driven out by Israeli forces in 1948. I began to find out about the barbaric methods used to rid the fledgling state of as many Palestinians as possible. The world recoils today at the thought of bacteriological warfare, but Israel was probably the first country to use it in the Middle East.

Jewish forces would empty Arab villages of their populations. To make sure the Arabs would not return, Israelis put typhus and dysentery bacteria into the water wells.[5]

Anti-Jewish riots in Tripoli remain one of my earliest childhood memories. I remember being taken to nursery school in army trucks by British soldiers because of the dangers. Thousands of Palestinian refugees later arrived as teachers and civil servants after Libyan independence.

I learned more about the exodus of Arab Jews to Israel from former members of the Black Panthers during my first stint in Israel-Palestine during October 2009 to January 2010 as a member of the World Council of Churches Ecumenical Accompaniment Programme for Palestine and Israel (EAPPI).

Whereas European Jews (the Ashkenazi) were settled mainly in the coastal cities of Israel, Arab Jews (the Mizrahi) were assigned to poor and dangerous areas where they became and remain Israel's underclass. In Jerusalem they were billeted in the district of Musrarah and other areas along the 'green line', and thus within firing range of Jordanian troops who, until the Six Day War in 1967, controlled the Old City.

Social frustrations inevitably boiled over. The Black Panther movement of Mizrahi youth erupted in the early 1970s in reaction to non-fulfilment of promises made to their parents. Teenagers decided to hold a demonstration outside Jerusalem Mayor Teddy Kollek's office to ask for a table tennis table for their youth centre.

Kollek eventually appeared, told the kids that they were scum and must get off his grass, and then had them arrested. They were detained and tortured at the nearby police headquarters and, as a result, the movement escalated and elicited public sympathy. The Black Panthers demanded a meeting with Prime Minister Golda Meir. She refused to meet them until they threatened a hunger strike in front of the Wailing Wall.

They were semi-literate kids meeting the prime minister, and she treated them with her typical grandmotherly disdain until they demanded reform of the government's education and housing policies. Taken aback, Meir asked them not to talk to the press whilst she arranged matters with her cabinet ministers. Then, that very evening, she announced on radio that she had met the Black Panthers, and arrogantly described them as 'not nice people'.

In response, the teenagers launched their 'not nice people' confrontation with the establishment. One campaign was to steal milk bottles in affluent areas of Jerusalem and to distribute free milk to poor people. The Black Panthers became the biggest social movement in Israeli history. Arab Jews by then were almost half of Israel's population, and outnumbered the Ashkenazi.

The implications terrified Meir's government, but then the movement collapsed with the Yom Kippur War in 1973. That war yet again diverted the country from social issues. The surprise Egyptian attack was repulsed with much difficulty, and Israel even threatened to drop nuclear bombs on Damascus before the US belatedly intervened with massive airlifts of armaments.[6]

In his drive to oust the Labour Party from office, Menachem Begin of the Likud Party embraced the Mizrahi with extravagant promises of social development. Their orientation switched from left wing to right wing, and eventually the Mizrahi were absorbed politically into the Shas Party. One of the original Black Panther leaders, Rubin Aberzer, who was born in Morocco and is now in his fifties, told me:

> After sixty years, the Zionists still have not fulfilled their promises. Our parents did not want to rock the boat, but by the 1970s we youth demanded delivery. Discrimination makes us a separate group. Zionist leadership plays off Palestinians and Middle East Jews. That ability to divide and rule enables the state of Israel to avoid peace in the Middle East. Once there is peace in the Middle East, the Zionists will have to address social discrimination against the Mizrahi.
>
> Any demands for reform, and the Ashkenazi go crazy. They insist that we must buy into their Holocaust narrative. We couldn't play our music in 1948. In order to be part of Israel we had to erase our identity. When the Russians came, they were financially supported. But when we set up radio stations, we are called 'pirates'.[7]

After the 1973 Yom Kippur War, an estimated one million Russians, many with very dubious claims to Jewish identities, settled in Israel. Aberzer argues that the Ashkenazi panicked when the Black Panthers organised, and were terrified that the Mizrahi, being Arabic-speaking, would align themselves with the Palestinians. Russian migration funded mainly by the US was promoted to dilute the numerical and political impact of the Mizrahi. Many of the Russians simply wanted to get out of the Soviet Union, and grabbed the opportunity.

During our orientation period, EAPPI arranged a number of briefings by Israeli peace activists. From Maya Wind, then working for the Israeli Committee Against House Demolitions (ICAHD), we learned:

> A two state solution has become a distant dream. Either we kill all Palestinians or we suppress them in a blatant apartheid state. The alternative, dreaded by

virtually all Israelis, is a one state solution.

Palestinians are thirty-six per cent of the population of Jerusalem. They pay forty per cent of the taxes, but only seven per cent of the municipal budget is spent in Palestinian areas.

There are major financial interests at stake. International and Israeli corporations are profiting hugely from the Occupation. These include not just construction companies, but also private security and surveillance companies. The weapons industry now accounts for thirty per cent of Israel's GDP.[8]

Highly articulate, Wind also told us about her own personal journey from the sheltered daughter of religious Jews to busy activist, and her consequent estrangement from her family. As in apartheid South Africa, any challenge to 'national security' comes at huge personal cost.

Capping all diplomatic difficulties in the Middle East, the continuing Israeli-Palestinian crisis remains pivotal. In particular, the status of Jerusalem is critical. The Israeli government insists that a unified Jerusalem will remain 'the eternal capital of the Jewish state'. The international community, including even the US government, still refuses to recognise Jerusalem as the capital of Israel, and also repudiates the annexation of Jerusalem's Palestinian neighbourhoods.

From the Palestinian perspective, East Jerusalem including the Old City as the capital of any future Palestinian state is simply non-negotiable. The Sheikh Jarrah district became a major flashpoint in October 2009 when Palestinians facing eviction from their homes held a demonstration outside the US Consulate. Their banner read: 'Dear Obama, we deserve your attention and protection.'

Media focus spanned the globe, and Israeli authorities were infuriated when the numbers of Israeli peace activists grew week by week. As EAPPI's team in Jerusalem, we were detailed to monitor the situation in Sheikh Jarrah. In my first report back to South Africa, I wrote:

> Mohammed Sabbagh and his family have lived in the Sheikh Jarrah area of East Jerusalem since 1956 in houses built for them by the UN. They had been evicted eight years earlier from their property in Jaffa during Israel's

1948 War of Independence, referred to by Palestinians as Al Nakbar (the catastrophe).

Twenty-eight families with similar histories live in Sheikh Jarrah. Three of them have already been forced out of their homes after long court battles. The Sabbagh family is scheduled to be the fourth. The reason: fundamentalist Jews claim the 'right of return' on the basis of a highly contested document that suggests the area was owned by Jews back in the 1880s.

Under Israeli laws, foreign-born Jews may claim such rights, but the Sabbagh family has no such rights to their property in Jaffa, now an extension of Tel Aviv. The family last week challenged the authenticity of the document in court, and the settlers have twenty-one days to prove the claim.

The traumatic circumstances of the three families already evicted from their homes have elicited worldwide media publicity. A delegation of ten European parliamentarians visited Sheikh Jarrah to voice their abhorrence of eviction of people from their houses.

To South Africans present, the evictions are ominously reminiscent of the notorious Group Areas Act. Similarly reminiscent of the apartheid era was the police announcement that the press conference was an illegal gathering, and people present had five minutes to disperse.[9]

Indeed, the parallels with apartheid South Africa are glaring, and blatantly contradict the carefully constructed perceptions of Israel as a democracy. Even the terms *apartheid* in Afrikaans and *hafrada* in Hebrew have identical meanings, namely separation.

The rate of unemployment amongst Palestinians is estimated at over fifty per cent. The parallels with apartheid are further illustrated by the annual per capita income of Israelis of US$20 000, compared with US$1 000 for Palestinians.[10] In fact, this ratio is even worse than the ten to one income differential between whites and blacks in South Africa during the apartheid era.

Rabbi Arik Aschermann of Rabbis For Human Rights wrote in despair:

> I see Jerusalem in flames – Armageddon straight ahead. The diplomats will write urgent reports, but we need effective pressure. The politicians will say that this is a matter for the courts, and that they cannot interfere. The courts

say the law takes precedence over personal consciences. The Police will prepare emergency plans. If nothing changes, Jerusalem will burn.

The US government issued statements condemning the evictions in Sheikh Jarrah, but Prime Minister Benjamin Netanyahu and his government provocatively ignored such declarations. Netanyahu told an American Israel Public Affairs Committee (AIPAC) conference in Washington DC in March 2010:

> The Jewish people were building Jerusalem three thousand years ago, and the Jewish people are building Jerusalem today. Jerusalem is not a settlement. It is our capital. Today, almost half of the city's Jewish population live in neighbourhoods beyond the 'green line'.
>
> All these neighbourhoods are within a five-minute drive from the Knesset. They are an integral and inextricable part of modern Jerusalem. Everyone knows that these neighbourhoods will be part of Israel in any peace settlement. Therefore, building them in no way precludes the possibility of a two-state solution.[11]

Everyone knows?

Even the US government regularly reiterates that Israeli settlements in East Jerusalem and the West Bank are illegal. Netanyahu's belligerence compares with P W Botha's mentality and behaviour when, as in his Rubicon speech of August 1985, Botha told the world to go to hell. Israeli politicians habitually use threats of war to deflect attention from Israel's social problems, and the economic dominance of the Ashkenazi elite who constitute only about ten per cent of Israel's population.

The columnist Carlo Strenger commented in *Haaretz*:

> Behind the immediate crisis, there looms a much deeper problem which pertains to a fallacy in Netanyahu's worldview that is reflected in all his actions. His reasoning implies that Israel can continue whatever it wants: He assumes that time is on Israel's side. The fallacy in Netanyahu's argument is fateful. His thinking and his policies have become a self-fulfilling prophecy, and are making peaceful coexistence of Israel with the Arab world impossible in the long run.

The result is catastrophic, because Netanyahu actually seems to believe that there is no connection whatsoever between how Israel conducts itself and the Arab's world's relationship to Israel. And he also seems to think that time is not of the essence and that Israel can stall further without weakening its position.[12]

Despite intense lobbying by the Zionist community, the US governments had all been extremely wary of entanglements with Israel. That stance changed dramatically when Henry Kissinger became Secretary of State in 1973 during the Nixon administration. The US was then reeling in shock over the fiascos of the war in Vietnam and the Watergate scandal. Cold War tensions with the Soviet Union were at their peak, and Kissinger was determined to project American power in the world.

The Middle East was and remains a ready flashpoint. In his book entitled *A World Of Trouble*, the American journalist Patrick Tyler writes:

> More than any other American official, Kissinger authored the notion that without disproportionate bias in American policy toward Israel, the Arab camp would sense a loss of American support for the Jewish state and would rush in to annihilate it. He seemed deaf to the advice of his more knowledgeable peers.
>
> By the end of the Nixon administration in 1974, Israel would be straining under the load of American arms that Nixon and Kissinger authorised, and the sheer size of the arsenal would lead Israeli generals, and their political patrons, to contemplate offensive military operations in the region, the invasion of Lebanon being the most devastating example.[13]

Commitment to the Zionist cause shaped Kissinger's view of the Middle East, but his ties to the Shah of Iran further compounded his prejudices and biases against Arabs. Tyler also reveals:

> Kissinger and the Shah, with Nixon's apparent approval, agreed to coordinate a secret contingency plan to seize control of Saudi Arabia and its massive oil wealth in the event of instability or a radical takeover of the kingdom. Here were Nixon and Kissinger ceding the American security role to a regional autocrat, the Shah, whose ambition to dominate the Arabs was growing

beyond his competence or capability, as events would later show. But that was the kind of intimate ally the Shah had become on the thinnest record of reliability, except that he was spending billions on American weapons.[14]

Arab members of the Organisation of Petroleum Exporting Countries (OPEC) retaliated with oil embargoes and massively increased prices. After initial hysteria, especially amongst American consumers, OPEC's oil embargoes backfired and actually played out to favour the US. Like most commodities, oil is priced in dollars, and producer countries stacked up huge credits and 'petrodollar' balances with the major American banks. These deposits in turn resulted in reckless lending practices by those banks, and led to future financial crises.

In fact, American banks, oil and armaments companies expanded hugely. In combination, these corporations became the new 'war business' that encouraged and profited from political turmoil. With massive increases in oil revenues after the 1973 Yom Kippur war and encouraged by the US government, Iran, Iraq and Saudi Arabia all squandered their new wealth on American-made armaments.

America's new style imperialism was premised upon a balance of terror and, in pursuit of 'democracy', in supporting dictatorial regimes. Given its own agenda of military hegemony from Iran to Morocco, with lavish American funding Israel willingly and eagerly became the US's surrogate in the Middle East.[15]

Yet the huge American arsenal in Iran finally proved useless in 1979 in defending the Shah's dictatorial regime from collapse. The repercussions continue to reverberate around the world. Iraq was encouraged to attack Iran in December 1980. In the ensuing eight years about one million people died in a war deliberately instigated to bleed both Iraq and Iran so that neither country might pose a threat to the Saudi monarchy.

Weapons were poured into Iraq by numerous countries, including South Africa, whilst both Israel and the Americans also surreptitiously supplied the Iranians. The then prime minister and future French President Jacques Chirac was so involved during the 1970s in arms export deals that his nickname became 'Monsieur Irak'. Author Kenneth Timmerman, in his book *The Death Lobby: How The West Armed Iraq*, describes those deals as:

> Petrochemical plants, desalinization plants, gas liquefaction complexes, housing projects, telecommunications systems, broadcasting networks, fertiliser plants, defence electronic factories, car assembly plants, a new airport, a subway system, and a navy yard, not to mention Exocet, Milan, HOT, Magic, Martel and Armat missiles, Alouette III, Gazelle and Super-Puma helicopters, AMX 30-GCT howitzers, Tiger-G radar, and a nuclear reactor capable of making the bomb. It was a multi-billion dollar relationship.
>
> The Franco-Iraqi Nuclear Cooperation Treaty committed the French to train six hundred Iraqi nuclear technicians, more than enough for a nuclear bomb programme. Others were to receive training at the Commissariat à l'Energie Atomique, including training of chemists because extracting military plutonium from spent reactor fuel required complex chemical processes.[16]

A financially exhausted Iraq then invaded Kuwait in 1990, intending to use Kuwaiti financial resources to repay the massive loans that had been taken out to buy weapons from virtually every arms producer in the world.

The first Gulf War in 1991 and the second War on Iraq of 2003 were both direct consequences of the armaments industry's controls over politicians in the US and Britain. With the collapse of the Soviet Union, a new enemy was quickly created in Islam. Samuel Huntington's thesis of a 'clash of civilisations' between Islam, Judaism and Christianity provided justification for still greater expenditure on armaments and war. The communist 'anti-Christ' was replaced by the 'war' against Muslim terrorists.

Belligerent alliances hinged on absurd but ingenious identifications of 'good and bad Muslims'. Vile dictatorships in Saudi Arabia, Egypt, Yemen and Jordan were extolled as 'moderate'. Dictatorships in Iran and Iraq (and Venezuela) were, however, condemned and labelled as 'the axis of evil' because they demanded payment for their oil exports in currencies other than the US dollar.

There is always someone who can be bribed and employed to do 'the dirty work'. Prince Bandar had been dispatched to England at the age of sixteen to be trained as an air force pilot. The illegitimate offspring born in 1950 of a Saudi prince and a Yemeni slave girl, Bandar has played a hugely malevolent role in world power plays since the late 1970s. His late father was Crown Prince Sultan, and his uncle is Saudi King Abdullah.

Bandar was sent to Washington in 1978 to buy ninety-one F-15 fighter aircraft for the Saudi Arabian Air Force.[17] It was the beginning of his long personal relationships over the next three decades with the political elites in the US, Britain and elsewhere around the world, including South Africa.

Bandar's extraordinary skills were in working the Washington political network. When Ronald Reagan became president, the Saudis convinced him that communist threats to the Arabian/Persian Gulf and the Horn of Africa regions could sever vital supplies of oil to the US and Europe.

Reagan came to office with typical American prejudice against Arabs, and commitment to Israel. Between 1979 and 1995, Israel received well over US$60 billion's worth of American weaponry and, in addition, special arrangements included subsidies for the Israeli armaments industry as well as refinancing of Israeli debt.

The destruction of the 'Evil Empire' was Reagan's foreign policy priority. The oil wealth of Saudi Arabia became the cash cow to fund destabilisation strategies in Afghanistan, Central America and Africa. Bandar became the 'bagman' for these operations. Saudi Arabia provided the money to circumvent US congressional and legal objections after the Soviet Union invaded Afghanistan in 1979. In Afghanistan alone, this funding annually amounted to US$500 million.

As in Vietnam, Iraq, Iran, Angola and numerous other countries, the people of Afghanistan and Pakistan were merely pawns in the barbarism that followed, and still continues thirty years later. Is it deliberate, one finally asks in exasperation, that the military-industrial complex has learned nothing from these disasters?

American Christian evangelists in conjunction with the CIA unleashed a jihad in Afghanistan amongst mujahedin groups to force a Soviet withdrawal. The 'jihad' succeeded in that objective by 1988, but there have been multiple blowback consequences of that blunder, including 9/11. Neighbouring

Pakistan now teeters on the brink of being a failed state equipped with nuclear weapons.[18]

The attack on the World Trade Center in September 2001 was just the opportunity for which the war business had been waiting. Within two months the US attacked Afghanistan, ostensibly to find Osama bin Laden even though the Taliban government was willing to extradite him to Pakistan to be held under house arrest in Peshawar.

Under pressure from Washington, Pakistan's military dictator Pervez Musharaf vetoed that proposal. Blair declared: 'No peaceful alternative was ever on offer. There is no diplomacy with Bin Laden or the Taliban regime. There is no compromise possible with such people, just the choice of defeat them or be defeated by them.'[19]

In addition to the F-15 fighter aircraft which Bander had negotiated in 1978, and over vehement objections from the Israeli lobby, another arms deal in 1981 supplied Saudi Arabia with five AWAC surveillance aircraft worth US$8.5 billion. It was the start of a massive network of operating bases and military installations in the Middle East, and that full package amounted to an estimated US$85 billion.[20]

By 1985 Saudi Arabia was demanding even more armaments. The Israeli lobby in Washington was furious, so Reagan referred the matter to British Prime Minister Margaret Thatcher. She ecstatically negotiated the notorious Al Yamamah deal for one hundred and twenty British Aerospace Tornado aircraft. With the Americans supplying the Israelis and the British the Saudis, the arms race in the Middle East was notched up dramatically.

Bandar's biographer William Simpson notes:

> The Al Yamamah contracts have always been shrouded in an incomparable degree of secrecy. After running the gauntlet of US congressional hearings, meddling reporters, and the Freedom of Information Act, Saudi Arabia welcomed the British climate of confidentiality in general and the Official Secrets Act specifically.
>
> The extent of the confidentiality blanketing Al Yamamah was reinforced by the deliberate suppression of the National Audit Office (NAO) report into the deal on the grounds of national interest.

Prompted by sustained speculation in the press over the payment of large commissions, the audit ... was suppressed in March 1992 by the House of Commons Public Accounts Committee (PAC). The decision to sit on the report was made by then Labour Chairman of the PAC, Robert Sheldon, who said there was no evidence of corruption or of public money being used improperly.

The unique barter deal – premised on one quarter of the world's oil reserves – generated a phenomenal amount of money through the Defence Exports Services Organisation (DESO) before being paid to BAE. In effect, Al Yamamah became a backdoor method of buying US arms without congressional oversight.

Although Al Yamamah constitutes a highly unconventional way of doing business, its lucrative spin-offs are the by-products of a wholly political objective. Al Yamamah is, first and foremost, a political contract. [21]

British authorities estimate that more than £6 billion was paid out in illegal commissions to numerous agents and middlemen, including Thatcher's son Mark. Bandar paid £11 million to buy the two thousand acre Glympton estate in Oxfordshire, and then poured another £42 million into upgrading the place. Bandar's American ninety-five acre estate in Aspen, Colorado, was for sale for two years for US$135 million. It was the most expensive private property ever listed in the US, but was withdrawn after the property market crashed in 2008.

Even more serious than the bribes and corruption are Al Yamamah's payment arrangements. Saudi Arabia delivers oil to BP and Royal Dutch Shell, which sell it on international markets and deposit the proceeds into an account at the Bank of England. The account is controlled by British and Saudi governmental officials. The amount of oil varies according to fluctuating oil prices from three hundred thousand to six hundred thousand barrels per day. By 2010, these deliveries were generating roughly US$25 million per day for the destabilisation fund.

After payments to BAE covering supplies of armaments to Saudi Arabia, massive surpluses have been generated over the years. These surpluses are estimated by analysts in the United States to be worth about US$160 billion. Their purpose is twofold; the first being to ensure British and American support for the Saudi royal family against domestic insurrection.

The second political objective is diabolical. It is to fund covert British and American destabilisation strategies in Asia and Africa to secure mineral resources such as oil. Afghanistan, Iraq, Libya, Sudan, Nigeria, Somalia, the Congo and Zimbabwe are but some of the countries devastated by these strategies. Given rising competition in future decades for access to African resources, this devastation will escalate unless exposed and halted.

Given its mineral wealth, South Africa is another, obvious target. The extreme length to which Blair went in December 2006 to halt the Serious Fraud Office (SFO) investigation of the Al Yamamah bribes illustrates the seriousness of the matter. In effect, the slush fund at the Bank of England is the largest clandestine war chest in history. It is protected by the British Official Secrets Act and beyond the scrutiny of British citizens, their elected representatives, or the courts.

Bandar and the destabilisation fund focused on South Africa long before the arms deal was signed. Having so casually and so easily obtained US$10 million from Indonesia's General Suharto in 1990, Mandela unashamedly solicited campaign funds for the ANC. His relationship with Bandar was so extraordinarily close that Bandar was the only foreigner present at Mandela's very private and secret wedding to Graça Machel in 1998.[22]

At least US$60 million flowed from Saudi Arabia, plus contributions from Morocco, Libya and others. Numerous presidential and ministerial visits to Saudi Arabia during both the Mandela and Mbeki eras confirmed that South Africa's foreign policies, including arms sales, were being determined according to payments to the ANC.

Even Bandar finally overreached himself. Reports from Iran in August 2009 announced that he had been placed under house arrest in Saudi Arabia. Bandar's reported crime: a failed coup d'etat to remove his uncle and to install his father as king. The alternative story was that he was under treatment for alcohol abuse and depression.

After decades of deceitful dealings by the British and US governments, there were huge hopes when Obama was elected and promised 'change'. People around the world anticipated a new era. Taking advantage of the

American interregnum between the election in November and Obama's inauguration in January 2009, Israel launched Operation Cast Lead against the people of Gaza in December 2008. Obama inexplicably remained silent.

The UN Human Rights Council (UNHRC) appointed South African Judge Richard Goldstone to lead investigations into allegations of war crimes perpetrated by both the Israeli army and by Hamas during the bombardment of Gaza. The essential findings of the Goldstone Report were confirmed by Amnesty International and Human Rights Watch that Israeli actions were disproportionate to provocation by Hamas, and thus constituted a war crime.

The UN General Assembly in November 2009 endorsed the Goldstone Report by one hundred and fourteen votes to eighteen. However, US abuse of its veto powers at the UN Security Council protects Israel from the consequences of war crimes.

Expectations that Obama would usher in a new world era soon evaporated. He inherited a meltdown of the American financial system as well as the wars in Iraq and Afghanistan. Instead of using the opportunity for military withdrawal, Obama poured even more American soldiers into Afghanistan. The wars thus became 'Obama's wars'.

Americans have assumed that the international role of the US dollar enabled the US to act unilaterally to impose its will around the globe. The Eisenhower Research Project by the Watson Institute for International Studies at Brown University finds that:

- The US wars in Afghanistan, Iraq and Pakistan will cost US taxpayers between US$3.2 and US$4 trillion. Because these wars have been financed almost entirely on debt, these figures excluding the future interest on war-related debt which alone will amount to another US$1 trillion by 2020.
- At least 225 000 people, including civilians and soldiers, have been killed, and the wars have created more than 7.8 million refugees amongst Iraqis, Afghans and Pakistanis.
- The medical and other expenses for wounded, but not killed, American soldiers will amount to between US$600 and US$950 billion, and these costs will not peak until the middle of the century.[23]

Even more bizarre, the man who was awarded the 2009 Nobel Peace Prize became America's greatest ever arms dealer. *Fortune* Magazine,[24] ABC News and other commentators were aghast. Matthew Mosk wrote in November 2010:

> The Obama administration has quietly forged ahead with its proposal to sell US$60 billion worth of fighter jets and attack helicopters to Saudi Arabia, unhampered by Congress, despite questions raised in legislative inquiries and in an internal congressional report about the wisdom of the deal.
>
> The massive arms deal would be the single largest sale of weapons to a foreign buyer in the history of the US, outfitting Saudi Arabia with a fully modernised, potent new air force.
>
> The Obama administration has touted the deal as a boon for American jobs, and as a move to solidify the alliance between the US and Saudi Arabia at a time when American intelligence is dependent on the Islamic nation for help in the war on terror.
>
> Morris J Amitay, a former head of the pro-Israel lobbying group, AIPAC,[25] told ABC News a chief aim of the sale is to insure that Saudi Arabia can serve as another regional military counterweight to Iran.
>
> 'It is an attempt to bolster the Saudis at a time when the Iranians are trying to be a hegemonic power for the entire region,' he said. Israel has not been raising significant objections to the deal, even though Amitay suspects Israel will push hard to insure that the aircraft are not equipped with weapons systems as advanced as those held by Israel's own military.
>
> 'As long as Saudi Arabia is stable and considers itself a friend of the US, there is not that much concern,' Amitay said. 'The problem is how stable is a regime run by people in their 80s, with unrest in the south, where neighbouring Yemen is harbouring Al Qaeda?'[26]

The so-called 'Arab Spring' caused panic in Washington and Jerusalem but, most especially, in Riyadh amongst the royal house of Saud. Tunisia's dictator Zine Ben Ali was the first to fall in January 2011. Egypt's Hosni Mubarak was next, in February. Mubarak and his corrupt family amassed a private fortune variously estimated at between US$35 and US$70 billion, much of that fortune apparently derived from selling Egyptian oil and gas from the Sinai to Israel at a forty per cent discount.

After an absence of almost two years, Prince Bandar was politically resurrected in March 2011. That Bandar might have instigated a coup in 2009 against his uncle had not quite made sense until CIA reports suggested that King Abdullah and his brothers had 'wobbled' in their loyalty to America. Abdullah had little respect for President George Bush, and his initial optimism for Obama also soon faded.

Bandar's covert intervention and bribery skills were urgently needed however, when a rebellion erupted in Bahrain and threatened to sweep away the Bahraini monarchy and Sunni dominance of the island. There, eighty per cent of the population is Shiite and thus susceptible to Iranian influences, so Saudi and UAE troops were dispatched to defend the monarchy and to suppress the uprising violently.

American analyst Bruce Riedel commented:

> As alarming as is the unrest in Arabia to the House of Saud, the American reaction is even more unsettling. The Kingdom has built its security on an alliance with Washington since 1945. But now the US seems to be betting that history favours change in Arabia that threatens the absolute monarchy.
>
> The Saudis think America is naive at best, untrustworthy at worst. They are also looking east for help to old allies in Pakistan and China. Bandar reportedly visited Islamabad in March 2011 to ask the Pakistanis for troops, and invoked a 1980 understanding when Pakistan provided ten thousand soldiers to protect Saudi Arabia after the Iranian revolution. He has also been in Beijing to promote more trade and to ensure that the Chinese communist dictators stand by their Saudi friends.[27]

Apartheid South Africa – Saddam Hussein – Osama bin Laden – or the Saudi royal family! Supporting apartheid South Africa in the face of international protests and domestic civil disobedience eventually had become just 'too much hassle'. Bin Laden was assassinated by the Americans in Pakistan in May 2011. British journalist Robert Fisk commented:

> A single shot to the head, we were told. But the body's secret flight to Afghanistan, an equally secret burial at sea? The weird and creepy disposal of his body – no shrines, please – was almost as creepy as the man and his

vicious organisation.

The Americans were drunk with joy. 'A resounding triumph,' Israeli Prime Minister Netanyahu boasted. But after three thousand American dead on 9/11, countless more in the Middle East, up to half a million Muslims dead in Iraq and Afghanistan and ten years trying to find Bin Laden, pray let us have no more 'resounding triumphs'.

'Justice,' Obama called his death. In the old days, of course, 'justice' meant due process, a court, a hearing, a defence, a trial. Like the sons of Saddam, Bin Laden was gunned down. Sure, he never wanted to be taken alive.

But a court would have worried more people than Bin Laden. After all, he might have talked about his contacts with the CIA during the Soviet occupation of Afghanistan, or about his cosy meetings with Prince Turki, Saudi Arabia's head of intelligence.[28]

Gaddafi was next. Flowery diplomatic language deplored the gross and systematic violation of human rights, including the repression of peaceful demonstrators, expressed deep concern at the deaths of civilians, and rejected unequivocally the incitement to hostility and violence against the civilian population made from the highest level of the Libyan government.[29]

The North Atlantic Treaty Organisation (NATO) began bombing operations, and almost ten thousand bombing sorties were carried out between March and October 2011.[30] Instead of humanitarian protection, NATO's operations had devastating consequences for Libya's people and its economic infrastructure. Between thirty thousand and fifty thousand people died, but some estimates range even as high as two hundred thousand people. Refugees poured out of Libya. Many lost their lives in rickety boats trying to cross the Mediterranean Sea to Italy.

Only months earlier, major European arms companies and their governments had competed to sell their wares to Libya. Reuters reported in an article entitled 'Libya is a showcase for the new arms race':

> To take out Muammar Gaddafi's air defences, western powers such as France and Italy are using the very aircraft and weapons that only months ago they were showing off to the Libyan leader. French Rafales flew the western alliance's very first mission. One of the Rafale's theoretical targets: Libya's

French-built Mirage jets which Paris has recently agreed to repair. The Libyan operation also marks the combat debut for the Eurofighter Typhoon, a competitor to the Rafale which is being built by Britain, Germany, Italy and Spain.

Almost every modern conflict from the Spanish Civil War to Kosovo has served as a test of air power. But the Libyan operation to enforce UN Resolution 1973 coincides with a new arms race – a surge of demand in the US$60 billion a year global fighter market and the arrival of a new generation of equipment. For the countries and companies behind those planes and weapons there is no better sales tool than real combat. As soon as an aircraft is used on operational deployment, that instantly becomes a major marketing ploy; it becomes 'proven in combat'.[31]

NATO's sudden aversion to Gaddafi's dictatorship allegedly had nothing to do with support for Libyan human rights or democracy. Instead, Gaddafi had signalled an intention to demand payment for Libya's oil in gold instead of dollars.[32] Regime change even by assassination became Washington's priority, just as it has been in Iran since the 1979 revolution that toppled the Shah, or in 2003 when Iraq's Saddam Hussein wanted payment in Euros, or when Venezuela's Hugo Chavez baulked at American imperialism. Maintaining dollar supremacy in the world is critical to US military power.

In a grotesque commentary on just how far US government policies have become removed from all norms of human decency, President Barack Obama immediately declared Gaddafi's death as 'a foreign policy success'.[33]

Just months before opting to attack Libya, Britain's Prime Minister David Cameron had sent a government team to Tripoli to negotiate yet another new arms deal with Gaddafi. The country was already awash with weaponry including vast stockpiles of long-range rockets and surface-to-air missiles.[34]

Gaddafi's death coincided with that of the Saudi Crown Prince Sultan at the age of eighty-five, a crucial figure in the geriatric Saudi political establishment, and Prince Bandar's father.

Perhaps the only positive aspect of the fiasco in Libya is a growing realisation that NATO's purpose has expired, and that the waging of war is not an effective method to achieve peace, justice or security.

Endnotes

1. Julia Werdiger and Rachel Donadio: 'Oil Companies Plan Evacuations From Libya', *The New York Times*, February 21, 2011.
2. 'I'd do it again – Blair on Iraq', BBC News, January 29, 2010.
3. Andrew Gavin Marshall: 'Flashback to 1953: Operation Ajax – Joint CIA/MI6 Military Coup in Iran', Global Research, August 19, 2010.
4. Naeim Giladi: *Ben-Gurion's Scandals*, Dandelion Books, Tempe, Arizona, 2003.
5. Ibid.
6. Israel Shahak: *Open Secrets: Israeli Nuclear And Foreign Policies*, Pluto Press, London, 1997, pp 48-51.
7. Interview with Rubin Aberzer, November 27, 2009.
8. Maya Wind, ICAHD, Jerusalem, October 23, 2009.
9. EAPPI Newsletter, November 2009.
10. Professor Mustafa Abu Sway, Al Quds University.
11. Transcript of Israeli Prime Minister Binyamin Netanyahu's AIPAC speech, AIPAC, March 23, 2010.
12. Carlo Strenger: 'The Fallacy Of Netanyahu's Worldview', *Haaretz*, March 24, 2010.
13. Patrick Tyler: *A World Of Trouble: America in the Middle East*, Portobello Books, London, 2009, pp 108-109.
14. Ibid, p 121.
15. Israel Shahak: *Open Secrets: Israeli Nuclear And Foreign Policies*, Pluto Press, London, 1997.
16. Kenneth R Timmerman: *The Death Lobby: How The West Armed Iraq*, Bantam Books, London, 1992, pp 60-62.
17. William Simpson: *The Prince*, HarperCollins Publishers, New York, 2006.
18. Mahmood Mamdani: *Good Muslim, Bad Muslim*, DoubleDay, New York, 2005, pp 119-177.
19. John Pilger: *The New World Rulers*, Verso Books, London, 2002, pp 103-104.
20. William Simpson: *The Prince*, HarperCollins Publishers, New York, 2006, pp 63-94.
21. Ibid, pp 133-151.
22. Ibid, pp 362-368.
23. 'Costs Of War', Eisenhower Research Project, at the Watson Institute for

International Studies, Brown University, June 29, 2011.

24. Mina Kines: 'America's Hottest Export: Weapons', *Fortune* Magazine, February 24, 2011.

25. American Israel Public Affairs Committee.

26. Matthew Mosk: 'Critics Slam Obama Administration For "Hiding" Massive Saudi Arms Deal', ABC News, November 19, 2010.

27. Bruce Riedel: 'Saudi Arabia On The Brink', *The National Interest*, April 6, 2011.

28. Robert Fisk: 'Was He Betrayed? Of course. Pakistan Knew Bin Laden's Hiding Place All Along', *The Independent*, May 3, 2011.

29. UN Security Council resolution 1970, February 26, 2011.

30. Laura Smith-Spark: 'What's Next For NATO in Libya?' CNN, October 21, 2011.

31. Tim Hepher and Karen Jacobs: 'West Shows Off Its Latest Firepower: Libya Is A Showcase For The New Arms Race', *Cape Times*, April 8, 2011.

32. 'The Gold Dinar: Saving The World Economy From Gaddafi', Global Research, May 5, 2011.

33. Ewen MacAskill: 'Obama Hails Death of Muammar Gaddafi as foreign policy success', *The Guardian*, October 20, 2011.

34. Con Coughlin: 'Will A Middle East Awash With Weapons Be Gaddafi's Final Legacy?' *The Telegraph*, October 23, 2011.

7 • BATTING FOR BRITAIN

Robert Clive in India in the eighteenth, Cecil Rhodes in South Africa in the nineteenth, and Basil Zaharoff and other warlords in the twentieth century had no compunctions about using bribes to grease the affairs of state or business. Before the discovery of diamonds in South Africa, they used poppy seed and opium to devastate China by drug addiction, a history that the CIA disgracefully continued in Vietnam, Afghanistan and Central America.

Even in the late 1970s, the chief of the state-owned car company British Leyland feigned bewilderment that his firm 'should be criticised for the perfectly respectable fact it was bribing wogs'.[1] Margaret Thatcher called it 'batting for Britain'.

The Matrix-Churchill case investigated by the Scott Commission confirmed that Thatcher's cabinet ministers in the 1980s encouraged the company's directors to sell high grade machine tools to Iraq to manufacture weapons, and then vehemently denied anything of the kind.[2] The John Major years were marked by one arms deal corruption scandal after another.

The Pergau dam scandal revealed how the British government in 1988 unashamedly tied financial assistance of £234 million for construction of the dam in Malaysia to the purchase for £1.3 billion of BAE Hawk fighter aircraft.³ Despite court actions and judicial criticisms of the behaviour of cabinet ministers, BAE and major contracting companies still plead that 'national security' trumps all other considerations. Alternatively, if the Brits don't supply the weapons, the French will …

The adage that patriotism is the last refuge of the scoundrel needs constantly to be remembered. Sadly, the lessons of British perfidy were ignored by the South African government that rushed headlong into the traps of the arms deal debacle. The journalist Allister Sparks describes the arms deal as 'the primary cancer [that] should have been surgically removed early. The failure to do so has allowed the cancer to metastasize to the point where the whole body politic is now riddled with it'.⁴

The royal family is regularly trotted out to open doors for arms deals. Prince Andrew in 2011 was unashamed about lobbying on behalf of BAE and for lifting a prohibition on arms exports to Indonesia.⁵ Oil and mineral rich but despotic and notoriously corrupt, Kazakhstan is evidently another of Prince Andrew's favourite destinations.⁶

A quarter of a century after the Al Yamamah deal, Thatcher's legacy continues to expose how corruption in Britain, especially relating to arms exports, oil and banking, extends to the highest in the land. British anti-corruption laws have been archaic, essentially dating back to the 1880s. They have assumed that foreigners are almost all corrupt, and that bribing them is a necessary cost of doing business.

Thanks to Thatcher, Britain now has virtually no manufacturing industry other than armaments. Even those jobs are shrinking as BAE transfers its operations elsewhere. The reality is that the armaments industry is a capital intensive, not labour intensive, business and that it is massively subsidised.

The international community is still reeling from the consequences of what she unleashed, in conjunction with President Ronald Reagan and Prince Bandar, ostensibly to save the world from communism. With the collapse of the Soviet Union, hopes were high that a 'peace dividend' would bridge the economic and political disparities between the 'first' and 'third' worlds. Instead, after the Cold War the war business quickly shifted its focus from confrontation in Europe to the Middle East.

Knowing some of that history, I wrote to Blair when he visited Cape Town in 1996 pleading for South Africa to be excluded from British arms exports. Poverty eradication was the priority in the post-apartheid era and, given the militarist obsessions of the past, South Africa was already hugely over-armed. The dismissive response I received from Blair's assistant was that arms exports were a perfectly legitimate activity, and were a source of job creation in England.

The Organisation for Economic Cooperation and Development in 1997 established the OECD Conventions Against Bribery of Foreign Officials. Not until the United States after 9/11 pressured for implementation of the conventions did the British government finally introduce implementing legislation but, even then, has still remained notoriously lax about enforcing international commitments.

That Britain's involvement with the US in the 2003 'War on Iraq' was driven by government and oil company determination to gain control over Iraq's oil reserves can no longer be denied. Over one thousand documents obtained in terms of the Freedom of Information Act reveal how twenty-year contracts covering half of Iraq's reserves were bought by BP and other foreign oil companies. BP's senior management were so close to Blair that the company was even sometimes referred to as 'Blair Petroleum'.[7]

A Foreign Office memorandum in November 2002 declared: 'Iraq is a big oil prospect. BP are desperate to get in there and anxious that political deals should not deny them the opportunity to compete.' In contradiction, four months later BP was still publicly insisting: 'We have no strategic interest in Iraq. If whoever comes to power wants Western involvement post the war, if there is a war, it should be on a level playing field.'

Blair himself described the 'oil conspiracy theory is honestly the most absurd. The fact is that if Iraqi oil were our concern, we could probably cut a deal with Saddam. It is not the oil that is the issue, it is the weapons.'[8]

Blair left unmentioned, of course, that Saddam was supplied with weapons by the West, including Britain, and then encouraged to attack Iran. The British government's claim that Iraq could deploy 'weapons of mass destruction' within forty-five minutes was subsequently thoroughly discredited by the

Chilcot Inquiry.

BAE has also profited hugely from Blair's support for the Bush administration's wars in Afghanistan and Iraq, and the so-called 'War on Terror'. The Stockholm International Peace Research Institute (Sipri) in April 2010 revealed that BAE is now the world's largest armaments company. With sales of US$32.4 billion in 2008, it briefly eclipsed even Lockheed Martin with which the Bush administration had particular affinity.[9]

The oil and weapons contracts that Blair negotiated with Muammar Gaddafi in 2004 illustrate the stranglehold that the war business holds over British governments. Manipulating UN Security Council resolutions, Britain and NATO blundered into Libya in March 2011 ostensibly to defend Libyans against 'Brother Leader'.

The Centre for Policy Studies estimated that British taxpayer guarantees and liabilities for the contracts that Blair negotiated amounted to £1.18 trillion.[10] *The Observer* newspaper commented:

> Go forth and flog Britain's wares is the message. The notorious Export Credit Guarantee Department (ECGD), responsible for some of the most economically foolish and unethical business deals of the past twenty years, has been boosted. From arms sales to Saudi Arabia and Indonesia, to oil and gas pipelines in central Asia, to mega-dams in sub-Sahara Africa, the ECGD has backed projects that have been implicated in corruption, environmental destruction and human rights abuses.
>
> Algeria, Egypt and Saudi Arabia have provided rich pickings for UK arms exporters. Of all the bilateral arrangements of recent years, perhaps the most despicable is the one with Libya. Colonel Gaddafi morphed from terrorist sympathiser to friend of the west, which then turned a blind eye to his internal repression. Libya is regarded as a priority partner.
>
> Equipment approved for export to Libya included wall-and-door breaching projectile launchers, crowd control ammunition, small arms ammunition, and teargas/irritant ammunition. No requests for licences were refused.[11]

The European Union's Code of Conduct on Arms Exports, which Blair in 1998 with great fanfare purported to sponsor, failed to meet its expectations. Of course, Britain is not alone in using bribes to obtain arms export contracts.

The French, Germans and Americans are equally hypocritical. The Swedish sale of Bofors artillery to India continues to resurrect allegations that the murder of Prime Minister Olav Palme in 1986 was somehow connected to bribes paid to Indian politicians and middlemen.

Despite Swedish pretensions of being 'squeaky clean', Prime Minister Göran Persson and Defence Minister Björn von Sydow were heavily involved in pressuring the South African government to buy BAE/Saab Gripen fighter aircraft. The Gripen was a financial and political disaster. The Swedish armaments industry and government were desperate to recoup some of the public monies that had gone into it.

South Africa was targeted as a prospective export market, and the Swedes had few hesitations about leveraging their previous financial and moral support for the ANC. Objections to the Swedish lobbying efforts were met with protestations that South Africa was now a democracy and could make its own decisions about its economic priorities.

The further twist was added that it would be racist for Sweden to refuse to supply highly sophisticated fighter aircraft way beyond South Africa's capacity to provide pilots to fly them or mechanics to maintain them. I attended a parliamentary breakfast that the ANC's chief whip Tony Yengeni hosted for Von Sydow in June 1998, and sat directly across the table from Yengeni.

Von Sydow talked at length about a long-term military relationship with South Africa that would follow selection of Swedish equipment. Yengeni responded that the decision on what equipment to buy 'would depend upon the generosity of the offsets'. His 'body language' screamed: 'How big are the bribes?'

Yengeni's associate Ntsiki Mashimbye continued in that vein. 'If Sweden really wants to be generous to the "new" South Africa,' he said, 'then the Gripens should be manufactured here so that South Africa can gain the benefit of exports to countries such as Brazil.'

In reply, Von Sydow declared that he had 'got the message'! 'That decision,' he said, 'is not mine to make. But I have got the message, and will take that message back with me to Sweden.'

Von Sydow was subsequently promoted to Speaker of the Swedish Parliament, and has since pleaded, unconvincingly, that perhaps he was naive in not suspecting the involvement of bribes. Although the Gripens have been developed and made in Sweden, BAE had a major equity interest in the programme and the responsibility for international marketing.

The sale of BAE/Saab Gripens to South Africa was intended to fit into BAE's arrangements with Saudi Arabia. The aircraft on several occasions failed South Africa's tendering criteria. Extraordinarily, Defence Minister Joe Modise then removed cost from consideration. Over objections by the Secretary for Defence Pierre Steyn, Modise announced that South Africa's armaments industry needed what he termed a 'visionary approach'.

Modise's 'visionary approach' was that the state-owned armaments company Denel would manufacture BAE armaments under licence in South Africa for export to Saudi Arabia. Denel and South Africa would thereby join the big league in the international war business. Corruption and human rights abuses in Saudi Arabia are notorious but, in the event of any public uproar, BAE and the British government could disclaim responsibility and shift the blame to South Africa.

Shop stewards of the National Union of Metalworkers of South Africa (Numsa) in December 1998 informed me that BAE bribes, described as 'funding for an industrial training school' were being laundered via two Swedish trade unions. A Swedish television journalist confirmed the payments, but could obtain no further details.

Accordingly, through the Campaign Against Arms Trade (CAAT) in London, I asked the British government to probe whether BAE was bribing South African politicians. The London Metropolitan Police were detailed to the task. The response, astonishingly, was that it was not illegal in Britain to bribe foreigners, so there was no crime for Scotland Yard to investigate.

A few months later Yengeni's infamous Mercedes Benz 4x4 became the talk around Parliament amid allegations that he was the recipient of BAE's £1 million 'first success fee'. Other evidence of bribes soon followed, but in July 1999 the South African media was too nervous to investigate. Only in March 2001 did the *Sunday Times* finally disclose Yengeni's 4x4 saga, plus thirty-one other Mercedes Benz vehicles used to sway support for the arms deal.

The Guardian newspaper in 2003 exposed a £60 million slush fund, which BAE maintained to pay for lavish hotel accommodation, prostitutes and other services in London for visiting Saudis. David Leigh and Rob Evans continued researching meticulously and published their findings. To the embarrassment of both BAE and the British government, Leigh and Evans revealed

> … that with the help of Lloyds Bank, BAE's Red Diamond Trading Company secretly channelled payments around the world. Typically the funds would be moved to another company in Panama or Liechtenstein, with a secret owner and a Swiss bank account. The cash ended up with BAE agents or consultants. Where the money went from there was designed, deliberately, to remain a mystery.[12]

In September 2006 the British Serious Fraud Office (SFO) summoned the courage to investigate the Swiss bank accounts of members of the Saudi royal family. The Saudis were furious, and threatened that unless the British halted the investigation within ten days, BAE, BP and Royal Dutch Shell would lose the next phase of the Al Yamamah deal.

The British ambassador in Saudi Arabia, Sir Sherard Cowper-Coles, lobbied on behalf of BAE, telling the SFO director that lives on British streets would be at risk.[13] Blair stepped up the Saudi and BAE pressure. He unctuously announced that on the advice of the Attorney General, he had recommended to the SFO that in the interests of 'national security' they call off their inquiry. In turn, the SFO buckled under Blair's pressure, declaring:

> This decision has been taken following representations made both to the Attorney General and the Director of the SFO concerning the need to safeguard national and international security. It has been necessary to balance the rule of law against the wider public interest. No weight has been given to commercial interests or to the national economic interests.[14]

The claim that no weight had been given to commercial interests was plainly a lie. Blair's biographer Anthony Seldon claims that Blair was motivated by fears about fifty thousand British jobs in the arms industry, and the damage that would be inflicted on Britain's relationship with Saudi Arabia. Cowper-Coles subsequently became a BAE director.

The Guardian revealed in June 2007 that BAE, in collusion with the British Department of Defence, had paid bribes of over £1 billion to Bandar via Riggs Bank in Washington DC.[15] So suddenly the Americans became involved, and wanted to know why the British government was laundering bribes through the American banking system. Other bribes were paid through Swiss banks.

Ironically, Blair's intervention put the focus on the South African deal, which was the second largest of numerous BAE contracts under investigation in eight countries. President Thabo Mbeki was livid and, a few weeks later at the World Economic Forum conference in Davos, angrily berated Blair as a hypocrite. *The Guardian* and civil society organisations persisted.

CAAT and the Corner House took the SFO to court, arguing that British obligations under the OECD's anti-bribery convention expressly forbid the termination of corruption investigations on grounds other than the merits of the case. The SFO had itself stated that its decision was based on the grounds that continuing the corruption investigation would damage relations with Saudi Arabia and thus the UK's national security.

CAAT and the Corner House won their case. On appeal to the House of Lords, the law lords decided that the government holds the prerogative to decide what does and does not constitute 'national security'. That, however, was not the end of the matter. The FBI in May 2008 detained BAE executives as they transited American airports.

In November 2008, just before they were disbanded, the Scorpions obtained court authority to raid BAE's premises around the country. The one hundred and sixty pages of affidavits presented to the court in Pretoria detail how BAE used a front company, Red Diamond Trading, to launder bribes of £115 million to South African bagmen.

The amount of the bribes tallied with what we estimated back in 2002 when I obtained a copy of the BAE loan agreements signed by Finance Minister Trevor Manuel. I subsequently learned that BAE had actually budgeted for £200 million, but the figures were scaled down after objections by the British government's Export Credit Guarantee Department (ECGD). Most of the bribes were distributed after Manuel signed the loan agreements.

I had written to the ECGD during October 1999 advising that very serious evidence of corruption had been forwarded to the Judge Heath Unit and that pending those investigations it would be fraudulent to finalise the financing arrangements. To my surprise, the same director of the ECGD with whom I was corresponding, Chris Leeds, was the very man who in January 2000 signed the loan agreements on behalf of the British government.

Minister Peter Hain insisted when I met him in Cape Town in February 2000 that there was absolutely no evidence of corruption. The one-time anti-apartheid activist but otherwise a politician with a chequered career, Hain was then minister in the Foreign and Commonwealth Office with particular responsibility for Africa.

In a letter to CAAT just a few months earlier, he had queried why anyone should object to sales of weapons to South Africa. The hypocrisy of British officials, and of Blair's government in particular, knew no bounds. BAE was said to 'own the key to number ten Downing Street'![16]

The late Richard Charter was a major beneficiary of the bribes. He died mysteriously in February 2004 in what was described as a heart attack during a canoeing accident on the Orange River. Other reports indicate that he was hit over the head with a paddle, and that his head was then held under water until he 'drowned'.

Charter's payments were laundered through Airborne Trust, which had been established by Basil Hersov, chairman of First National Bank and the Anglo-Vaal Group, and of which Modise was a patron. As the *Mail & Guardian* noted, the Trust was funded

> ... by Alan Curtis, one of the grey eminences of the British arms trade ... the so-called 'Savoy Mafia', a group of arms brokers, intelligence officers and bankers who gathered regularly at the Savoy Hotel in London during the Thatcher era.
>
> They were the key architects of British arms sales to Saudi Arabia, as well as to Iraq during the Iran-Iraq war. Curtis was a close friend of Thatcher's husband Denis and, according to security writer RT Taylor, one of the

Savoy Mafia's recruits was her son Mark, reputed to have made £12 million out of the infamous BAE-Saudi al-Yamamah arms deal.

The M&G understands that the SFO is investigating whether Curtis may have also received commission payouts on the South African deal.[17]

Over £40 million was paid to another company in the British Virgin Islands called Kayswell Services Ltd, which was sixty per cent owned by John Bredenkamp who was BAE's main agent for southern Africa.

A third major beneficiary of the bribes was Fana Hlongwane to whom BAE between September 2003 and January 2007 paid more than £10 million through Hlongwane Consulting. Hlongwane received more than R51 million from Sanip, a South African-registered company owned by Saab, the Swedish manufacturer of the BAE/Saab Gripen fighter aircraft. Another R30 million was due for payment during 2011.[18]

The affidavits revealed that through various other vehicles the payments to Hlongwane amounted to over R280 million. Hlongwane was Modise's adviser during the arms deal negotiations. Amongst numerous allegations requiring investigation is whether the arms deal was the payback to Modise from Mbeki for removing Chris Hani as a candidate to succeed Nelson Mandela as president. It also provided huge enrichment opportunities.

Persistent allegations in the public domain link the murder in April 1993 of Chris Hani to Modise, and beyond to BAE. There was long-time animosity between Hani and Modise that had dated from Camp Quattro days. Hani was then only saved from execution because of intervention by the late Oliver Tambo. These allegations are highly controversial, and are still shrouded in unproven claims but are regularly resurrected by the Communist Party and others. For some days after Hani's murder the country hovered on the brink of anarchy and South Africa's transition to democracy was very nearly aborted.

The Truth and Reconciliation Commission's (TRC) investigation into Hani's assassination was, at best, inconclusive. At worst, it was a deliberate cover-up by factions within the ANC. Mbeki and Hani had been rivals for leadership of the ANC. Modise backed Mbeki, and orchestrated the 'dirty tricks' that removed both Hani and Cyril Ramaphosa from contention.

The allegations include Bredenkamp as the mastermind behind the assassination, and that the Conservative Party's Clive Derby-Lewis was merely a useful red herring and idiot to shift the blame to white right-wing extremists. It is alleged that co-assassin Janusz Walus was employed by BAE and Bredenkamp, the latter having made little secret of his propensity for 'third world procedures'.

Bredenkamp is allegedly a top British intelligence operative and a tobacco and arms sanctions buster during the Rhodesian UDI days. He is reputedly one of the main money men behind Zimbabwe's President Robert Mugabe.[19] He is also, perchance, amongst a handful of whites who have continued to prosper in Zimbabwe.

Before going into exile to become the leader of Umkhonto we Sizwe, Modise had been a gangster in Alexandra township and he ran drug trafficking, car theft and diamond rackets to maintain his lavish lifestyle in Lusaka. He was allegedly protected by an espionage network that included South African as well as American and British intelligence agencies. Even before the ANC was unbanned in February 1990, BAE was already preparing for the arms deal and had Modise in its clutches.

I was informed six weeks before he died in November 2001 – ostensibly after a short battle against cancer – that Modise was in fact being poisoned. The ghosts from Camp Quattro had finally taken revenge. There was nothing at the time that I could do about this. Besides, I was not particularly sympathetic. Nonetheless, in April 2004 I submitted a report to the police in the Western Cape but, predictably, no action was taken.

During 2008 I had been cooperating with senior investigative journalists at the *Sunday Times* newspaper. They had asked for my assistance in ridding the country of Mbeki by exposing bribes he had accepted from German paymasters. I appreciated the risks involved, but I also had no hesitation in agreeing to help.

For three weeks in succession, the newspaper published details about the arms deal. The first were revelations that Mbeki had received R30 million from MAN Ferrostaal, of which he paid R28 million to the ANC and gave R2 million to Jacob Zuma.[20] The newspaper also focused on economic warnings given to Mbeki and cabinet ministers by the arms deal affordability study which, irrationally, they ignored.

MAN Ferrostaal has subsequently become the subject of a massive corruption scandal in Germany, which may eventually eclipse even the sensational Siemens case. For years, Europe's largest and most prestigious engineering company paid bribes to secure contracts in 'third world countries', including South Africa. Eventually in 2008 after US pressure on the German government, Siemens paid fines of US$1.6 billion to settle the investigations.[21]

The allegations against Ferrostaal include astonishing claims that it actually made a business of fronting for other German companies and of arranging requisite bribery payments.[22] South Africa was just one of a dozen countries where bribes were paid totalling Euros 336 million (R3.4 billion). Indeed, the Greek and Eurozone financial crisis in part relates back to German, French and US pressures on successive Greek governments to buy armaments way beyond Greece's requirements.[23]

Ferrostaal boasted that it was one of the world's leaders in the use of offsets for government procurements. The offsets for South Africa's purchase of three German submarines were touted as a stainless steel plant at Coega that would create over sixteen thousand jobs. Predictably, the plant never materialised, and the company has dismally failed to meet its commitments.

The Debevoise & Plimpton report in April 2011 revealed that the bribes to secure the submarine contracts were at least Euros 36 million (R350 million), and that the offset contracts were merely vehicles to pay bribes. In facilitating these contracts, Greek tycoon Tony Georgiadis's role was as conduit to politicians, including Mbeki and Nelson Mandela.[24] As recently as September 2010 MAN Ferrostaal announced that it would provide funding of R75 million towards making the film of Nelson Mandela's biography, *Long Walk To Freedom*.[25]

The *Sunday Times* provided me with the final version of the affordability study. The Cape High Court back in March 2003 had ordered Finance Minister Trevor Manuel, within ten days, to provide discovery to me of the financial working papers pertaining to the arms deal. He refused to comply with that ruling, despite having unsuccessfully argued in court papers that it was not in the national interest to disclose how the government conducts its financial business. It took two applications against Manuel for contempt of court before, in November 2003, I received what eventually proved to be just a draft copy of the affordability study.

At that time, I had emailed my lawyers:

> The documents received yesterday are very uneven and incomplete. Of two hundred and twenty-four pages, fifty-one relate to three steel projects, the opening paragraph says South Africa doesn't need another steel mill. After comparison with chapters eight and nine of the JIT report, it is evident that we've only got part of the IONT and financial working group documents. The Cabinet most certainly did not approve of the arms deal on the basis of the documents we've got, given the repeated and unambiguous warnings they contain about the risks involved. If they did, they most certainly did 'not apply their minds'. Having ignored these warnings and signed the loan agreements, Manuel should be facing criminal charges.[26]

The version of the affordability study provided by the *Sunday Times* was even more scathing about the arms deal risks than the draft I had obtained five years earlier. With the more complete version, I calculated that Manuel had provided me with less than three per cent of the documentation the court had ordered him to hand over. Accordingly, he had committed perjury when certifying in November 2003 that he had complied with the court order.

Whether Manuel was himself a recipient of bribes is irrelevant. As finance minister, he had a constitutional obligation to ensure that the arms deal was not tainted by bribes. As Andrew Feinstein commented, the weapons procurement 'was pushed through in spite of massive risks to the fiscus, a most likely negative impact on all aspects of the macroeconomy and a clearly negative impact on the major social services'. [27]

The Prevention of Organised Crime Act (1998) also requires any person who even suspects money laundering or bribery to report his suspicions. Under this legislation, and as confirmed by South Africa's commitments to the OECD Convention Against Bribery of Foreign Officials, any person convicted of money laundering is liable to a fine of R100 million or to imprisonment for a period not exceeding thirty years.

Failure to report suspicion of money laundering and bribery is also a crime, persons convicted of such an offence being liable to a fine, or to imprisonment for a period not exceeding fifteen years.

I agreed with the *Sunday Times* to file charges of money laundering and perjury against Manuel, and was assured that the full story of his complicity would be exposed. Just before deadline, however, I was informed that the revelations had been dramatically watered-down on the orders of the newspaper's management, and had been relegated to the inside pages.[28] The two journalists were profuse in their apologies to me.

Manuel's response was rapid, alleging that my vindictive attitude towards him was compromising South Africa's international standing. He sought a two-year suspended jail sentence for my refusal to abide by an interim gagging order he had obtained in March 2008.

With hindsight, I should have based my defence upon the money laundering and perjury charges. In an error of judgment, I held my tongue and accordingly my conduct was raked over the coals by the judge. Lacking funds for legal representation, I had to represent myself. It was a nightmare.

Instead, however, of the suspended jail sentence that Manuel sought, Judge Burton Fourie refused to pass sentence for three years. The arms deal loan agreements that bear Manuel's signature are in my opinion a textbook example of third world debt entrapment by European banks and government agents. They have never been submitted for scrutiny or approval by South Africa's parliamentarians.

As I left the court and faced a press barrage, I declared my confidence that I would be vindicated long before three years elapsed. True enough, the revelations led to Mbeki's dismissal as president just one month later. The *Sunday Times* had achieved its objective. Manuel resigned with him, but then retracted his resignation.

My previous book *Eye On The Money*, published in August 2007, records my objections to Manuel's involvement in the arms deal. Feinstein's *After The Party* came out in October 2007. Feinstein describes how Manuel invited him to lunch near parliament, and at the end of the meal came to the real point of the meeting:

We all know JM [as Joe Modise was known]. It's possible that there was some shit in the deal. But if there was, no one will ever uncover it. They're not that stupid. Just let lie. Focus on the technical stuff, which was sound.

I responded that there were even problems with the technical aspects, and warned that if we didn't get to the bottom of the deal now, it would come back to haunt us – a view I expressed over and over again within the ANC.

Another senior member of the ANC's National Executive Committee invited me to his house one Sunday. Sitting outside in the sunshine, he explained to me that I was never going to 'win this thing'.

Why not? I demanded.

Because we received money from some of the winning companies. How do you think we funded the 1999 election?[29]

Quite clearly, Manuel suspected that Modise had been bribed. The two ministers had been members of the cabinet's arms deal subcommittee. As the affordability study confirmed, the arms deal was unaffordable. The only logical conclusion was that the cabinet decision was driven by bribes paid by the arms suppliers. The Debevoise & Plimpton report confirms that the corruption was on a scale beyond what even I had estimated.

As Finance Minister, Manuel's responsibility in the arms deal was its affordability and financing arrangements. He was known to have opposed the arms deal during its early stages. Yet it is his signature on the loan agreements that gives effect to the contracts. Feinstein had been the ANC's senior representative in the parliamentary Standing Committee on Public Accounts (Scopa). He was eventually drummed out of parliament when his commitment to clean and transparent public administration brought him into conflict with Mbeki and the ANC's hierarchy.

For many years the ANC was insolvent and salary and other expenses often had to be met by Tokyo Sexwale and other wealthy members. Then to South Africa's astonishment, Mendi Msimang announced at the ANC's congress at Polokwane in December 2007 that the party had assets worth R1.75 billion.

Msimang had been South Africa's High Commissioner in London when the arms deal contracts were negotiated. Subsequently and curiously, he was still included in many of the arms deal negotiations even after he became the ANC's treasurer.

Equally dramatically, it was at the Polokwane congress where Jacob Zuma turned the tables on Mbeki, and humiliated him. He and his closest cabinet colleagues were booed and voted off the National Executive Committee (NEC).

Manuel, who five years earlier had been voted into first place on the NEC, only just 'made the cut' in fifty-seventh place in the sixty-member body. I wrote a letter to the *Cape Argus* expressing delight that Manuel might be one of the first ministerial casualties of the Polokwane conference. Manuel applied to the Cape High Court and won a gagging order against me.

The arms deal was the underlying issue for the internal coup d'etat in the ANC. In sensational and protracted court cases, Mbeki tried unsuccessfully to scapegoat Zuma to divert attention from his own far greater complicity.

Mbeki chaired the committee which had oversight over acquisitions of warships and warplanes, and as early as January 1995 had been irregularly scheming with German Foreign Minister Klaus Kinkel and ThyssenKrupp executives.[30] Mbeki's positions on Aids, Zimbabwe and the arms deal became the three defining issues of his unlamented presidency.

Commenting on the *Sunday Times* revelations, Mbeki's biographer Mark Gevisser wrote:

> If the arms deal has become the poisoned well of post-apartheid South Africa politics, then it was Thabo Mbeki who initially contaminated the water. And as the allegations multiplied, he became increasingly strident in his defence of it.
>
> Nothing in the South African transition illustrates this more trenchantly than the spectacle of an ANC government committed to redistribution and 'a better life for all' dropping nearly R60 billion on submarines, frigates and fighter jets at a time when it was trying to cap spending on everything else. We live with the consequences.
>
> The government was forced to admit in 2006 that only thirteen thousand of the promised sixty-five thousand jobs had materialised, and it became clear that many of the offsets would be rolled out entirely at the discretion of the sellers. In the end, arms companies seemed to find it cheaper to be fined

for non-compliance than to have to deliver on their promises.

Manuel was opposed to the arms deal from the start, because it ran so counter to Gear principles and because he was convinced that the rand would depreciate and this would raise the [sic] value (cost) of the deal considerably – something on which he was ultimately proven correct.

It has not yet been alleged that Mbeki is personally corrupt, although it is clear that he played a key role in steering the state away from the navy's original preference for Spanish corvettes, which were much cheaper, and towards the German ones. The German media revealed that a R130 million bribe was paid in this deal, but authorities there have dropped their investigation – apparently because of lack of co-operation from the South Africans.

Now the *Sunday Times* has alleged that Mbeki received a R30 million kickback for the submarine contract, and that he channelled the money to the ANC and to Zuma. Of course, if Mbeki did hand a kickback on to his movement, or to a comrade in financial trouble, this makes it no less corrupt.[31]

Manuel's refusal to put his pen to paper, as finance minister, would have vetoed the arms deal. Like his predecessor Owen Horwood, who notoriously signed the 'Infogate' cheques, Manuel simply 'closed his eyes'. When I tried previously to have the loan agreements set aside, the Cape High Court ruled that Manuel was merely implementing a cabinet decision. The judges ducked the issues. They ruled that I had sued the wrong person and, in effect, decided that the finance minister was merely a messenger boy. The alarming implication was that every cabinet minister was above the law.

The consequences were predictable. Almost every government department became dysfunctional and most repeatedly received qualified audits from the Auditor General's office. Corruption in government departments was rife, and the public at large was by now increasingly vocal about 'non-delivery' of social services. Manuel's functions included not only tax collection, but also oversight on how monies are spent.

In particular, despite huge financial resources poured into them, South Africa's public education and health services are even worse than they had been in the apartheid era. The number of people living in shacks in the most appalling conditions was, and remains, a national disgrace. These failures by the ANC government are inexcusable, and unforgivable.

After removing Mbeki and his allies, the ANC's next priority at Polokwane was the disbandment of the Scorpions, South Africa's counterpart of the FBI.

The Zuma camp insisted that investigation by the Scorpions into Zuma's involvement with Schabir Shaik and the arms deal represented a political agenda, and that they had abused their authority. General Siphiwe Nyanda, himself a major beneficiary of the arms deal and a Zuma ally, brazenly declared that the Scorpions had 'acted outside the strictures of the Constitution and national legislation, compromised the security of the Republic, exceeded their legal mandate and operated without oversight'.[32]

Even the Constitutional Court was initially reluctant to get involved. In rejecting Hugh Glenister's application in 2008 that disbandment of the Scorpions deprived South Africans of an effective crime-fighting unit, the Court cited the doctrine of separation of powers, and that it could not therefore interfere in parliament's intentions to bring corruption investigations under the control of the police.[33]

South Africa's constitutional democracy seemed likely to follow the tragic example of neighbouring Zimbabwe. Abuse of power by governments and politicians is obviously nothing new, but new concerns could be sensed amongst some citizens. Corruption and the arms deal scandal were back on the front pages.

The mood was sombre. St George's Cathedral in Cape Town in November 2008 became the venue for a protest meeting reminiscent of the 1980s during the struggle against apartheid. Paul Holden was talking about his recently published book, *The Arms Deal In Your Pocket*. The activist Zackie Achmat had organised a huge turnout of people concerned about Aids, corruption and xenophobic rioting directed against Zimbabwean and other refugees.

Seated a few rows behind me, Advocate Paul Hoffman SC suggested that the president's refusal to appoint a commission of inquiry into the arms deal should be judicially reviewed. A few months earlier, Hoffman had relinquished a successful and lucrative career at the Cape Bar in protest against racist and corrupt behaviour on the part the Judge President of the

Western Cape, John Hlophe.

Hoffman was then establishing the Institute For Accountability in Southern Africa (Ifaisa). He challenged the Judicial Services Commission's support for Hlophe, and encouraged Glenister to resume his campaign against disbandment of the Scorpions. Hoffman was subsequently successful with both cases before the Constitutional Court. Ifaisa has set itself the mission of:

> ... Upholding constitutionalism in Southern Africa through inculcation of the values of accountability and responsiveness to the needs of the people of the region in its governments, parastatal organisations and civil society, including business and industry. Accountability is the obligation of those with power or authority to explain their performance and justify their decisions.[34]

Two weeks after that meeting in St George's Cathedral, the Scorpions raided BAE premises around the country. It was their last action before being disbanded. A week later Archbishop Emeritus Desmond Tutu and former President F W de Klerk agreed to petition interim President Kgalema Motlanthe to appoint a commission of inquiry into the arms deal. In their open letter, Tutu and De Klerk stated:

> We write to you as concerned citizens and in conjunction with the organisations listed, all of whom are deeply troubled about the state of the rule of law, accountability and constitutionality in our country. We address you with the request that you appoint an independent and public judicial commission of inquiry into the arms deals in terms of your responsibilities under section 84 (2) (f) of the Constitution.[35]

Despite the affidavits and Scorpions raids, the dismissive response from Motlanthe was that parliament's Scopa committee, having studied the documents brought before it had decided against requests for a new investigation, 'without new, substantive and compelling evidence'.[36]

It was evident that Menzi Simelane was appointed as Director of Public Prosecutions so that he could block corruption investigations of prominent ANC members. In scathing condemnation of Simelane's previous behaviour as Director General of the Justice Department, the Ginwala Commission stopped just short of declaring him unfit to hold public office.[37] The whole thrust of the new Zuma administration was to block any investigation into the arms deal. The same was also true in England with the British government.

Fana Hlongwane had become one of South Africa's wealthiest 'black diamonds'. In misuse of his position, Simelane in March 2010 blocked prosecution of Hlongwane, and refused to seize bribe money paid into Hlongwane's bank accounts in Liechtenstein. Despite affidavits detailing why and how Hlongwane was the recipient of BAE bribes, Simelane claimed the case against him had been abandoned because of a lack of evidence.[38]

In February 2011 the British government and BAE negotiated a plea bargain agreement and a fine of £30 million arising from BAE's 'failure to keep reasonably accurate accounting records' of bribes it had paid in Tanzania. No reference was made to the bribes that BAE had paid in South Africa.

In conjunction with this agreement, the US authorities allowed BAE to plead guilty to 'one charge of conspiracy to make false statements', and fined BAE US$400 million. The Americans fined BAE another US$79 million in May 2011 for more than two thousand, five hundred regulatory violations on arms exports.[39]

Again, no reference was made to the South African bribes. The heavy fines were hailed as 'a deterrent for future improper conduct', but one that 'would not threaten the defendant's core business'. Nor was BAE blacklisted from the American weapons market.

Despite the lack of will in England to prosecute BAE, church organisations in Sweden had taken a renewed interest in the matter. An op-ed piece that I helped to draft was published simultaneously in Sweden and South Africa in March 2010, and called upon:

- The South African government to initiate an independent judicial inquiry into the allegations of corruption,
- The Swedish government to cooperate fully in these inquiries, to suspend the sale of arms to South Africa until the review process is complete, and to urge the British, German and Italian governments and suppliers to take similar action, and on

- Churches and non-government organisations in both countries to challenge their respective governments to accelerate demilitarisation, to abandon arms production, to devote public resources to the reduction of poverty, and to resolve conflicts without violence.[40]

Resulting from the Gothenburg Process initiative to reduce Sweden's role in the armaments industry, three Swedish organisations in September 2010 filed charges of corruption against Saab. They noted that Sanip had made payments to Hlongwane, and that he had close connections with the ANC.[41] Saab's chief executive officer finally admitted in June 2011 that, without its knowledge, BAE had used Saab's accounts to make irregular payments to Hlongwane.

Meanwhile, under pressure from the media and in an effort to redeem its badly tarnished image, Scopa in September 2010 summonsed Simelane and General Anwar Dramat, the chief of the newly created 'Hawks' for explanations about the status of the arms deal investigation.

A month earlier I had furnished the chair of Scopa, Themba Godi, with copies of the BAE affidavits, plus the loan agreements signed by Manuel, and also the complaints of perjury and money laundering that I filed against Manuel in August 2008.

The Democratic Alliance's representative on the committee, Mark Steele, commented that the political interference and foot-dragging on the arms deal scandal was unconscionable, and asked whether Simelane had the necessary will to take the matter forward. In response, Simelane declared:

> ... the matter will be dealt with in accordance with the law, not to suit some political parties. I will not rush the matter, and it will be conducted in the appropriate normal manner of doing business.

Dramat acknowledged that the Hawks had inherited three investigations from the Scorpions into the frigate, submarine and BAE contracts.[42] Astonishingly, he then revealed that the huge quantity of BAE information seized by the Scorpions amounted to four hundred and sixty boxes and 4.7 million computer pages of evidence.

It would take ten years to investigate, he said, given that there was only one person assigned to the task. Dramat then announced two weeks later that all three investigations had been abandoned.

I returned to Palestine a few days later, but through my lawyers lodged an application in the public interest to the Constitutional Court. I requested the Court to overrule the president's refusal to appoint a judicial commission of inquiry into the arms deal.[43] The Court scheduled a hearing for May 5, 2011.

Our heads of argument set out my contention that:

> ... under South Africa's system of government, the President is obliged to ensure accountability, responsiveness and openness. Conduct inconsistent with these foundational values is invalid. Obligations include the responsibility of the President to appoint a commission of inquiry ... and that refusal to appoint a commission of inquiry [in the circumstances of the arms deal] is constitutionally invalid.

The next development was the Constitutional Court's ruling in March 2011 that the legislation that abolished the Scorpions and established the Hawks was unconstitutional because the Hawks were not politically independent. The Court noted:

> Corruption threatens virtually everything that the country holds dear in its hard-won constitutional order. It blatantly undermines the democratic ethos, the institutions of democracy, the rule of law and the foundational values of our nascent constitutional project. When corruption and organised crime flourish, sustainable development and economic growth are stunted.[44]

The Glenister judgment was a huge boost to our confidence. Tutu again wrote to President Zuma asking him urgently 'to appoint a commission of inquiry now as a first step towards rooting out the cancer of corruption in South Africa'.[45] The *Cape Argus* newspaper followed up with an editorial entitled 'The Case For An Inquiry':

> President Jacob Zuma's reaction to Archbishop Emeritus Desmond Tutu's challenge to him to set up an independent commission of inquiry into the

now infamous multibillion rand arms deal will be a telling measure of South Africa's commitment to open government. It is to be hoped that the president considers carefully the plain argument the Archbishop has presented.

The risk of not dealing openly and decisively with the myriad claims of corruption associated with the arms deal is not only that those specific instances will remain untested – and potentially, unpunished – but that an implicit legitimacy is unwittingly conferred on corrupt habits and impulses throughout society as long as those engaged in them can get away with it.[46]

Endnotes

1. Andy McSmith: 'The Firm With The Back Door Key To Number 10', *The Independent*, October 2, 2009.
2. 'The Scott Report', BBC News, April 27, 2004.
3. 'Arms And The Dam', *The Economist*, February 1997, and dissertation by Alexander Gordy: 'The Implications Of The Pergau Dam Scandal', April 2004.
4. Allister Sparks: 'The Law Of Creeping Corruption', *Business Day*, April 14, 2010.
5. David Brown: 'Prince Andrew Attacked For Opening Door To Arms Dealers', *The Times*, April 11, 2011.
6. Robert Mendick and Andrew Alderson: 'Prince Andrew And The Kazakhstan Connection', *The Telegraph*, May 30, 2010.
7. Kim Sengupta: 'Tony Blair's Former Iraq Envoy Lobbied For BP Oil', *The Independent*, May 19, 2011.
8. Paul Bignell: 'Secret Memos Expose Link Between Oil Firms And Invasion of Iraq', *The Independent*, April 19, 2011.
9. Richard Norton-Taylor: 'BAE Tops Global List Of Largest Arms Manufacturers', *The Guardian*, April 12, 2010.
10. 'Libyan Massacre That Should Shame Blair', Mail OnLine, Febuary 21, 2011.
11. John Kampfner: 'When Tyrants Want Teár Gas, The UK Has Always Been Happy To Oblige', *The Observer*, February 20, 2011.
12. David Leigh and Rob Evans: 'BAE And The SFO And The Inquiry That Refused To Go Away', *The Guardian*, October 1, 2009.
13. Anthony Seldon: *Blair Unbound*, Simon & Schuster, London, 2007, p 526.
14. www.controlbae.org
15. David Leigh and Rob Evans: 'BAE Secretly Aid More Than £1 billion Via US Bank To Saudi Prince, Sanctioned by MOD', *The Guardian*, June 7, 2007.
16. Andy McSmith: 'The Firm With The Back Door Key To Number 10', *The Independent*, October 2, 2009.
17. Adriaan Basson, Sam Sole and Stefaans Brummer: 'Arms Probe Reopened', *Mail & Guardian*, March 20, 2008.
18. 'New Light Over Shady Aircraft Deal', *Stockholm News*, May 17, 2011.
19. 'John Bredenkamp puts his foot in it', *EIR*, June 7, 2007.

20. Megan Power and Jocelyn Maker: 'The R30 million Bombshell That Points Fingers At Both Mbeki And His Former Deputy', *Sunday Times*, August 3, 2008.

21. Catherine Hickey: 'Siemens Bribes Leave Von Pierer Unbowed In CEO Memoir', Bloomberg, January 27, 2011.

22. Jorg Schmitt: 'Germany's Ferrostaal Suspected Of Organising Bribes For Other Firms', *Der Spiegel*, March 30, 2010.

23. Christopher Rhoads: 'The Submarine Deals That Helped Sink Greece', *Wall Street Journal*, July 10, 2010.

24. Debevoise & Plimpton: 'Ferrostaal Final Report Compliance Investigation', April 13, 2011.

25. 'Ferrostaal Draws Anger Over Funding For Mandela Film', *Mail & Guardian*, November 3, 2010.

26. Email message to Charles Abrahams and Paul Eia dated 19 November 2003.

27. Megan Power and Jocelyn Maker: 'Hefty Price Tag: What The Boffins Say', *Sunday Times*, August 10, 2008.

28. Megan Power and Jocelyn Maker: 'Now Manuel Faces Arms-Deal Charges', *Sunday Times*, August 17, 2008.

29. Andrew Feinstein: *After The Party*, Jonathan Ball Publishers, Johannesburg and Cape Town, 2007, p 177.

30. Jean le May: 'Corvettes – Thabo All At Sea', *Weekend Argus*, May 21, 1995.

31. Mark Gevisser: 'Why Mbeki Went For The Arms Deal', *Cape Argus*, August 10, 2008.

32. 'ANC Defend Scorpions Disbandment,' Independent newspapers website, August 7, 2008.

33. 'Glenister Fails In Scorpions Court Appeal', *Mail & Guardian*, October 22, 2008.

34. www.ifaisa.org website.

35. Letter to President Kgalema Motlanthe dated 1 December 2008.

36. Reply from President Motlanthe dated 12 December 2008.

37. Adriaan Basson and Sello Adcock: 'The case against Simelane', *Mail & Guardian*, December 4, 2009.

38. Rob Rose: 'How Arms-Deal Man Escaped with R200 million', *Sunday Times*, March 21, 2010.

39. Stephen Foley: 'BAE To Pay "Final" $79m fine over US Violations', *The Independent*, May 18, 2011.

40. 'Stop The Arms Deal', *Dagens Nyheiter* and *Sunday Times*, March 13, 2010.
41. 'Saab Charged Over Sale Of Gripens To SA', *Mail & Guardian*, September 9, 2010.
42. CAS 914/11/2009, CAS 915/11/2009 and CAS916/11/2009.
43. CCT 103/10.
44. Ernest Mabuza: 'Hawks ruling: Victorious Crusader Seeks Truly Independent Corruption-Buster', *Business Day*, March 18, 2011.
45. 'Archbishop Tutu To President Zuma: Do The Right Thing On The Arms Deal', *Cape Argus*, April 12, 2011.
46. 'The Case For An Inquiry', *Cape Argus*, April 13, 2011.

'There is no hope for Al Walaja,' was the response from Jerusalem City Councillor Meir Margalit to my question in October 2010. 'The United States government,' he explained, 'proposes a land-swap-for-peace deal. Al Walaja will be incorporated into the Gush Etzion enclave, and then annexed into Israel. Al Walaja has no future.'

The area of two hundred and fifty square kilometres of Palestine known as Gush Etzion was occupied by Israel after the 1967 war. About fifty-five thousand settlers now live in twenty-two communities, the two largest being Betar Illit and Efrat. That settler population is projected to increase to ninety thousand by the year 2020.

The Palestinian population in the region numbers about eighty-five thousand people. Their livelihoods and their lives are continually threatened by the settlers. American-born Bob Lang of the Efrat Religious Council and previously adviser to Israeli Prime Minister Benjamin Netanyahu unapologetically insists upon the biblical right of Jews to live there.[1]

Belief in military service and national security for Israel from the Jordan

River to the Mediterranean trumps all ethical considerations. Lang declares that Gush Etzion is vital strategically for the survival of Israel. He challenges his listeners to look at a map of the Middle East, and to appreciate just how small Israel is by comparison with some twenty Arabic-speaking countries to which Palestinians should willingly emigrate.

The houses and streets in Efrat remind one of suburban California. In fact, a large proportion of Efrat's residents are English-speaking Jews, including recent South African, American and Australian immigrants – known in Israel as 'Anglos'. Lang adds thoughtlessly in a manner so reminiscent of whites in apartheid South Africa, 'We have good relationships with our Palestinian neighbours, and we give them our cast-off clothing.' I left the meeting gasping at the parallels with South Africa during the 1980s.

I had been placed in Jerusalem by the Ecumenical Accompaniment Programme For Palestine and Israel (EAPPI) during October 2009 to January 2010. Our duties then focused on monitoring checkpoints, house demolitions and evictions and in liaising with Israeli peace groups. It was a life-changing experience, so I had no hesitation when EAPPI invited me to return to Palestine in October 2010.

This time I was placed in Bethlehem, where four of us shared a house near the checkpoint that controls the movement of Palestinians from Bethlehem to Jerusalem. My housemates were Ulrich Kadelbach from Germany, Aimee Kent from Australia and Mathilda Lindgren from Sweden. Our primary commitment was to monitor the checkpoint and, secondly, to support the villages in the area.

There is also the huge variety of churches in Bethlehem – Greek Orthodox, Syrian Orthodox, Armenian Apostolic, Latin Catholic, Roman Catholic, Lutheran, Baptist, Presbyterian – that need encouragement given the heavy emigration of Palestinian Christians. As a German pastor who remains acutely conscious of the Holocaust, the crime of silence for a second time by German Christians is an especially heavy burden. Uli has recorded his experiences in his book entitled *Bethlehem: Zwischen Weihrauch und Tränegas* (*Bethlehem: Between Incense And Teargas*).[2]

It was a privilege, the day after returning to Palestine, to visit the

Lutheran-inspired 'Tent of Nations' project near Bethlehem. There, an inscription affirms 'we refuse to be enemies'. The Nassar family has owned the property since 1916, and have the title documents to prove it. They have spent over US$1 million in legal fees during the past twenty years to defend their ownership, but the Israeli government is still determined to evict them.

The farm is atop the highest point in the region and sometimes on a clear day one can see the Mediterranean Sea. Every structure on the property, even a chicken coop, has been served with demolition orders. The family lives below ground in caves supplied with solar-generated electricity. They conduct courses in passive resistance and conflict resolution skills for schoolchildren in the region around Bethlehem.

That same day, after dinner with a Muslim family in the nearby village of Nahalin, the men amongst us were invited to join evening prayers in the mosque, whilst the women of our team taught English to the girls. Nahalin is a very conservative rural community, and is threatened by four Israeli settlements. Much of Nahalin's agricultural land is severely polluted and now unusable because of wastes dumped on to it by settlers in Betar Illit.

October is also the season for olive harvesting when, sadly, it is not uncommon for Israeli settlers to cut down or set fire to the trees. A few days later, we received a phone call that settlers from Betar Illit had set fire to olive trees in Husan and that for 'security reasons' the Israeli army refused to allow the Palestinian fire brigade on to the land.

We immediately informed a news agency, which promptly sent a television crew to document the incident. On their arrival the army squad quickly reversed its decision but by then the trees had been destroyed.

Another village is Tuq'ua, beneath which is an aquifer supplying water to both Palestinians and Israelis. Tuq'ua is home to twelve thousand people, and the boys' high school has an enrolment of seven hundred and fifty. Bi-weekly visits by EAPPI were requested because the army regularly harasses the boys on their way to school. In fact, on my first visit I met several boys who, just a few days earlier, had been released after six months' 'administrative detention'.

Typically, the army targets thirteen-year-olds they accuse of throwing stones, and who are then jailed without trial. The purpose is to terrify the youngsters, and to turn them into informers against their older brothers. It is estimated that one-third of Palestinian boys have been jailed, usually on trumped-up charges. One day, when we were not there to witness it, the army stormed the school and fired tear gas into several of its classrooms. One of the boys, however, made a video of the incident.

The Palestinians are almost without exception hugely grateful for what little can be done by international observers to document and publicise the atrocities being committed against them.

Perhaps most moving of all the welcomes I experienced in Israel-Palestine was at a synagogue in the old Palestinian seaport of Jaffa. There, the female rabbi preached about the yearning for peace that transcends all religions. As we broke bread and shared wine and greeted one another with Shabbat Shalom, the cantor closed the service by singing John Lennon's 'Imagine', first in Hebrew and then in English:

> You may say that I'm a dreamer,
> But I'm not the only one,
> I hope someday you'll join us,
> And the world will live as one.

Strategically critical to the US intentions to annex Gush Etzion into Israel, Al Walaja is a Palestinian village two kilometres west of Jerusalem and four kilometres north of Bethlehem. Before 1948 its extensive agricultural fields and olive groves straddled the railway track between Jerusalem and Jaffa which, in terms of the 1949 Rhodes armistice agreement, then became 'the green line'. In the intervening years, successive Israeli governments have confiscated most of the village lands.

Title to ninety-two per cent of all land in Israel is held by the State. This with few exceptions is land that has been confiscated from previous Palestinian owners. The Israel lobby rigorously denies that Israel practises apartheid. Yet in practical terms, use of such land is now restricted to people only of Jewish faith.

All ninety houses in Al Walaja, even the school, have been served with demolition orders. A five-thousand-year-old olive tree, claimed to be the oldest olive tree in the world, is also to be bulldozed. Meir Margalit is a member of the Maretz Party, and is one of few Israelis still prepared to speak out about his country's theft of Palestinian land and water. He explained:

> Palestine will be allocated a similar area of land south of Hebron somewhere in the Negev. But no consideration will be given to the respective quality of the land or to the opinion of the International Court of Justice in 2004 that Israeli settlements beyond the 'green line' are illegal in terms of international law.

Israel has repeatedly ignored findings that the 'apartheid wall' is illegal. The Wall is intended to strangle Al Walaja and Palestine economically, and thus force inhabitants to leave. About forty-five thousand Israeli settlers will be housed on stolen Al Walaja land.

Margalit continued: 'The villagers' lives will become intolerable. They will be surrounded by multi-storey buildings, without farm land, with no options for developing or constructing. Ultimately, they will have to move elsewhere.'

The Hajajla family property – eighteen dunams (two hectares) and one hundred olive trees – is amongst those scheduled for demolition. In August 2010 Anas Omar Hajajla was a seven-year-old Palestinian boy who joined a small group of older boys and men in the village in a peaceful demonstration. The villagers had decided, Gandhi-style, to sit on the ground. A two-minute video taken at the protest shows Anas being carried away after a soldier hit him with a rifle butt, cutting open his head. He is heard in the video desperately telling his father: 'I can't breathe, I can't breathe.'

The soldier is shown arrogantly walking away, seemingly unconcerned by the suffering he has inflicted on the young boy. Fortunately, Anas recovered physically, and now runs around like others of his age. The psychological trauma he suffered may yet be another matter.

Soldiers of the Israeli army deployed at the protest that day were in the mood for violent confrontation. Older men were sprayed with pepper spray,[3] which is deliberately intended to inflict considerably more pain than tear gas and – in terms of article 1.5 of the Chemical Weapons Convention – is designated a banned weapon.

The demonstrators were arrested, forced to sit down, and then handcuffed back-to-back. In addition to the terrorising effects of pepper spray, sound bombs were dropped next to them. They were jailed for a day and then released.

The consequences of pepper spray include the temporary loss of vision, convulsions, a body rash and sometimes, albeit rarely, even permanent blindness and death. Israel has signed the Convention, but still refuses to ratify it or to implement its provisions.

The views from Al Walaja across the steep slopes of the valley to Jerusalem are spectacular. One can walk there in twenty minutes, a trip that some men still risk in search of work. The lavish Jerusalem shopping mall and the Teddy Kollek soccer stadium are clearly seen, but the impression also gained is that of a city ready to expand again at any price, including even war.

Below, along the floor of the valley, trains run to and from Jerusalem and Tel Aviv/Jaffa on the old railway line built during the days of the Ottoman Empire. The railway marks the 'green line'.

Although far slower than road transport, I have twice taken a train from Jerusalem to Tel Aviv just for the experience. As the trains wind their way slowly through the valley, the ruined remains can still be seen of houses of the pre-war village of Al Walaja. They stand out amongst pine trees planted by the Jewish National Fund to obscure the past Palestinian ownership of the land.

Beyond the train track is Jerusalem's 'Biblical Zoo', which Anas is not permitted to visit even though it is also visible from his home.

The Al Walaja villagers are incensed that the Vatican has cut a deal at their expense with the Israeli government to preserve its ownership of the adjacent Cremisan Theological College and Winery. The monastery has been a landmark in Palestine since the mid-nineteenth century.

The villagers feel betrayed, so I paid a visit. Cremisan's Deputy Vicar, Father Luciano Nordera, agreed to my request for an interview, but only against the strict proviso of 'nothing political and for the sake of ecumenical relationships'. An Israeli military outpost overlooks the monastery, illustrating the political sensitivity of Cremisan's position in Israel and Palestine.

It was founded in 1863 by an Italian missionary, Father Antonio Belloni, who described Cremisan as 'a gift from God'. He planted vineyards and olive groves to generate income and financial support for his ministry. The sixty-five hectares of land are dramatically terraced and meticulously cultivated. They have spectacular views of Jerusalem and a mountain known to Palestinians as Mount Everest and to Israelis as Har Gilo.

Israel annexed half of the Cremisan property after the 1967 war, but left half of it within Palestine. Israel also supplies the water necessary for irrigation of grapes and olives. The property is soon to be separated from both Bethlehem and Al Walaja by the 'apartheid wall', and a newly cleared dirt road connects Cremisan to Jerusalem.

Father Nordera says that the Second Intifada was a disaster for Cremisan. The theology college was closed in 2004 and its library of seventy thousand books was transferred to Ratisbonne, another Salesian institution in the Rehavia neighbourhood of Jerusalem.

Production of Cremisan wine has since declined in both quantity and quality, but the two thousand olive trees continue to flourish. There are ambitious new plans to reinvigorate Cremisan. A winemaster has recently been employed who will replant the vineyards with modern cultivars. The huge old monastery will be renovated as a place of reflection and new hope, and to provide retreat accommodation for the worldwide Salesian movement.

Nearby, route 60 is an 'apartheid road' under construction which will cut Al Walaja's access to Bethlehem. Against penalties of six months' imprisonment, Palestinians are even prohibited from travelling on 'apartheid roads' reserved for settlers. In the extraordinary topography that is Palestine the tunnels of route 60, which run beneath districts of Bethlehem, enable Israelis to travel from Jerusalem to the settlement towns of Gush Etzion without encountering Palestinians.

Back in 1946, ninety-three per cent of land in Palestine belonged to Palestinians and only seven per cent to Jews. Palestine has a long history of welcoming refugees from Asia, Europe and Africa, including Jewish refugees from Europe. Ignoring both morality and law, the United Nations in 1947 voted to divide Palestine and to allocate more than half of it to a Zionist state. Not surprisingly, Palestinians rejected the proposal to give away their country.

From 1947 to 1949, Zionist militias violently forced Palestinians from their homes and towns. Hundreds of Palestinians were killed, and many thousands more were forcibly rounded up, threatened with execution and evicted from their homes. The hills around Jerusalem, including Al Walaja, witnessed some of the worst atrocities. When some refugees attempted to return to their properties, they were shot as 'infiltrators'.

Israel declared statehood in May 1948, and only then did neighbouring Egypt and Jordan intervene ineffectually. Resulting from that war, Israel captured seventy-eight per cent of Palestine, Egypt occupied Gaza, and Jordan annexed 'the West Bank'. The 'green line' established during the 1949 Rhodes armistice negotiations marks the internationally recognised demarcation between Israel and Palestine.

In 1949 the UN declared, in terms of the Geneva Conventions and other instruments of international law, that Palestinian refugees had a right of return to their land.[4] Then, in 1967, Israel invaded the remaining twenty-two per cent of Palestine, and so began its occupation and colonisation of Jerusalem, the Gaza Strip, the West Bank and Syria's Golan Heights.

More than two hundred illegal Israeli settlements in the West Bank have confiscated a further forty-four per cent of Palestine. Given 'A zones', 'B zones' and 'C zones' following the 1993 Oslo negotiations and subsequent 'peace talks', the land area of the proposed independent state of Palestine in terms of the 'two-state solution' would amount to only eight per cent of the country.

It is still considered 'politically incorrect' amongst Europeans or North Americans to refer to the situation in Israel-Palestine as 'apartheid'. Israeli apologists object that there are no 'whites only' signs. We South African EAs had no such compunctions. Land thefts in South Africa by conquest and by apartheid legislation allocated eighty-seven per cent of the country to whites, whilst the remaining thirteen per cent would be independent states – the so-called Bantustans.

In the South African analogy, humiliating segregation laws were described as 'petty apartheid', and were supposedly just a temporary necessity that would disappear once 'grand apartheid' was implemented. Within Israel itself as the 'Jewish State', citizenship, language and property laws automatically reduce Christian and Muslim Israelis to second-class citizens.

Reminiscent of South Africa's anti-miscegenation laws and the notorious Immorality Act, Jews may not marry non-Jews in Israel. Illustrating this iniquity, a Jewish woman in 2010 seduced a man on a street in Jerusalem. He happened to speak fluent Hebrew, so she assumed he was Jewish. Within fifteen minutes of meeting they were having consensual sex. Three months later, she tracked him through his cellphone number and only then realised that he was Palestinian and not Jewish. She filed charges of rape. An Israeli court found him guilty, and sentenced him to two years' imprisonment.

As regards 'grand apartheid', the Bantustans in South Africa were in theory a well-intentioned agenda towards decolonisation and the problems inherited from the British Empire. The Bantustans were never internationally recognised, except by Israel, because the partition was so grossly unequal. The whites allocated the best areas to themselves and the impoverished labour reserves to the 'native' population.

Yet even the apartheid Bantustans in South Africa had more going for them as independent states than could a future Palestine split into twelve or fifteen non-contiguous pieces of land. South Africa's notorious pass laws were also crude by comparison with the surveillance and identity systems which Israelis now apply so viciously against Palestinians.

Nor were there any 'apartheid roads' in South Africa, and the 'apartheid wall' is an illegal and physical monstrosity that eclipses the Berlin Wall and the walls of the Warsaw Ghetto.

It extends seven hundred and fifty kilometres, the distance from Cape Town to Port Elizabeth. About eighty-five per cent is not actually a 'wall' but a series of fences. The fences actually cause even greater economic devastation because they cut a swathe one hundred and twenty metres wide through rural areas and agricultural land.

In the Bethlehem area, the Wall is nine metres high and is capped by three-metre high security towers. It blocks the former four-lane main road from Jerusalem to Hebron, and weaves capriciously around the town. The Anastas family, whose house abuts the Hebron road, are now surrounded on three sides by the Wall. Their friends are afraid even to visit them because all movements are recorded by surveillance cameras.

Although situated on the Palestinian side of the Wall, the Israeli army has determined that the Anastas family's use of their third floor constitutes a 'security risk'. When it rains, the flood waters rebound from the Wall into the ground floor of the Anastas home.

Graffiti adorning the Wall, much of it highly imaginative and even artistic, draws the parallels with apartheid and, worse still, to Nazi Germany. At the entrance to the checkpoint, a daubed slogan reads: 'Gas Bombs Now – Gas Chambers Tomorrow – Rise Up Whilst You Still Have Breath.'

EAPPI's primary task in Bethlehem is to monitor the CP 300 checkpoint four days per week from 4am until the lines clear, usually by about 7:30. We would arrive fifteen minutes early to find about five hundred people already waiting for the checkpoint to open. Many of the men would have slept there from 2am to be the first to get through.

CP 300 is deliberately dehumanising. Although I was familiar with the Qalandiya checkpoint from my previous three-month assignment in East Jerusalem, my first reaction was 'Oh God, can I really survive this for three months? Pull yourself together, these people face this every day of their lives,' I immediately told myself.

The men in the main line along 'the Wall' are barricaded into cages that serve as holding bays. For elderly men, women, the sick and tourists, there is the adjacent 'humanitarian lane' but when that is open, the main line for workers and family breadwinners is closed. A soldier, barricaded into a bullet-proof glass booth, electronically opens and closes the turnstiles according to the capacity of the main terminal to process the crowds.

Checkpoint duty is one of the nightmare assignments for Israeli conscript soldiers. The turnstiles very often remain closed for an hour and longer. Our function included phoning the 'humanitarian hotline' at army headquarters and other contact numbers to try to fix whatever problem in the terminal was causing delay. Our purpose was to collate figures and reports for the UN and other international organisations.

There are three metal detector machines in the terminal building. Usually only one and sometimes two, but never three, machines is in operation. The typical excuse is not enough soldiers available to supervise the machines. On one occasion I was told: 'Oh, it's the Russian squad on duty today. They all got drunk last night and overslept.'

All metal objects have to be removed, even shoes and belts. The soldiers often adjust the sensitivity of the machines just to 'play games'. Privatised security guards, machine guns at the ready, patrol the gantries above the metal detectors. In a bizarre situation, they also guard the soldiers from the Palestinians. Several hundred people can often be waiting at the turnstiles to the metal detector machines. Tempers fray quickly under these circumstances.

It is mainly construction workers who need to get through the checkpoint in the early morning. They have already been extensively vetted by the Israeli secret service, and it is almost impossible for a Palestinian male under the age of thirty to get a permit.

After the metal detectors, the next stage in the terminal is computer verification of the permit and the bearer's handprints. The terminal has twelve verification booths but, again, usually only one or two are in use. A soldier is directed by a computer, against which there is no recourse or appeal. 'The computer says …'

Should the computer reject either the handprints or permit, the worker will get no pay until the matter is remedied or will perhaps lose his job. Of the two thousand, four hundred people who typically pass through the checkpoint in the early morning, all but fifty are men.

We decided to institute daily spot checks after we were told repeatedly that without EAPPI's watching presence the behaviour of the soldiers was even worse. Friday, we learned, was usually the worst day of the week when the Israeli army took particular vehemence in humiliating elderly Palestinians.

Here is a report I wrote to EAPPI and the South African Council of Churches in Johannesburg soon after arriving in Bethlehem:

Muslims around the world faithfully observe prayers on Fridays, and the tradition in Palestine of praying at the Al Aqsa mosque in East Jerusalem is most especially revered. Fridays are the days however, when Bethlehem Checkpoint 300 – only seven kilometres south of Al Aqsa – is frequently at its most chaotic.

Repeated difficulties at the checkpoint during the week of Eid al Adha resulted in a decision that, in addition to our 04:00 checkpoint duties, we EAs should conduct daily spot checks.

There were about two hundred and fifty people waiting in the main line when I arrived at 08:30 and joined the queue. A phone call to the humanitarian hotline reached only a recorded message, an inappropriate greeting of Shalom. Another call at 08:49 to the District Commissioner's office to report the situation seemingly caused the turnstiles to be opened for just a minute. It would be 09:39 before the lines moved again.

The people were remarkably patient and good humoured. Women were dressed in their finest embroidered coats, and many men wore traditional Palestinian headdresses.

An elderly woman allowed me to photograph the permit allowing her to be in Jerusalem for Friday prayers between the hours of 05:00 and 16:00. How perverse that an official permit is required in the Holyland – of all places – before people can pray at the place of their choice!

We watched as tourist buses with foreign Christians poured into Bethlehem through the vehicle checkpoint, their pilgrim passengers oblivious to the shambles just thirty metres away. We waited for an hour and a half just to get through the turnstiles, and then into the terminal itself.

The next stage was the metal detection machines, none of which was operating, and abusive shouting by Israeli soldiers over the intercom system. About three hundred people were waiting there, some now impatient and angry. Again I phoned the DCL office, this time to no effect.

Risking possible confiscation of my camera for photographing a military installation, I took surreptitious pictures and video footage of the turmoil. Decisions at the checkpoint to allow people to enter Jerusalem can be capricious and arbitrary. I left at 10:30, and returned to Bethlehem. It might be hours before the people got through, their precious day in Jerusalem wasted at the checkpoint.

That evening, as dusk fell, I joined a handful of Catholic Caritas sisters, clerics and laypeople at the weekly Friday evening vigil walking beneath the Wall, just beyond the checkpoint. One of the regular worshippers is Clemence Handal, our Arabic teacher, part of whose property was confiscated for construction of the Wall. We prayed the 'Stations of the Cross' in Arabic, English and Latin; it was a most moving and calming experience.

Yet even here during the brief fifteen-minute vigil, soldiers sometimes intervene under the pretext of 'security'. The road alongside the Wall, which leads only to a convent, is deemed to be 'zone C'. Although on Clemence's land and on the Palestinian side of the Wall, the road remains under control of Israeli military authorities.

A couple of weeks after returning to Palestine, I received an email message from six Israeli peace activists. It was headlined 'Any South Africans Here? We Need Help Circulating This And We Don't Have Much Time'. It read:

It behoves all South Africans, themselves erstwhile beneficiaries of generous international support, to stand up and be counted among those contributing actively to the cause of freedom and justice ... we know too well that our freedom is incomplete without the freedom of the Palestinians.
Nelson Mandela, Pretoria, 4th December 1997

Dear singers, musicians and other members of the Cape Town Opera,
As Israeli citizens who are active against our government's apartheid policies, we find it distressing that the Cape Town Opera has agreed to perform at the Tel Aviv Opera House starting 12/11/10. The Tel Aviv Opera House is state sponsored, and serves Israel's 'We are a Civilised Democracy' propaganda narrative. This institution is complicit in Israel's policy of colonisation and apartheid. Therefore, we are asking you to postpone your performance to a future time when Israel no longer practices these policies.
Please do not perform Porgy and Bess in Apartheid Israel.

Time was indeed short, less than three weeks until the CTOC was scheduled to open its performance of George Gershwin's 'Porgy and Bess' at the Tel Aviv Opera House. My wife and I had in fact seen the show in Cape Town, and had thought it excellent.

The CTOC is a progressive organisation that has taken township kids, and trained them into world-ranking opera singers. Almost all its repertoire is highly politicised in favour of human rights, and has included a performance of the opera 'Fidelio' on Robben Island. Archbishop Tutu, as if in full voice and song, is depicted on one of the CTOC's most memorable banners. Why on earth would such an organisation be performing in Israel?

I immediately forwarded the appeal to the Archbishop 'with the request that you consider, as patron, asking them to call off their engagement in Tel Aviv next month'. At the time he was actually on board a ship in the Pacific Ocean off the coast of Japan, and was lecturing American students in the University of Virginia's Semester-At-Sea programme. Overnight, he forwarded the message to his office in Cape Town.

Neither he nor I had any inkling of the uproar within days after the *Cape Times* newspaper ran the story in front page headlines. In an open letter published in newspapers all over the world, the Chief Rabbi of South Africa, Warren Goldstein, declared:

> Dear Archbishop Desmond Tutu, I write to you with a heavy heart.
> You are a revered leader in South Africa, but recently have added your iconic voice to the campaign for sanctions against Israel.
>
> Archbishop, I believe you are making a terrible mistake. I am convinced that the sanctions campaign against Israel is morally repugnant because it is based on horrific and grotesquely false accusations against the Jewish people.
>
> The truth, Archbishop, is that Israel is simply not an apartheid state. In the State of Israel all citizens – Jew and Arab – are equal before the law. Israel has no Population Registration Act, no Groups Areas Act, no Mixed Marriages and Immorality Act, no Separate Representation of Voters Act, no Separate Amenities Act, no pass laws or any of the myriad apartheid laws.
>
> Israel is a vibrant democracy with a free press and independent judiciary, and accords full political, religious and other human rights to all people, including its more than one million Arab citizens. All citizens vote on the same roll in regular, multiparty elections, there are Arab parties and Arab members of other parties in Israel's parliament.
>
> Arabs and Jews share all public facilities, including hospitals and malls,

buses, cinemas and parks. And, Archbishop, that includes universities and opera houses. The other untruth is the accusation of illegal occupation of Arab land. Like the apartheid libel, this is outrageously false.[5]

The Israeli *hasbara* (propaganda) machine is extremely well organised, and lambasts all criticisms of Israel as anti-Semitic. Consequently, the CTOC rejected the Archbishop's appeal, and opened at the Tel Aviv Opera House to flash mob demonstrations that, to the astonishment of Israeli viewers, were carried on television and then around the world by YouTube.

Talented musicians and dancers parodied the iconic song 'Summertime' with:

PALESTINE – Where The Living Ain't Easy –
APARTHEID – And The Wall Is So High …

The organisers had invited me to attend, but I decided on discretion. Nonetheless, I emailed Michael Williams, the CTOC's general manager, and challenged him to bring the company through the Bethlehem checkpoint between four and six in the morning, so that they might see apartheid in Israel-Palestine for themselves.

To my surprise, he telephoned me to say that he was leaving Tel Aviv and would be at the Bethlehem checkpoint within two hours. Williams and two assistants duly arrived, and were genuinely appalled by what they saw of the checkpoint and of the apartheid wall.

Williams explained that he and the CTOC had naively walked into a minefield. The tour had been four years in negotiations. Therefore to cancel it at such short notice would have left the CTOC vulnerable to a financial lawsuit, which would have bankrupted it and would mean that the singers would be unemployed and 'on the streets' by Christmas.

The controversy erupted again in January 2011 when certain members of the South African Zionist Federation (SAZF) sought to have Archbishop Tutu and Judge Goldstone removed as patrons of the Cape Town and Johannesburg Holocaust Centres. A letter of mine published in the *Cape Times* declared:

As the culprit who forwarded the appeal by Israeli activists to Archbishop Tutu to stop the Cape Town Opera Company performances of 'Porgy and Bess' in Tel Aviv, I challenge anyone – Jew or Christian – who labels criticisms of apartheid Israel as 'anti-Semitic' to take the blinkers off their eyes.

After 62 years of military occupation of Palestine, every aspect of Israeli society is corrupted – political, legal, economic, religious, social. Israel is a military dictatorship masquerading as a democracy, where everything is trumped by 'national security'.

The 'rule of law' is a farce. There is massive war profiteering by Israeli and international corporations. The 'West Bank' and Gaza are Bantustans, even less economically viable than the Bantustans of apartheid South Africa. The parallels between apartheid South Africa and apartheid Israel are glaring.

The Holocaust was a crime against humanity. Sadly, the Zionist descendants of its victims have become the perpetrators of another crime against humanity in Palestine.

The good news is that the apartheid 'two-state solution' is fast collapsing, and a bi-national state will emerge in which Palestinians will form the majority. Even ardent Zionists within Israel now recognise that 'Israel as a Jewish state' has no future.

A counter-petition supporting Tutu garnered twelve times as many signatures. The SAZF backpedalled, and the Holocaust Centres in due course pleaded with Tutu and Goldstone to remain on as patrons. Next, the University of Johannesburg in March 2011 decided to sever its ties with Ben-Gurion University in Beer'sheva because of the latter's active engagements and research for the Israeli army.

Successive Israeli governments for many years have encouraged settlements in the West Bank to create 'facts on the ground'. Property prices are dramatically lower than in Tel Aviv or West Jerusalem, and there are numerous other incentives to lure new immigrants – most of whom are deliberately kept ignorant of the fact that they live on stolen land. The 'green line' has been obliterated, and apartheid roads create the impression that the settlements are integral parts of Israel itself.

There are now over seven hundred thousand Israelis living illegally, in terms of the Geneva Conventions, in the West Bank and East Jerusalem. One of the first measures after the 1967 war was to incorporate huge areas of East Jerusalem and beyond into the 'eternal capital of the Jewish state'.

The Mayor of Jerusalem, Nir Barkat, intends over the next twenty years to build fifty thousand more housing units. He declares that he does not support splitting the city between east and west. 'Jerusalem is a united city, one capital under Israeli sovereignty.'[6]

Most highly contentious is Barkat's plan to demolish dozens of Palestinian homes in the Silwan valley to make way for an archaeological theme park for foreign tourists. Silwan has been inhabited for thousands of years because of its arable land and supplies of water. It lies just outside the walls of the Old City and in close proximity to the Haram al Sharit and Al Aqsa mosques.

It is therefore also close to the western wall, and thus the presumed site of the Second Temple built by King Herod. Road signs for Silwan have already been replaced by signs announcing the City of David. The impression is created for tourists that this is a Jewish rather than Palestinian neighbourhood.

The Israeli government in 1997 handed control of the site to a private right-wing organisation, Elad. Professional archaeologists are highly critical of Elad's operations and its political agenda. So contentious are its activities that Netanyahu's planned visit in October 2009 was cancelled because of angry Palestinian protests. There were concerns that just his presence at the City of David would provoke rioting, and even the 'third intifada'.

Archaeologists agree that the site is where Jerusalem began some three thousand years ago, and is thus a highly important world heritage. Yet the city has also been destroyed by earthquakes many times, and so is layered by numerous civilisations. Artefacts of non-Jewish history are allegedly disregarded in Elad's quest to achieve Israeli dominance of the entire area. The courts have held that Elad cannot be prevented from searching for Jewish history. Scholars in private moments question whether King David ever lived there. Others query whether he even existed and suggest that he was just one of the myths of Jewish history.

Another of Netanyahu's political allies is the American bingo billionaire Irving Moskowitz who allocates profits from his bingo operations to 'charities'. Under peculiar tax-deduction provisions of California law, Moskowitz funds an agenda to judaise Sheikh Jarrah and other areas of East Jerusalem. The intention is no less than ethnic cleansing and eviction of Arab residents, and the transformation of Jerusalem so that it can never again be divided or become the capital of a Palestinian state.

Over many years Moskowitz has made no secret of his hostility towards Palestinians. He specialises in redevelopment of strategically positioned properties such as the old Shepherd's Hotel in Sheikh Jarrah, which he bought for US$1 million in 1985 after it had been confiscated from its Palestinian owners.

Another of Moskowitz's favourite charities is Ateret Cohanim, which runs a prominent yeshiva on the Mount of Olives. Beit Orot calls for rebuilding the Holy Temple. Its website unashamedly announces its agenda to promote judaisation of Jerusalem:

> Beit Orot represents the first living Jewish presence in two millennia on Har Hazeitim, the Mount of Olives, in Yerushalayim, filling an integral role in the reclamation and development of crucial historic areas of the Jewish capital. The Irving Moskowitz Yeshiva and Campus, a hesder yeshiva, is the nucleus of a new Jewish neighbourhood on the strategically crucial northern ridge of Har Hazeitim.
>
> In addition to its core educational and reclamation objectives, Beit Orot aims social activities to helping various sectors of Israeli society. By virtue of its location and philosophy, Beit Orot is at once defending the sacred traditions of our nation, the physical security of Eretz Yisrael and the integrity of Yerushalayim as the undivided capital of Israel and the Jewish people.[7]

These property developers have close political connections with both the Israeli and US governments. War profiteering is rife. Israeli banks, earthmoving equipment and cement companies are making massive profits from Israel's illegal occupation of Palestine, and the construction of settlements. Peace is the last item on their agenda.

It was therefore no surprise to me when the 'peace process' – including the land-swap-for-peace deals – brokered by the US collapsed just days after

I interviewed Meir Margalit. The release by Al Jazeera and *The Guardian* newspaper in January 2011 of more than one thousand, six hundred documents, immediately referred to as the 'Palestine Papers', merely confirmed what for years has been glaringly evident to local and foreign observers. *The Guardian* commented:

> It is hard to tell who appears worst: the Palestinian leaders who are weak, craven and eager to shower their counterparts with compliments; the Israelis who are polite in word but contemptuous in deed; or the Americans whose neutrality consists of bullying the weak and holding the hand of the strong. Together they conspire to build a puppet state in Palestine, at best authoritarian, at worst a surrogate for an occupying force.[8]

Robert Fisk described the disclosures 'as damning as the Balfour Declaration' and noted:

> The PA was prepared, and is prepared, to give up the 'right of return' of perhaps seven million refugees for a 'state' that may at best be only ten per cent of Palestine. It is clear that the representatives of the Palestinian people were ready to destroy any hope of the refugees going home. It is an outrage for the Palestinians to learn how their representatives have turned their backs on them.[9]

The documents show that Palestinian negotiators were even willing to yield jurisdiction over Haram-al Sharif – the Muslim holy sites in Jerusalem – to international control. Former British Prime Minister Tony Blair predictably and immediately denounced the leaks, and accused those responsible of 'wanting to seriously damage the peace process'.[10] The duplicity of the Quartet's mission was confirmed in a statement released in March 2010 reiterating

> ... that Arab-Israeli peace and the establishment of a peaceful state of Palestine in the West Bank and Gaza is in the fundamental interests of the parties, of all the states in the region.
>   The Quartet calls for a solution that addresses Israel's legitimate security

concerns, including an end to weapons smuggling into Gaza; promotes Palestinian unity based on PLO commitments and the re-unification of Gaza and the West Bank under the legitimate Palestinian Authority.[11]

The Quartet routinely denounces Hamas's refusal to renounce the use of violence whilst remaining essentially silent about the Israeli violence in the West Bank and Gaza. As Fisk suggested, ill-considered British interventions in the Middle East date back to the 1917 Balfour Declaration, and earlier. At stake have been oil supplies.

In the new age of electronic communications, the Palestine Papers expose the realities that deceit and betrayal remain the way that governments still do business. As the world's only superpower, in succession to the British Empire of a century ago, it is the credibility of the US that has suffered most from the disclosures.

Whatever the rights or wrongs of history, there are five million Jews and five million Palestinians living in the same, small country. As the American-Palestinian commentator Ali Abunimah writes:

> The fact is that today there are two communities who have a right to life, freedom, and absolute equality no matter what happened in the past or continues to happen in the present. If we start from this premise, reconciliation becomes conceivable, even possible.
>
> It is also the fundamental principle behind the post-apartheid dispensation in South Africa. The white government could have decided to use its overwhelming military resources to preserve its power for perhaps five, ten or twenty more years. It might have led to millions of deaths and reduced the country to an ungovernable failed state of warring enclaves. At some point, some critical number of white South Africans, under intense internal and external pressure, realised that giving up power was the best way to secure their future.
>
> The hope held out by South Africa is that when Israelis and Palestinians finally do conclude that separation is unachievable, there is an example of an alternative to perpetual conflict.[12]

I was in Bethlehem when Dudu Masango at the SACC in Johannesburg suggested I should attend the Russell Tribunal on Palestine in London in November 2010. I recalled that Lord Bertrand Russell was the mathematician, philosopher, the 1950 Nobel laureate for literature, one of the great intellectuals of the twentieth century, and the political activist who organised a tribunal in Sweden and Denmark to investigate American war crimes during the Vietnam War.

Russell had been a conscientious objector even during the First World War. For all his life, he remained the bane of militarists and their use of war to resolve conflicts. The war in Vietnam is the exemplar where the US jettisoned all pretences of innocence or the 'rules of war', and targeted civilians.

The US government smeared the Russell Tribunal as a kangaroo court without legal standing. The reality, however, is that the hearings in Stockholm and Copenhagen made a huge impact in galvanising public opinion and eventual American withdrawal from Vietnam.

An eminent panel of jurists unanimously found that the US government had been judged guilty of war crimes. Americans remain deeply traumatised and wounded by the experiences of that war – the first war they ever lost.

My wife and I visited Vietnam in 2009. The terrible consequences of the use of napalm, phosphorus, Agent Orange and other chemicals are still evident generations later in births of grotesquely deformed and mentally handicapped babies. About twenty per cent of Vietnam's land area was sprayed with Agent Orange to defoliate the trees and to prevent the growing of crops.

Yet given massive implications for the American economy, the US Supreme Court has blocked legal action against Monsanto, Dow Chemicals and other corporations, and financial claims by their victims. The perverse reasoning for the Supreme Court's ruling was that Agent Orange was not defined as a 'poison' during the Vietnam War.

The Russell Tribunal was resuscitated after the Israeli attack on Gaza in December 2008 and January 2009 to consider the situation in Palestine. More and more Israelis are testifying about human rights abuses during army operations. To the acute embarrassment and increasing anger of the government, an organisation of former soldiers, Breaking The Silence, has revealed that the Israeli army is neither trained nor operationally equipped for the Occupation.

Hearings held in Barcelona in March 2010 agreed that the European Union and its member states had been complicit in not holding successive Israeli governments to the obligations of the United Nations Charter, Geneva Conventions and other instruments of international law. The International Court of Justice (ICJ) in 2004 found that the construction of the wall is illegal, and that Israel is obligated to end its breaches of international law.[13] Instead, the Israeli government continues with its construction. Given the ICJ's finding, the Tribunal's session in London eight months later in November 2010 considered whether:

- International corporations are complicit in Israeli violations of international law?
- What are the legal consequences of their activities in aiding and abetting Israeli violations?
- What are the remedies available, and the obligations of states regarding corporate complicity?

I submitted a paper, and was invited to speak about the role of the international banking community in facilitating Israeli profiteering. I spoke for ten minutes on the complicity of both Israeli and international banks, and the possibility of a Belgian court order against the Society for Worldwide Interbank Financial Telecommunication (SWIFT) to suspend international payments to and from Israeli banks.

I pointed out that Israel's economy is most especially vulnerable to sanctions given its heavy dependence upon imports and exports. Without access to the international payment system facilitated by SWIFT for imports or exports, Israel's economy would rapidly collapse.

The intention of sanctions is to 'balance the scales' so that negotiations between Israel and Palestine could even become possible. Although access to New York banks remains pivotal, interbank transfer instructions are now conducted through SWIFT, which is domiciled in Belgium. SWIFT links nine thousand financial institutions in over two hundred countries.

My presentation was extremely well accepted by the jurors. They grasped the remedies that SWIFT sanctions offer as a non-violent instrument to pressure the Israeli government to enter into meaningful negotiations with Palestinian leaders. I continued:

> If international civil society is serious about the Israeli-Palestinian conflict and in ending the Occupation, then suspension of SWIFT transactions for international payments to and from Israeli banks offers an instrument to bring about a peaceful and non-violent resolution to the conflict.
>
> Rather than the poor and politically voiceless, this strategy would impact rapidly upon the political and financial elites who are profiting hugely from the present situation but also have the clout to effect political change. Such a suspension would not affect domestic banking transactions within Israel and Palestine.
>
> It is economic warfare using weapons of non-violence, and makes redundant the use of armaments, including Israel's nuclear weapons. It is a strategy that can however be reversed as soon as its measurable political objectives have been achieved and without inflicting long-term structural economic damage.
>
> SWIFT, rightly, will take action against Israeli banks only if ordered to do so by a Belgian court, and only in very exceptional circumstances. Such exceptional circumstances are now well documented. SWIFT is outside American jurisdiction, but also beyond the reach of Israeli military retaliation.
>
> I propose that the Russell Tribunal should recommend and lead a SWIFT sanctions campaign against Israeli banks. What is required is an urgent application in a Belgian court ordering SWIFT to reprogramme its computers to suspend all transactions to and from Israeli banks until:
>
> - The Israeli government agrees to end its occupation of the West Bank including East Jerusalem, and that it will dismantle the 'apartheid wall',
> - The Israeli government recognises the fundamental rights of Arab-Palestinians to full equality in Israel-Palestine,
> - The Israeli government acknowledges the right of return of Palestinian refugees.

Endnotes

1. Meeting, November 8, 2010.
2. Ulrich Kadelbach: *Bethlehem Zwischen Weihrauch und Tränegas*, Gerhard Hess Verlag, Bad Schussenried, 2011.
3. PAVA, desmethyldihydrocapsicum.
4. UN Resolution 194.
5. Warren Goldstein: 'An Open Letter To Tutu', *Jerusalem Post*, November 3, 2010.
6. Tim Marshall: 'Jerusalem Mayor defiant over new settlements', Sky News, March 22, 2010.
7. Beit Orot website www.beitorot.org
8. 'The Palestinian Papers: Pleading For A Fig Leaf', *The Guardian* editorial, January 23, 2011.
9. Robert Fisk: 'A New Truth Dawns On The Arab World', *The Independent*, January 26, 2011.
10. Andrew Sparrow: 'Blair Says Leak Of Palestine Papers "Destabilising" For Peace Process', *The Guardian*, January 28, 2011.
11. Press release: 'Quartet Meeting in Moscow urges Israelis and Palestinians to engage in proximity talks', Blair Office, East Jerusalem, March 19, 2010.
12. Ali Abunimah: *One Country: A Bold Proposal to End the Israeli-Palestinian Impasse*, Metropolitan Books, New York, 2006, pp 10-11 and 144.
13. 'Legal Consequences Of The Construction Of A Wall In The Occupied Palestinian Territory', International Court of Justice, The Hague, July 9, 2004.

9 • A CIVIL SOCIETY IMPERATIVE

Cecil Rhodes's imperialist vision in 1877 of the British Empire 'so powerful and so overwhelming as to render all wars simply impossible' has been overtaken by history, but the consequences of imperialism still shape events in Africa and the Middle East.

Rhodes's intention was the conquest of Africa from Cape to Cairo funded by South African diamonds and gold, and settlement by European immigrants. In terms of geopolitical theories of those times, the country that controlled the 'African heartland' would control the world.

The resultant arms race between Britain and Germany made the twentieth century the bloodiest in history. Even after the Second World War, the world hovered on the brink of nuclear annihilation for another forty-five years during the so-called 'Cold War'.

The machinations of the war business during the twenty-first century could yet lead to the planet Earth's destruction. It is appropriate to recall the warning just before the First World War when British parliamentarian Philip Snowden declared:

We are in the hands of an organisation of crooks. They are politicians, generals, manufacturers of armaments and journalists. All of them are anxious for unlimited expenditures.[1]

With the addition of bankers who fund the war business, what has replaced 'Pax Britannica' is even more dangerous. It is a new empire expressed in the Judaic-Christian alliance of fundamentalist Christians and Israeli nationalists. It is a menace to the whole international community – Jews, Christians, Muslims and others.

In the United States alone, an estimated fifty million Christian Zionists believe that the war of Armageddon will precede the second coming of Christ. Christian fundamentalists insist on the literal biblical veracity of Jews as God's chosen people, but also that the geographical extent of the state of Israel extends from Iraq to Egypt.

Stephen Sizer, in his book *Christian Zionists: On The Road To Armageddon*, writes:

> The belief that the Jews remain God's chosen people leads Christian Zionists to a justification for Israel's military machine in Palestine. Israel belongs exclusively to the Jewish people, therefore land must be annexed and settlements adopted and strengthened. Jerusalem is the eternal and exclusive capital of the Jews, and cannot be shared with Palestinians.
>
> Since Christian Zionists are convinced that there will be an apocalyptic war between good and evil in the near future, there is no prospect of lasting peace between Jews and Arabs. Indeed to advocate Israel compromise with Islam or coexist with Palestinians is to identify with those destined to oppose God and Israel in the imminent battle of Armageddon.[2]

Closely related to Christian Zionism was the influence within the Bush administration and neo-conservatives of the Project For the New American Century (PNAC). Key members within the Bush administration promoted the notion that American global leadership is 'good for America and good for the world'.

PNAC was lobbying for regime change in Iraq as early as 1997, and within days of 9/11 urged President George Bush 'to remove Saddam Hussein from power even if evidence does not directly link Iraq to the attack'.

The perceived joint destiny of Israel and the US is conveyed by declarations by Christian fundamentalist theologians that only one nation, Israel, stands between terrorist aggression and the complete decline of the US as a democratic world power. Israel is supposedly the key to America's survival in an evil world dominated by communism and Islam, both of which are considered antithetical to Judeo-Christian democratic values.

With peculiar perversity, some Christian Zionists are driven by acute anti-Semitism. In the wacky and weird prophecies of the 'Rapture' to accompany the battle of Armageddon at Megiddo near Haifa, two thirds of Jews will be slaughtered and the one third to be 'saved' will be converted to Christianity.

For believers in this cult, only those who have accepted Jesus Christ as their lord and saviour – the so-called 'born-agains' – will be beamed up to heaven. Wars with Iraq and Iran are therefore deliberately instigated to speed the process of Christ's second coming.

What is both dangerous and extraordinary is the control that right-wing Christians in conjunction with the Israeli lobby hold over American politicians of all parties, as illustrated by the twenty-nine standing ovations that Benjamin Netanyahu received during a joint sitting of Congress in May 2011. No senator or congressman in Washington dares to denounce the Israeli lobby because of almost certainty of defeat at the next election.

The co-founder of the PNAC Robert Kagan answered critics of US imperialism with the highly dubious assertion that, contrary to the exploitative purposes of the British Empire, the genius of American power is:

> ... that it always makes money for its partners. America has not turned countries in which it intervened into deserts. It enriched them. Economic expansion does not equal imperialism, and American intentions of spreading democracy and individual rights are incompatible with the notion of an empire.[3]

This obscene agenda of waging wars to 'make money' was reflected in expectations within the Bush administration that seizure of Iraq's oil resources would result in massive reductions of the oil price to only five dollars per barrel. In fact, the price of oil soared and has severely impacted upon the world economy as attested by food riots in many countries.

The major American oil companies, however, have declared spectacular profits. Five companies – BP (now more American than British), Chevron, Conoco-Phillips, Exxon Mobil and Shell – made profits of US$952 billion in the decade ended 2010, but yet demand still more taxpayer subsidies over the next decade of US$36.5 billion.[4]

Halliburton and corporations associated with the Bush administration unapologetically also profited hugely from the war against Iraq. Privatised military companies, such as Blackwater and Aegis Defence, are increasingly even more important than official armies. Executive Outcomes, apartheid South Africa's firm of diamond mercenaries in Namibia, Angola and Sierra Leone, provided the model for this highly dangerous and politically unaccountable practice. Their annual revenues now exceed US$100 billion.

In pursuit of its hegemonic agenda, the US remains on a permanent war footing to ensure 'full spectrum dominance' of the world. The assassination of Osama bin Laden highlighted the contempt that the US holds for the rest of humanity. President Barack Obama's ratings and prospects for re-election in 2012 immediately rose by eleven per cent. As Noam Chomsky commented:

> It is increasingly clear that the operation was a planned assassination violating elementary norms of international law. In societies that profess some respect for law, suspects are apprehended and brought to fair trial. We might ask ourselves how we would react if Iraqi commandos landed at George W. Bush's compound, assassinated him and dumped his body in the Atlantic.[5]

The fiction of Flash Gordon or James Bond or Star Wars or innumerable Hollywood disaster films could become reality in the 'Rapture' driven by profit. Notwithstanding the disasters in Iraq and Afghanistan, deliberate US-Israeli confrontation with Iran could escalate into a conflagration from China across Asia and Africa to Nigeria.

The Bible, guns and diamonds are a bizarre combination. Diamonds play a critical role because the Israeli armaments industry has developed the next generation of laser weapons, spy satellites, surveillance systems and unmanned aerial vehicles (UAVs), otherwise known as drones. Israeli surveillance equipment is used at almost every airport around the world, in streets, shopping malls, and soccer stadiums.

In addition to collaboration on nuclear weapons, Israel and South Africa during the 1970s and 1980s also jointly developed a range of drones. South Africa funded those projects, including supplies of uranium and industrial diamonds. Indeed, a former Israeli ambassador, Alon Liel, acknowledges that South African financial support was critical in those days for the very survival of Israel:

> The Israeli security establishment came to believe that the Jewish state may not have survived without the relationship with the Afrikaners. We created the South African arms industry. They assisted us to develop all kinds of technology because they had a lot of money. We gave the know-how, and they gave the money.[6]

Israeli expertise in identity authentication and surveillance cameras is an outgrowth of that close collaboration. Subsequent Israeli drones carry an array of hi-tech equipment, including cameras, mapping devices, electronic jamming equipment and even missiles.[7]

With the Israeli economy having been on a war footing since 1948, its armaments industry was perfectly positioned to take full advantage of the growth in the surveillance business that followed the attack on the World Trade Center. Security is the boom industry of the present era. We are told that inconvenience and huge expenditures are only 'insurance' against terrorists most of whom, we are encouraged to believe, are Muslims.

The justification is always that Israel is under attack from neighbouring countries. The mantra is continually repeated: 'if you want peace, prepare for war'. There is no debate in Israel about what actually constitutes national security. Patriotism is manipulated by a cabal of army generals, politicians, armaments companies and bankers. The opportunities for war profiteering are immense.

Obsessed with security, the US spends trillions of dollars waging wars that it cannot win but, in the process, makes the world a lot more dangerous.

Bloated on public taxes, Lockheed Martin, Carlyle Industries and Raytheon are the beneficiaries. Their counterparts in Israel are Elbit, Raphael, Israel Aerospace and other armaments industry companies, the banks and the diamond industry.

Elbit boasts that it leads the world in battle command technology to provide comprehensive C4ISR solutions – Command, Control, Communications, Computers, Intelligence, Surveillance and Reconnaissance – for space, air, sea and ground warfare.

The war business, plainly, is out of control. Rough diamonds of gemstone quality may fetch more than US$38 000 per carat but industrial diamonds, some as cheap as only US$1 per carat, are essential for armaments. In addition to precision machine tools, high-tech uses for industrial diamonds include electronic circuitry and high energy laser technology.

The US uses drones in Afghanistan and Pakistan to attack the Taliban and Al Qaeda. Israel uses them in Gaza and the West Bank to 'eliminate' Hamas and other so-called terrorists. The use of pilotless drones and remote-controlled weaponry is even more grotesque than traditional warfare. As if acting out a Hollywood movie, the 'enemy' is eliminated by a young computer programmer sitting thousands of kilometres away in Nevada or California in air-conditioned comfort.

It is a perverted mentality even more diabolical than the hatred spawned in Sierra Leonean child soldiers or Palestinian suicide bombers or, indeed, the operators of the gas chambers and ovens at Auschwitz. Killing people for profit has become just a game that is rightly described as a 'PlayStation mentality'. Even fighter aircraft flown by highly skilled and expensively trained pilots have become redundant.

The assumption is purveyed that modern technology is unfailingly accurate, and that a few civilian casualties are just unfortunate 'collateral damage'. The reality is that the ratio of civilian deaths to terrorist leaders targeted by drones too often is about fifty to one. Industrial diamonds are essential in this new era of laser weapons, and in homing devices often planted by local informants.

A report presented to the United Nations Human Rights Council noted that unmanned American Predator and Reaper drones in Afghanistan and Pakistan have killed hundreds of innocent civilians. It declared:

> Intelligence agencies, which by definition are determined to remain unaccountable except to their own paymasters, have no place in running programmes that kill people in other countries. The world does not know when and where the Central Intelligence Agency (CIA) is authorised to kill, its criteria for choosing targets, whether they are lawful killings, and how it follows up when civilians are illegally killed.[8]

The reckless Israeli war agenda previously focused on Iraq was directed against Iran until the Arab Spring changed the balance of Middle East politics. Only months before publication of the Palestine Papers that so devastatingly discredited US policies, Israel and Saudi Arabia were reportedly scheming to attack Iran to destroy its nuclear programme. The Israelis and Saudi royal family, in common, are paranoid about Iran. Peace historian, Antony Adolf in June 2010 reported:

> It is like playing with rubber ducks in the bath, except if one of them explodes the Third World War starts. Increasingly isolated Israel is now stationing three German-built submarines in the Persian Gulf off the coast of Iran, all equipped with cruise missiles capped with nuclear warheads.
>
> And if that weren't enough, Saudi Arabia has conducted tests to ensure that it can stand down its air defence if Israel were to launch a nuclear attack against Iran's nuclear development sites. Most shocking of all, the US State Department is in collusion with this Saudi-Israeli nuclear attack plan. The Saudis have given permission for the Israelis to pass over, and they will look the other way.[9]

Israel's arsenal of up to three hundred nuclear warheads[10] can be launched from drones that have a range of one thousand, five hundred kilometres. Given diplomatic protection by the US, Israel refuses any international supervision of its nuclear capacities, and refuses to sign the non-proliferation treaty. The war on Iraq in 2003, the attack on Lebanon in 2006 and continuing operations in Gaza were but preliminary rehearsals.

The Irish Nobel peace laureate, Mairead Corrigan Maguire declares:

> Israel started the nuclear arms race in the Middle East, and is still the only country in the region that has nuclear weapons. A brave whistle-blower, Mordechai Vanunu told the world about twenty-five years ago about Israel's nuclear weapons programme. He was imprisoned for eighteen years, twelve of which he spent in solitary confinement. He remains subject to stringent conditions and travel restrictions, and is not permitted to talk to foreigners.
>
> He remains in virtual imprisonment. He is watched constantly and is unable to make a living, or leave Israel. The Israeli government's treatment of Vanunu is its way of telling Israelis: 'if you step out of line, this will happen to you.' He is kept as a reminder to the Israeli people that they must not criticise their government. He is a man who is totally non-violent, totally peaceful, who believes in global nuclear disarmament, and is being punished for following his conscience. We must never forget what we owe Vanunu because he wanted to save the Israeli people from a nuclear holocaust.
>
> He was following his conscience, and now is paying a very high price. He is a brave man and one of the heroes in the world today. We have to keep remembering him, be grateful to him, and keep pressuring our own governments to tell the Israeli government that it is time to let Vanunu go.[11]

US abuse of its veto powers at the UN Security Council to shield its Israeli client state has become the pre-eminent world issue of our time. Numerous resolutions and decisions regarding Israel's policies in the Palestinian territories have simply been ignored. This includes the advisory opinion in 2004 by the International Court of Justice that the 'apartheid wall' is illegal and should be dismantled. The World Court considered and found on five questions:

a. The construction of the wall being built by Israel, the occupying power, in the occupied Palestinian territory, including in and around East Jerusalem, and its associated regime, are contrary to international law.

b. Israel is under an obligation to terminate its breaches of international law; it is under an obligation to cease forthwith the works of construction ... and to dismantle forthwith the structure.

c. Israel is under an obligation to make reparation for all damage caused by construction of the wall.

d. All states are under an obligation not to recognise the illegal situation resulting from construction of the wall, and not to render aid or assistance in maintaining the situation created by such construction.

e. The UN, and especially the Security Council and the General Assembly, should consider what further action is required to bring to an end the illegal situation resulting from construction of the wall and its associated regime.[12]

More than forty years have elapsed since the 1967 Six Day War and, with it, Israeli military occupation of the West Bank and Gaza. In addition, the Israeli government unilaterally annexed more than seventy square kilometres of East Jerusalem and adjacent areas, which it declared to be part of the united capital of the Jewish state.

Israel complains that the UN is biased against Israel just as apartheid South Africa complained about the UN. Israel also declares that the UN has no credibility amongst countries regarded as 'democratic'. Yet it was the US and British governments that until 1990 repeatedly flouted UN decisions such as the 1977 arms embargo, and undermined sanctions initiatives by civil society to end apartheid.

This complicity enables Israel deliberately to stall on peace negotiations whilst expanding illegal settlements. Whilst constantly pretending and loudly declaring it seeks peace, Israeli intentions are to annex the whole area from the Jordan River to the Mediterranean. The Palestinians are expected simply to move elsewhere by emigrating.

With more than seven hundred thousand settlers now living 'beyond the Green Line',[13] the two-state solution promoted by the US, including land swaps, is a farce. The Israeli government itself does not support the notion of an independent Palestinian state. Ironically, a one-state solution is the likely outcome, albeit as the ultimate Israeli nightmare of a one state in which Palestinians are the majority.

Given unconditional American protection and support, the Israeli government has no reason to negotiate an equitable settlement with Palestinians. Israel is by far the largest beneficiary of American foreign aid. The US not only pours armaments into Israel but also hugely subsidises its armaments industry.

In the context of the global community, Israel's economy is tiny. Its arms trade, however, as an offshoot of its diamond cutting industry, now rivals Russia's, Britain's or Germany's. About eighty per cent of Israel's arms production is exported, usually with complete disregard for possible consequences. Sales in 2010 amounted to US$7.4 billion.[14]

Undeterred by such repercussions and despite massive American supplies of weapons to Pakistan, Israel in 2009 replaced Russia as the largest supplier of weapons to India, and the relationship between Israel and India allegedly includes nuclear fuel agreements. Israel is also the second largest supplier of weapons to China. Whilst the US pours weapons into Taiwan, Israeli arms exports to China include state-of-the-art American technology for surveillance aircraft.[15]

The historian Avi Shlaim declares:

> Israel has become a rogue state with an utterly unscrupulous set of leaders. A rogue state habitually violates international law, possesses weapons of mass destruction and practices terrorism – the use of violence against civilians for political purposes. Israel fulfils all of these criteria. Israel's real aim is not peaceful coexistence with its Palestinian neighbours, but military domination.[16]

In December 2009 the OECD noted that whilst the Israeli government has dedicated considerable efforts to fighting domestic corruption, there is a lack of commitment to tackling international corruption, especially in the armaments industry. Use of bribes to promote these exports is standard practice. It declared:

> Israel should be more proactive in detecting, investigating and prosecuting foreign bribery cases, notably those involving the defence industry, which is an area recognised to be at high risk of bribery solicitation.[17]

The report also confirmed that military censorship prevents publication of information about foreign bribery and money laundering by Israeli defence companies, and that there was a low level of understanding and detrimental effects inflicted on Israel's reputation and to the country concerned.

Even the US Ambassador to Israel in May 2009 described his host country as 'a promised land for organised crime', and noted that in recent years there had been a 'sharp increase in the reach and impact of organised crime networks'.[18]

Beyond Africa, major Israeli involvement in the Colombian and Panamanian drug trafficking in collusion with the CIA has long been established.[19] In January 2011, the Colombian government applied for extradition of former Israeli Army Colonel Yair Klein who was convicted in absentia by a Colombian court for training drug lord assassination squads.

Klein had been jailed for sixteen months in Sierra Leone in 1999 because of his role in the diamonds-for-gun trade, and also spent three years in a Russian prison after 2007 pending extradition to Colombia. He was freed in November 2010 when the European Human Rights Court ruled that Colombia could not guarantee his safety because of its poor human rights record, and he returned to Israel.[20]

In a lawsuit before the US District Court in New York, a former executive and whistleblower at JP Morgan Chase alleges that she was dismissed following her repeated warnings about an Israeli client's alleged mail fraud, bank fraud and money laundering transactions with Colombia.[21]

JP Morgan Chase, the second largest bank in the US, is also defending a US$19.9 billion lawsuit, which alleges that the bank ignored 'red flags' about the fraudster Bernard Madoff, who was a major client for more than twenty years. Madoff was sentenced in 2009 to imprisonment of one hundred and fifty years. Amongst the issues requiring further scrutiny are allegations that Madoff siphoned tens of billions of dollars to Israeli banks.

Human rights abuses and money laundering are invariably interconnected. In turn, money laundering is now regarded as a major international security problem. The UN estimates that global money laundering in various forms last year exceeded US$1 trillion.[22]

Yet in Israel 'national security' trumps all considerations of legality, morality or economic reason. The operations of the so-called 'Israeli mafia' are not only immensely profitable, but are politically protected and encouraged. Assassinations, corruption, money laundering and outright terrorism are all thereby 'justified'.

Given the pervasiveness of the military establishment, Israel is in effect a gangster state masquerading as a democracy. This opens unlimited potential for organised crime. That Israel misuses and abuses religion to rationalise such unlawful behaviour compounds the travesty.

Who Profits? is a computer website maintained by the Women's Coalition For Peace. The Coalition takes a critical position against the militarism which dominates Israel, and advocates for radical social and political change. The website documents the hundreds of international and Israeli companies that illegally profiteer from the Occupation, such as construction of the Wall and settlements, to agricultural produce grown on confiscated Palestinian land.

The banking industry is an essential element in such profiteering simply because banking is the lifeblood of any economy. As well as facilitating their clients' businesses, Israeli banks are shareholders in corporations that operate illegally in the West Bank. More importantly, war profiteering requires access to the international payments transfer system. A report published by Who Profits? in October 2010 confirmed that:

> ... there are five categories of operation in which Israeli banks provide financial services to occupation-related activity. Banks give mortgage loans for homebuyers in settlements; they provide financial services to Israeli local authorities in the West Bank and the Golan Heights; banks offer special loans for building projects in settlements; they operate branches in Israeli settlements; and they provide financial services to businesses in settlements.[23]

The Israeli activist Jeff Halper writes:

> The Occupation challenges us all – governments, faith-based communities, trade unions, human rights organisations, activist groups and concerned individuals alike. The Israeli-Palestinian conflict is far more than a localised war between two peoples in a remote land. It is nothing less than conflict

with fundamental significance for the global community.

Being emblematic for the Muslim world as a whole – the 'clash of civilisations' from a Muslim point of view, an American and western-backed occupation and not merely an Israeli one – it is inconceivable that stability be restored to the broader Middle East and security to the West unless this conflict is resolved.

No less important, Israel's occupation represents a profound challenge to a global system based on international law and universal human rights. What does it mean to peoples the world over if a regime of control, displacement, a denial of fundamental rights and repression actually prevails, in defiance of international law and more than two hundred United Nations resolutions?[24]

Israeli and Palestinian activists look to South Africa as a beacon of hope as a country that somehow averted catastrophe. The Boycott Divestment and Sanctions (BDS) campaign terrifies the Israeli government and its supporters because of its successes since 2005 in delegitimising the occupation. Omar Barghouti writes:

> Our South African moment has finally arrived! The Israeli lobby repeatedly claims that by advocating Palestinian rights, including full equality for Palestinian citizens of Israel and the UN-sanctioned right of Palestinian refugees to return to their homes, the BDS movement is 'de-legitimizing' Israel and threatening its very 'existence'. Such claims attempt to deny legitimate analysis of Israel's occupation, denial of refugee rights, and institutionalized system of racial discrimination, which basically fits the UN definition of apartheid.
>
> One can only wonder, if equality ends Israel's 'existence', what does that say about Israel? Did equality destroy South Africa? Did it 'delegitimize' whites in the southern states of the US after segregation was outlawed? The only thing that equality, human rights and justice really destroy is a system of injustice, inequality and racial discrimination.
>
> The 'delegitimization' scare tactic has not impressed many in the West, particularly since Israel's most far-reaching claim against BDS is that the movement aims to 'supersede the Zionist model with a state that is based on the "one person, one vote" principle'. This is hardly the most evil or disquieting accusation for anyone even vaguely interested in democracy, a just peace, and equal rights.

The job of defending Israel and guaranteeing the ongoing flow of billions of US taxpayers' money into its coffers despite its multi-tiered system of oppression has only become more precarious in view of the Arab democratic spring and Israel's loss of its most loyal ally in the region, the former Egyptian dictator Hosni Mubarak.

The Israeli government is terrified at this prospect, as it would further undermine its status as a state above the law of nations. The myth that US and Israeli interests fully converge is starting to crack. Instead, there is growing recognition in both countries that their interests are diverging. Even the former head of Mossad declared in the Knesset last year that 'Israel is gradually turning from an asset to the US to a burden'.[25]

The Israeli Defence Minister Ehud Barak has evidently also grasped the parallels with apartheid South Africa, saying:

> A UN declaration of Palestinian statehood without a prior Israeli political initiative will paint Israel into a corner previously occupied by South Africa during the apartheid era. There are quite powerful elements in the world, in trade unions, among academics, consumers, political parties, and this impetus has culminated in the BDS movement, which is what was done with South Africa.
>
> There are people in the European Union that deal with imports and exports, and they are capable without any government decision of inflicting significant damage on the Israeli economy. This uncontrollable process looks more dangerous than the Israeli public yet perceives. The political far right is exposing Israel to dangerous and unwarranted isolation.[26]

In apartheid South Africa during the 1980s, conscripted white soldiers, many of them still teenagers, were coming home either in body bags or, alternatively, were mentally and physically scarred for life. The End Conscription Campaign (ECC) became one of the most effective organisations opposed to apartheid. Increasing numbers of young white men left the country, some went to jail. Their defiance and refusal to serve in the army terrified the military establishment.

Defence Minister Magnus Malan declared: 'It is disgraceful that the South African Defence Force, but especially the country's young people, the pride of the nation, should be subjected to the ECC's propaganda, suspicion-sowing and misinformation.'[27] The ECC was 'banned' in 1988, yet in 1989 the register of conscientious objectors passed the one thousand mark.

The war in Namibia was South Africa's own Vietnam but, for me, it was also an insight of how young men, still only teenagers, are misused and brainwashed by the war machine. The traumas of South Africa's history are still reflected in the country's abnormally high levels of violent behaviour and crime, and will take generations to heal.

When the townships erupted in 1983 after the referendum for the Tricameral Parliament, South Africa was fast careening towards civil war. I feared that millions of people might die, and also that the country's infrastructure would be so destroyed that it would never recover either socially or economically. I was consequently one of the first signatories to the Kairos document when it was circulated at the Western Province Council of Churches (WPCC) in September 1985. It declared:

> The time has come. The moment of truth has arrived. South Africa has been plunged into a crisis that is shaking the foundations, and there is every indication that the crisis has only just begun, and that it will deepen and become even more threatening in the months to come. It is the Kairos, or the moment of truth not only for apartheid but also for the Church.
>
> The State in its oppression of the people makes use again and again of the name of God. Military chaplains use it, police chaplains use it, cabinet ministers use it in their propaganda speeches. This god is an idol. It is the god of supremacy, of the casspirs and hippos, the god of teargas, rubber bullets, sjamboks, prison cells and death sentences.
>
> The oppressive South African regime will always be particularly abhorrent to Christians precisely because it makes use of Christianity to justify its evil ways. The Bible describes oppression as the experience of being crushed, degraded, humiliated, exploited, impoverished, defrauded, deceived and enslaved. And the oppressors are described as cruel, ruthless, arrogant, greedy, violent and tyrannical, and as the enemy.
>
> A tyrannical regime cannot continue to rule for very long without becoming more and more violent. A regime that has made itself the enemy of the people has thereby also made itself the enemy of God. People are made in the image and likeness of God, and whatever we do to the least of

them we do to God.

It remains true that the Church is already on the side of the oppressed because that is where the majority of its members are found. The Church should not only pray for a change of government in South Africa. We must begin to look ahead and begin working now with firm hope and faith for a better future.

The moral illegitimacy of the apartheid regime means that the Church will have to be involved at times in civil disobedience. A Church that takes its responsibilities seriously in these circumstances will sometimes have to confront and to disobey the State in order to obey God.

And finally we also call upon our Christian brothers and sisters throughout the world to give us the necessary support so that the daily loss of so many young lives can be brought to a speedy end.[28]

What non-violent action and civil disobedience could I undertake, as a middle-aged banker, to bring down such a government? Six weeks later, the SACC sent me to New York and Washington to launch the international banking sanctions campaign against apartheid. I drafted an appeal by (then) Bishop Desmond Tutu and Dr Beyers Naudé, which declared:

The emergency in the country is now such that we consider it necessary as church leaders to urge that effective international and domestic financial leverage is applied to bring about an end to the unjust rule of apartheid, and to minimise further bloodshed and structural damage. Consequently, we urgently request of the banks participating in the rescheduling process that rescheduling of South Africa debt should be made conditional upon the resignation of the present regime and its replacement by a government responsive to the needs of all of South Africa's people.[29]

To my own amazement, I was not arrested or detained when I returned to Cape Town. The military hierarchy was evidently so confident of its supremacy that it could not conceive of non-violent or non-military challenges to its power. There was no prospect that apartheid South Africa could retaliate against international banks with its nuclear weapons. That arsenal, developed with Israeli assistance and with massive squandering of financial resources, therefore proved utterly useless.

The appeal was taken up by American church leaders and politicians and a year later, over President Ronald Reagan's attempted veto, in October 1986 became part of the Comprehensive Anti-Apartheid Act (C-AAA). The UN and Commonwealth subsequently acknowledged that banking sanctions was where the government was most vulnerable, and eventually set June 1990 as the deadline to end apartheid.

In particular, the banking sanctions campaign proved to be the single most effective strategy. It was premised on the realisation that because the US dollar is the settlement currency of the foreign exchange system, any significant economy would collapse without access to the New York bank payments system.

With the help of American churches, we developed an 'Adopt-A-Bank' strategy. Major church denominations threatened to withdraw their pension fund business if their bankers continued to transact international payments for South African banks. Similarly, the Municipality of New York told its bankers they must make a choice of the City's payroll account, or the business of apartheid South Africa.

A couple of the New York banks soon buckled under that pressure, and severed their correspondent banking relationships. *Business Day*'s Washington correspondent Simon Barber wrote that I must have become mentally deranged if I really expected an end to apartheid by June 1990.

Yet it was increasingly evident by mid-1989 that the government was fast losing control and was bewildered by its inability to suppress the unrest in the country. A 'palace coup' within the National Party in August that year removed P W Botha from the presidency, four years to the day after his Rubicon Speech.

After weeks of public protests against the violence of the apartheid system, on September 13, 1989, Archbishop Tutu led thirty-five thousand Capetonians in the 'March For Peace' from St George's Cathedral to the City Hall. The next day eighty-five thousand people marched in Port Elizabeth. Tutu is fond of recalling that 'we marched for peace in Cape Town, and the Berlin Wall fell down two months later'.

The sanctions campaign against apartheid was fortunate in its timing.

The Soviet Union was also collapsing, and the smear of communism that the government had so successfully applied since the early 1950s had lost its potency. Even the new President George Bush wanted to distance himself from the Reagan era, and in May had offered support.

The Archbishop flew to Washington in early October 1989 and, two days after his meeting with Hank Cohen, the Under Secretary for African Affairs, the Bush administration issued an ultimatum. The loopholes in the C-AAA would be closed early in the next year unless, with the opening of parliament, the government met the first three of our five conditions. These were:

- The end of the state of emergency
- Unbanning of political organisations
- Release of political prisoners

The South African Reserve Bank had earlier conceded that it was virtually powerless to counteract the pressures in New York and was extremely vulnerable. President F W de Klerk's announcement on February 2, 1990 was therefore not unexpected. Had he actually undergone a 'Damascus experience'? Or did De Klerk believe that, in releasing Mandela, a streamlined apartheid system could still be reimposed at a later date?

Prime Minister Margaret Thatcher tried to intervene by negotiating an extension of South Africa's foreign loans until 1993, but the die was already cast. Not even the 'Iron Lady' could save the apartheid regime. Bankers who participated in the rescheduling of loans told me that 'they got a good deal'. Intercepting the payments system was more critical than preventing the rescheduling of South Africa's foreign debt. That was the real pressure point.

Our fourth condition of the repeal of apartheid legislation was achieved in July. Nonetheless, four years elapsed before our fifth condition of constitutional negotiations towards a non-racial and democratic society was finally irreversible. Activists in New York insisted that banking sanctions would remain in place 'until Mr Mandela says so'!

Some of our antics were quite bizarre. They included a prayer breakfast with the Reverend Jesse Jackson outside Citibank's headquarters on Park

Avenue before we stormed the bank's annual general meeting. Ultimately they achieved their purpose – peaceful resolution of South Africa's racial conflict. For decades the world had predicted a bloodbath.

Three decades later banking technology has advanced dramatically. I believe international banking sanctions can now offer a unique opportunity to resolve crises without resorting to war. Indeed, despite the support of the US government, Israel is today far more vulnerable than was apartheid South Africa.

South Africa remains the only instance where sanctions worked. Cuba and Iraq are particular examples, confirmed by Zimbabwe and Burma, where sanctions have proved a dismal failure. Has it been the deliberate intention that governments can pretend to address the issues of repression in military dictatorships but, in fact, deliberately do nothing?

Whenever governments, especially the US, have applied sanctions they have inflicted further disasters upon the victims of oppression. The chasm between rich and poor in the world has widened alarmingly.

Banks are the means by which money laundering 'legitimises' the proceeds of blood diamonds, drug trafficking and other criminal activities. Israeli organised crime is disproportionately involved under the guise of 'national security'.

A heavy Israeli footprint can repeatedly be discerned and confirmed, most especially in Africa where law enforcement is weak. The Democratic Republic of Congo lurches from one catastrophe to the next, but the pattern has emerged of privatised armies plundering natural resources required by the Israeli armaments industry.

The operations of the so-called 'Israeli mafia' are not only immensely profitable, but are politically protected and encouraged. Banking is the lifeblood of any economy. This gives the Palestinian BDS campaign an opportunity to leverage bank transfers into political demands to end the Israeli occupation. Without access to SWIFT and the international payment system, Israeli banks would 'cease to exist', and the Israeli economy would implode. Given the crisis facing the banking industry, the last thing with which bank executives need to be identified is turning a blind eye to money laundering by

Israeli organised crime.

The war business could become obsolete, freeing financial resources for poverty eradication and social upliftment. The term 'apartheid' no longer applies just in South Africa, but has global implications.

South Africa's Human Sciences Research Council (HSRC) in 2009 released the results of a fifteen-month investigation, and found:

> Israel bears the primary responsibility for remedying the illegal situation it has created. In the first place, it has the duty to cease its unlawful activity and dismantle the structures and institutions of colonialism and apartheid that it has created. Israel is additionally required by international law to implement duties of reparation, compensation and satisfaction in order to wipe out the consequences of its unlawful acts.
>
> But above all, in common with all states, whether acting singly or through the agency of inter-governmental organisations, Israel has the duty to promote the Palestinian people's exercise of its right to self-determination in order that it might freely determine its political status and freely pursue its own economic policy and social and cultural development.[30]
>
> No serious attempt is made to compel Israel to comply with its international obligations. Israel has been exempted from sanction for breaking international legal norms. In this respect, the response of the international community differs substantially from its response to apartheid ... when states, corporations and civil society imposed various forms of sanctions. This is an issue that must be addressed if the credibility of the rule of law is to be maintained.[31]

After completing my second three-month assignment with EAPPI in Bethlehem, I headed home to South Africa in time for Christmas 2010. A couple of months later I was invited to join the organising committee for the third session of the Russell Tribunal on Palestine scheduled to meet in Cape Town in November 2011, and was then elected as secretary. The Cape Town session was obviously going to be hugely contentious for both the Israeli government and the Zionist community in South Africa. Yet it would also represent a massive leap forward in holding governments and the war business to account. For all the pitfalls and shortcomings, the world has made progress since 1977 when the UN Security Council determined that apartheid in South Africa was a threat to international peace and security.

The highly symbolic District Six Museum readily agreed that we could use its premises as the venue for the two-day event. The Museum, established in 1994 in the former Methodist Church for 'Coloureds' in Buitenkant Street, commemorates the apartheid era forced removal of about sixty thousand people from the precinct just outside the Cape Town central business district.

District Six was originally created in 1867 as a mixed community of freed slaves, merchants, artisans, labourers as well as immigrants. It was close to the employment prospects offered by the harbour and the clothing factories. A large proportion of the immigrant population was composed of Jews who had fled to South Africa to escape the pogroms of eastern Europe in the late nineteenth and early twentieth centuries.

District Six was declared a 'white area' in 1966. By 1982, its houses and business premises had been flattened by bulldozers. The population was scattered around barren outlying areas known as the 'Cape Flats', but street signs rescued from the rubble form a memorial to the trauma.

It is a devastatingly emotional portrayal of psychological wounds inflicted upon communities demolished by apartheid policies, either in South Africa or in other countries where a dominant community displaces the weak. Seated beneath the memorial, a panel of eminent jurists for two days listened to testimony from more than twenty witnesses.

The Cape Town session was opened by Archbishop Tutu who, in his inimitable fashion, declared:

> If our experience in South Africa contains lessons for other regions experiencing seemingly intractable conflicts, lesson number one must be our collective willingness to reconcile – our willingness to say sorry, to accept the apology, to forgive.
>
> How different would the world be today if Al Qaeda apologised for 9/11 and America accepted the apology? Or if instead of responding militarily, America had responded to 9/11 with introspection and humility?
>
> Forgiveness is much more than attributing blame or winning arguments. This is not just spiritual gobbledegook: it is realpolitik. Think of what

happens when you quarrel with your spouse. It does not matter what language you speak, or your culture. The most difficult words you have to say are 'I'm sorry. Forgive me.' Otherwise there is no future in the relationship.

There can be no future without forgiveness, whether in your domestic relationships or in the Holy Land.

My charge to the Russell Tribunal is thus: Please ensure that your deliberations contribute to peace and reconciliation in Israel and Palestine. Please be careful to leave the door open for forgiveness, for a better future for Israelis and Palestinians. Please remember you are dealing with your brothers and sisters here. For no matter where you come from or what you wear on your head – even if you wear no headdress at all – we are members of one family, the human family, God's family.[32]

The Zionist community went crazy with angry denunciations of the Tribunal as a 'kangaroo court'. They avoided the daily realities of Israel-Palestine as highlighted by more than twenty witnesses, and the Israeli government ignored an invitation to participate.

Most significantly, it is a holocaust survivor who leads the Tribunal. Stéphane Hessel is the extraordinarily iconic leader of the Russell Tribunal on Palestine. He was born in 1917 in Berlin, the son of a German Jew. He was outraged when he visited Gaza in 2009 in the aftermath of Operation Cast Lead, and saw for himself the devastation of the Israeli bombardment.

With the outbreak of the Second World War, Hessel joined the French Resistance. He was captured by the Gestapo, and was sentenced to death by hanging at Buchenwald concentration camp. The night before his scheduled execution, another inmate died of typhus. Hessel assumed his bunkmate's identity, and thus survived.

He then became one of the last drafters of the 1948 Universal Declaration of Human Rights, and is hugely celebrated in France. Hessel declares that Israeli behaviour in Palestine violates all basic Jewish and democratic values. At the age of ninety-three, Hessel published a forty-page booklet entitled *Time For Outrage* in October 2010.[33]

The sales of this little book have already exceeded more than three and a half million copies. It has become a publishing sensation around the world. It laments the betrayal of democratic values, and the power of financial and political lobbyists to negate the social and economic rights of ordinary people.

Publication preceded the 2011 'Arab Spring' and the Occupy Wall Street movements. Hessel, as a philosopher with an optimistic view of history, challenges the youth to be outraged by the devastation of the planet, and encourages them to use non-violence to overthrow tyrannical governments. He says:

> I was worried that in striving for material wealth so many young people had forgotten their responsibilities for values. Yet even wealth will be jeopardised if basic democratic values are not fought for. Resistance has always been a minority act. We need minorities.
>
> The worst attitude is indifference. Indifference is widespread in so many countries, reflecting discouragement, failure and lack of confidence. Have confidence. Trust your strength. If you go to the streets in a determined way, you will see that governments will have to listen to you. You have to be confident and brave.[34]

Endnotes

1. John T Flynn: *Men Of Wealth*, Simon & Schuster, New York, 1941, pp 337-372.

2. Stephen Sizer: *Christian Zionists: On The Road To Armageddon*, Presence Ministries International, Colorado Springs, Colorado 2004, p 102.

3. Debate on 'The United States Is, and Should Be, an Empire'. American Enterprise Institute, Washington DC, July 17, 2003.

4. Edward J Mackey: House Committee on Natural Resources, US Congress, Washington DC, February 3, 2011.

5. Noam Chomsky: 'My Reaction To Osama Bin Laden's Death', Znet, May 7, 2011.

6. Chris McGreal: 'Brothers In Arms – Israel's Secret Pact With Pretoria', *The Guardian*, February 7, 2006.

7. Simon McGregor-Wood: 'New Israel Drone Can Fly To Iran', ABC News, February 22, 2010.

8. Stephanie Nebehay: 'UN investigator calls for halt to CIA drone killings', Reuters, June 3, 2010.

9. Antony Adolf: 'With Israeli Nuclear Subs Off Iran's Coast, Saudis and US Give Green Light,' June 22, 2010.

10. Yaakov Katz: 'Israel Is The World's 6th Largest Nuclear Power', *Jerusalem Post*, April 11, 2010.

11. Hanan Chehata: 'Nobel Peace Laureate Mairead Maguire Speaks About Palestine, Political Prisoners And Nuclear Weapons, *Middle East Monitor*, December 1, 2011.

12. 'Legal Consequences of the Construction of a Wall in the Occupied Palestinian Territory', International Court of Justice, The Hague, July 9, 2004.

13. Yori Yalon: '722 000 Israelis Live Beyond The Green Line', Yisrael HaYom, January 14, 2012.

14. 'Israeli Arms Companies Target Third World', *United Press International*, April 8, 2011.

15. P R Kumarasswamy: 'At What Cost Israel-China Ties?' *Middle East Quarterly*, Spring 2006, pp 37-44.

16. Mark Braverman: *Fatal Embrace: Christians, Jews and the Search for Peace in the Holy Land*, Synergy Books, Austin, Texas, 2010, p 246.

17. OECD Directorate For Financial & Enterprise Affairs: 'Israel Should Ensure

That Remaining Concerns Do Not Undermine The Progress On Foreign
Bribery, Says OECD', Paris, December 16, 2009.

18. Yuval Mann: 'Promised Land For Organised Crime?' YNet News.com,
December 2, 2010.

19. Israel Shahak: 'What Israelis Know And Americans Don't About The Drug
Triangle', October 1989, plus chapter 10 of Shahak's book *Open Secrets: Israeli
Nuclear And Foreign Policies*, Pluto Press, London, 1997.

20. Frank Bajak: 'Colombia Asks Israel To Extradite Mercenary', Associated
Press, January 28, 2011.

21. Jonathan Stempel: 'Judge Rejects JP Morgan's Bid To Dismiss
Whistleblower's Retaliation Claim', Reuters, August 22, 2011.

22. Michael Stothard: 'Money Laundering On The Rise', *Financial Times*,
August 18, 2011.

23. 'Financing The Israeli Occupation', Who Profits? Coalition Of Women For
Peace, Tel Aviv, October 2010.

24. Jeff Halper: *Obstacles To Peace*, Israeli Committee Against House Demolitions,
Jerusalem, 2009.

25. Omar Barghouti: 'Peace Demands Challenging Israel's Exceptionalism',
Huffington Post, May 5, 2011.

26. Joseph Dana: 'Ehud Barak Acknowledges The Impact Of BDS', *Haaretz*,
May 6, 2011.

27. Gavin Evans: 'Calling Up Old Memories', *Mail & Guardian*, October 23,
2009.

28. Extracts from the Kairos Document, September 1985.

29. The saga of the international banking sanctions campaign is recorded in my
book *Eye On The Money*, published by Random House-Umuzi, Cape Town,
2007.

30. 'Occupation, Colonialism, Apartheid: A re-assessment of Israel's practices
In The Occupied Palestinian Territories Under International Law', Human
Sciences Research Council of South Africa, Cape Town, May 2009.

31. Ben White: *Israeli Apartheid: A Beginner's Guide*, Pluto Press, New York, 2009,
pp xv and xvi.

32. Archbishop Desmond Tutu's opening address to the Russell Tribunal On
Palestine, Cape Town, November 5, 2011.

33. Stéphane Hessel: *Time For Outrage*, Quartet Books, London, 2011.

34. Stéphane Hessel being interviewed by Juan Gonzales, 'Democracy Now',
October 10, 2011.

10 • BLACK DIAMONDS

Writing in the *Mail & Guardian* in October 2008, Shaun de Waal reviewed Thabo Mbeki's legacy:

The arms deal appears to have thrown the Mbeki presidency off course right from the start; certainly its ramifications contributed to his fall and to the ascendancy of Jacob Zuma. Mbeki was the man to modernise the ANC, to turn it from a liberation movement into a modern political party capable of running a developing democracy.

But even before Mbeki took up the presidential mantle he was deeply involved in the arms deal – and diverting it to reach desired outcomes, particularly in terms of 'offsets' that he and others seem to have imagined would compensate by way of investment into South Africa for the billions spent on military hardware we didn't really need. The 'offsets' barely materialised.

It's not a great stretch to see the arms deal, and what went wrong with it, as a key factor in the Mbeki presidency's slide into secretiveness, paranoia and denialism, not to mention its vicious attitude towards any dissent or revelations of wrongdoing. The manipulation of bodies designed to create checks and balances on the executive began with the emasculation of Scopa, and has carried through into the debacle around the National Prosecuting Authority.[1]

Just under twelve years had elapsed since Archbishop Njongonkulu Ndungane in August 1999 first called for a judicial commission of inquiry into the arms deal and the hearing at the Constitutional Court in Johannesburg on May 5, 2011. I was the applicant in the public interest in Terry Crawford-Browne against the President of the Republic of South Africa as first respondent and the Government as second respondent.[2]

Citing a long list of allegations of corruption against the then Deputy President Jacob Zuma, the official opposition party, the Democratic Alliance, in December 2002 had also called on then President Mbeki to appoint such an inquiry. His dismissive reply was they were 'mere allegations'.

Zuma's financial adviser Schabir Shaik was eventually sentenced to fifteen years' imprisonment. Mbeki dismissed Zuma in 2005 but, in an amazing political resurrection, Zuma turned the tables. The reasons for not charging Zuma himself are themselves still in the process of litigation.

Mbeki was 'recalled' by the African National Congress in September 2008. His dismissal as president was prompted, in large part, by the disclosures in the *Sunday Times* newspaper one month earlier that MAN Ferrostaal had paid Mbeki R30 million, of which he gave R2 million to Zuma and the rest to the ANC.

Zuma became president in 2009, and continued the ANC's efforts to squelch the saga. Like the Watergate scandal that eventually toppled United States President Richard Nixon, the cover-up has proved even worse than the original crime. It has been a long, gruelling and bruising debacle. The arms deal scandal has undoubtedly killed many people along the way, sadly probably including Bheki Jacobs at the age of forty-six. Whether Chris Hani and Joe Modise are other casualties also needs to be investigated.

The culture of corruption that the arms deal unleashed, and of which Jacobs warned, has exceeded even his or my worst fears. Jacobs was the original whistleblower, but his work was also crucial in exposing Jackie Selebi's involvements with Brett Kebble and other gangsters.

Selebi was eventually jailed for fifteen years. That the chief of the police was corrupt and colluding with thugs was bad enough. What made matters much worse was Mbeki's blatant misuse of his power to protect his friends and cronies. He did his damnedest not only to block investigation of the arms deal, but also to prevent prosecution of Selebi.

According to Jacobs, Mbeki deliberately encouraged his colleagues to enrich themselves, including Zuma, so that he might then control their political ambitions. His unscrupulous Machiavellian manipulations eventually unravelled. But at what price to South Africa's still fragile democracy and for the majority of people still living in abject poverty?

Most despicable of all was the behaviour of successive British governments, especially Prime Minister Tony Blair, in colluding with Mbeki to sell armaments which the country did not need and could not afford. When South African church leaders complained, they learned that it was not illegal in British law to bribe foreigners. It seems evident that the whole history of the British Empire was built on this premise.

The Defence White Paper of 1996 acknowledged that eradication of poverty was South Africa's overriding priority, and that there was no conceivable foreign military threat to the country. The only logical conclusion for buying warships and warplanes was bribery and corruption.

Bheki Jacobs was the nom de guerre given to him by the ANC in 1985 after he fled from South Africa and the security police. He was born in Durban as Hassan Solomon in 1962, and it was under that name that he was buried in Cape Town. In the tortured complexities of South Africa's obsessions with racial classifications, he was born 'coloured' but got himself reclassified as 'Indian' so that he might attend a better school.

He was highly trained as an intelligence operative at Moscow State University and returned to South Africa in 1994 to work under Mbeki at the ANC's international affairs department. The ANC was then trying to break the De Beers diamond cartel and sought assistance from Russian and Russian-Israeli diamond dealers. The old Soviet Union and De Beers from apartheid South Africa had perversely collaborated under the guise of 'market stability' to inflate diamond prices.

The simultaneous collapse of the Soviet Union and apartheid South Africa became the opportunity for Russians and Israelis such as Lev Leviev's to break the diamond cartel. De Beers and the ANC were in due course reconciled by the sale of a twenty-six per cent ownership in De Beers to party stalwarts including Manne Dipico and Cheryl Carolus.

For over a century De Beers was South Africa's corporate icon. Its practices in Kimberley and elsewhere and its political manipulations laid the basis of apartheid's migrant labour policies. The Truth and Reconciliation Commission in 1997 recommended a modest wealth tax to fund poverty eradication. Anglo American and De Beers, not individual white South Africans, had indisputably been the prime corporate beneficiaries and fulcrum of the apartheid system. They were to apartheid what BAE and BP are to the British government.

Instead, but inexplicably and despite exchange controls, Anglo American and De Beers in 1998 were permitted to transfer their domiciles from South Africa to Europe. They argued that the country was too small for their talents, and that they now needed to expand internationally.

The signal conveyed to the world was that post-apartheid South Africa was on the point of collapse. The rand crashed on foreign exchange markets. How much 'South Africa Inc' paid surreptitiously into the ANC's electioneering coffers and other expenses has yet to be revealed. The ANC pleads that as a political party it is a 'private entity' and therefore refuses to open its books to public scrutiny or to disclose the names of its donors.

In lieu of a wealth tax as modest restitution for apartheid, another of Mbeki's ill-considered decisions was Black Economic Empowerment (BEE) to create a black middle class. It was pursued for short-term political manoeuvring and manipulation rather than sound economic reasons, and must inevitably end in tears.

In the process, South Africa has lost its century-long control over the diamond industry. To support the Mugabe dictatorship, even blood diamonds from Zimbabwe have since June 2011 been certified under the Kimberley Process as 'conflict-free.'[3] The implications for the world diamond industry are dire when diamonds are again identified with gross abuses of human rights.

Similarly, South Africa's century-long dominance of gold mining has been eclipsed by China. Hundreds of thousands of jobs have been lost, but a handful of party cadres quickly became salivating sycophants and yes-men. Anglo American Corporation and BHP-Billiton are now foreign owned, and South Africa is again a neo-colonial dependency of the 'first world'. Mbeki's eagerness to play the game of 'world statesman' with the leaders of the G8 confirmed that power had gone to his head, and his eloquent charm was revealed as a sham.

Parliament's constitutional oversight over the executive was reduced to the function of a rubber stamp. Even worse, the BEE (otherwise known as black enrichment of the elite) deliberately reinstated race classifications which had been such a despicable feature of the apartheid era. Nelson Mandela's carefully constructed racial reconciliation policies were also discarded for short-term advantage.

Jacobs and Mbeki parted company because of the arms deal and, secondly, because of Kebble's influence within the ANC party hierarchy and youth league. Unfortunately, Jacobs did not live to see the days when Mbeki was finally removed from office, or when Selebi at long last was imprisoned. As Paul O'Sullivan commented:

> In the eight years that Selebi ran it, he corrupted the police force from top to bottom. So you end up with a force where twenty-five per cent are corrupt, twenty-five per cent are lazy and incompetent, twenty-five per cent do an average day's work and twenty-five per cent are bloody good cops. In my opinion, it was Mbeki's gutless and criminal conduct that resulted in the delays in bringing Selebi to book.[4]

As Kebble's embezzlement of his mining companies unravelled, he became more and more desperate to raise cash from smuggling operations, which he conducted through Johannesburg airport with Selebi's assistance. Such shipments, according to Jacobs, included rough diamonds from the Congo and Zimbabwe to be cut and polished in South Africa, and then exported as 'conflict free' in terms of the Kimberley Process.

That aspect of the Kebble saga was, unfortunately, never tested in the prosecutorial shambles of both the Selebi and Glenn Agliotti trials. Nor, it seems, will we ever know whether Kebble's death in September 2005 was 'assisted suicide' or cold-blooded murder.

There were many members of the ANC who were penniless before 1994, but who used their new political credentials to amass sudden wealth. They became known as 'black diamonds' and revelled in ostentatious consumption funded by heavily leveraged bank loans that made no economic sense. Mbeki's communications director Smuts Ngonyama infamously commented that he had not joined the ANC to be poor.

The banks and financial institutions colluded in these scams, just as they had in funding the Bantustans and state institutions such as Armscor during the apartheid era. For instance, funding for the R3.7 billion BEE stake in De Beers was provided by Standard Bank, but contributed nothing either to poverty alleviation or job creation.

Nicky Oppenheimer gushed in a press statement that it represented the 'most significant change of ownership since the formation of De Beers in 1888'. BEE significantly drives up interest rates for small businesses and crowds out much more worthwhile ventures for South Africa's economic development. It results in catastrophic unemployment amongst those who are not politically connected.

Kebble made his move in 1995 right after the transition to democracy when he teamed up with ANC activist Mzi Khumalo to take control of one of South Africa's largest and oldest mining houses, Johannesburg Consolidated Investments (JCI). Khumalo had spent twelve years on Robben Island and when he was released in 1990 he was determined to rebuild his life as an entrepreneur. He dabbled in insurance broking in the townships.

JCI had been established in 1888 by Barney Barnato, Rhodes's even wealthier rival who also made his fortune from Kimberley diamonds. Barnato then doubled his money after discoveries of gold in Johannesburg in 1887. He died at sea in 1897, aged forty-seven, en route to England in what also remains an unsolved mystery of suicide or murder.

Anglo American and De Beers were happy to be paid out for their thirty per cent shareholding in JCI, and in due course to disinvest from South Africa.

Mbeki's wife Zanele was one of the BEE beneficiaries. When the gold price slumped in 1999, Khumalo and Kebble were in deep trouble. They parted company in 2000. During the next five years JCI's assets were stripped by more than R2 billion.

Khumalo continued for a while as one of the 'new' South Africa's high flyers, ostentatiously chartering luxury yachts in the Mediterranean and spending money like water. That also all fell apart in 2010 when Khumalo's companies were placed into liquidation, and at last some people began to question the greed and madness that BEE inflicted on the country.

Kebble's bizarre funeral at St George's Cathedral in Cape Town was attended by about one thousand people, all of them, with few exceptions, 'black diamonds'. Mbeki sent his hatchet-man, the Minister in the Presidency, Essop Pahad, to deliver the eulogy. Pahad hailed Kebble as a 'great South African', noting his great generosity to political parties and the arts, and accusing the media of violating Kebble's fundamental right to be deemed innocent until proven guilty.

Saki Macozoma, Tokyo Sexwale, Ebrahim Rasool, Tony Yengeni, Andile Nkuhlu, Nomaindia Mfeketo, Mo Shaik, Dali Tambo and hundreds more were all there to pay their obeisances. Some parishioners questioned what connection Kebble had to the Cathedral. The response from the clergy was that a very substantial donation had been made.

It was a flamboyant funeral, only previously eclipsed at the Cathedral when Cecil Rhodes died in 1902. Then, Rhodes's body had lain in state at parliament before the funeral service, and afterwards was conveyed by train to Rhodesia for burial. All public buildings in Cape Town were closed, and draped in black. The archbishop of the day even declared that 'while some men collect butterflies and old china, Rhodes's hobby had been to open up central and South Africa to British enterprise'.[5]

BEE was a tried-and-proven ploy by which the Oppenheimers had co-opted the apartheid government in the 1960s. By the 1990s, their goldmines were old and played out, and were even losing money. Like the diamond fields in Namibia, they had been cherry-picked before the transition to democracy. What better way to shirk responsibility and financial liability for social and environmental damage? Add in an arms deal, and South Africa's hard-won constitutional democracy would quickly flounder.

Before long the vultures could then pick over the carcass, as they have in the rest of Africa. Sexwale, whose ambitions to be president repeatedly surface, is a prime example of meteoric transformation from a penniless prisoner on Robben Island to billionaire. He and his investment vehicle, Mvelaphanda Holdings, were mentored by no less than the Oppenheimers and Kebble. Sexwale had his fingers in the diamond industry and, it was repeatedly rumoured, much else, including Wingate Capital and its links to BAE and the British MI6.[6] Right from inception, the arms deal was just the tip of the iceberg by which politically well-connected members of the ANC would line their pockets, and on which Jacobs 'blew the whistle'.

Jenny Cargill, author of *Trick or Treat*,[7] finds that the ANC has become so enmeshed in political patronage that about R450 billion was wasted in the years until 2009 on non-productive BEE deals that should, instead, have been invested in infrastructure and social development. The gap between rich and poor, as measured by the GINI coefficient, is consequently now even wider than it was during the days of apartheid. The word 'tenderpreneur' entered South Africa's political dictionary.

Indeed, the arms deal numbers seem like 'petty cash' compared with the trillions yet to be spent on rebuilding South Africa's electricity network. Kickbacks through Chancellor House and Hitachi will unfairly provide the ANC with substantial funding and thus undermine our democracy, but that is a future battle for a younger generation. The plundering of Africa by rapacious foreigners, local warlords and rent-boys has been perfected by the war business, and there is evidently no end in sight.

The arms deal placed the eleven Constitutional Court judges in an embarrassing dilemma. Obviously preferring to avoid a constitutional con-frontation with President Zuma they were, nevertheless, visibly exasperated by Advocate Muromo Moerane's refusal to move beyond legal technicalities.

They finally challenged him to 'elect' whether the case should proceed on the basis of the evidence I had submitted. Instead of addressing issues of substance around the arms deal, the president's lawyers tried to bludgeon the judges with legal point-taking that there was no presidential obligation to appoint a judicial commission of inquiry.

In the preliminary exchanges of court papers, his lawyers had refused to deal with the merits of the case. They insisted that the president alone has discretion to decide whether to appoint a judicial commission of inquiry. By contrast, my argument was that South Africa is now a constitutional democracy where the Constitution is the supreme law of the land.[8]

I had argued for years that Zuma was only a small fish in the arms deal saga, and that his personal weaknesses had made him the perfect target for blackmail – too much sex and not enough money! The use of honey traps is legendary in the war business.

There is a massive volume of evidence of corruption around the arms deal. General Anwar Dramat confirmed in parliament in September 2010 that the Hawks had inherited from the Scorpions four hundred and sixty boxes and 4.7 million computer pages of evidence against BAE. In addition, there is much other evidence against the German Frigate and Submarine Consortia as well as about how BAE had sucked the Swedish Saab company into the scandal.

Nonetheless, I could only look on and observe a Kafkaesque battle between the legal eagles. Whose nerve would break first? Advocate Paul Hoffman remained calm. Moerane finally succumbed to pressure from the judges, and 'elected' for a postponement. We debated whether to go for the jugular and to demand an immediate review on the merits of the issue, but decided such a course might alienate the judges.

Business Day blandly reported:

> The Constitutional Court yesterday postponed until September 20, 2011 an application by arms deal campaigner Terry Crawford-Browne to force President Jacob Zuma to appoint a commission of inquiry into the arms deal.
>
> The court granted the postponement to the president's lawyers to allow Mr Zuma to answer allegations of fact made by Mr Crawford-Browne in his application. In their written argument and other papers before the Constitutional Court, the president's lawyers did not deal with the facts raised by Mr Crawford-Browne but confined their argument to the legal

issues.

The Constitutional Court judges said yesterday it would be difficult to deal with the constitutional issue of whether the court had the power to compel the president to appoint a commission relying only on facts provided by Mr Crawford-Browne.

One of the questions the parties were expected to answer was whether the constitution obliged the president to exercise his power to appoint a commission of inquiry whenever there were indications of corruption, malfeasance and misfeasance over public procurement. While Mr Crawford-Browne believed the president was obliged to appoint the commission, the president said he was not.[9]

The Constitutional Court itself and its building are both hugely symbolic of the changes in South Africa since 1994. The Court is constructed on the site of the old Johannesburg Fort built during the 1890s to protect the city and Transvaal Republic from British invasion. The Fort later became one of the most notorious of the jails of the colonial and apartheid eras.

Mahatma Gandhi was jailed there for two months in 1908 after confrontations with the British government of the Transvaal colony. Gandhi developed into the world's most outstanding proponent of non-violent civil disobedience, and the lessons he learned in South Africa equipped him to confront and defeat the British Empire in India. Nelson Mandela was also, briefly, an inmate of the Fort in 1962 on his way to Robben Island.

Instead of conveying the traditional message of the oppressive might of the law, the architecture of the new court deliberately embodies the constitutional requirement of openness and transparency of public administration. The Constitutional Court even houses a collection of over two hundred artworks by South Africa's leading artists. Judge Albie Sachs confirms:

> The architecture is intended to symbolise the continuity of the new constitutional order, just as the surrounding prisons will serve as museums to remind us never again to allow people to be treated as they were in the past. South Africa over the last one hundred and fifty years has had colonial conflict, industrial class warfare, battles between language communities, even religious strife.

The term imperialism was coined to extol British colonial policy in our area. The Anglo-Boer War gave rise to the phrase 'concentration camps'. We also contributed the word 'apartheid'. Indeed, no other country can claim that a whole international convention had been drawn up just to eliminate a policy which it, uniquely, had developed.[10]

The British Empire was at its zenith when the Fort was built. When he died, Barnato had been on his way to England to attend Queen Victoria's Diamond Jubilee festival. That commemoration relied on all the pomp and ceremony that the English could muster to convey the message of benign but determined supremacy.

As Sachs implies, South Africa is the victim of too much history, but it also has made a uniquely disproportionate impact on world events. The Constitution and the Constitutional Court were intended to make a decisive break from that past, and to usher in a new era in which human rights would be the arbiter.

The Court's landmark decisions include the abolition of the death penalty and the Irene Grootboom case. This challenged post-apartheid South Africa to give effect to the lofty intentions of socio-economic rights contained in the bill of rights. Grootboom was a destitute woman, one of almost one thousand adults and children living in the open on a soccer field because they had been evicted from their shacks. They desperately needed their constitutional right of access to adequate housing.

A street was named after her in Cape Town in honour of her struggle for a place to live. Yet Grootboom died in 2008 still destitute, and still without a house. Nothing so appallingly illustrates the chasm between rich and poor as the hovels in Crossroads, Nyanga and Khayelitsha with the mansions in Clifton and Bishopscourt. The new 'black diamonds' are merely following the examples of ostentatious behaviour exhibited by Barnato and other randlords who were known as the 'Hoggenheimers of Park Lane'.

The failure to redress the crises of poverty inherited from the apartheid era is repeated time and time again. There are impressive plans and good intentions, but appallingly poor implementation. Non-delivery protests throughout the country reflect public anger that the provision of services for education, health and housing has been abysmal. For that we must blame the culture of corruption that the arms deal unleashed, and to which every cabinet minister was repeatedly alerted.

About seven million people might have been modestly housed for the cost of the arms deal. Studies estimate that more than six hundred thousand houses could have been built for the cost of twenty-eight BAE/Saab Gripen fighter aircraft. The aircraft remain grounded because there are not enough qualified pilots to fly them, or mechanics to maintain them, or even the money to fuel them. Highly sophisticated BAE Hawk and BAE/Saab Gripen warplanes are useless for peacekeeping operations in the Congo or other African countries.

Of the three submarines, one was inadvertently connected to the wrong power supply, which destroyed its electrical system and batteries. It is now in Simon's Town naval dockyard being cannibalised for spare parts. Alternatively, over one hundred schools could have been built for the cost of just one German-supplied submarine.

Frigates and submarines are worthless for fisheries protection or other coastguard operations along the South African coast. Anyway, the frigates seldom go to sea, and are confined to port simply because the South African Navy cannot afford to operate them. Naval admirals have recently started boasting that the frigates and submarines are being used to combat piracy off the coasts of Mozambique and Somalia. One wonders if they actually believe they are fooling anyone other than themselves.

It is extraordinary that Mbeki, who has a master's degree in economics, the minister of trade and industry and the minister of finance could swallow the economically nonsensical proposition that expenditure of R30 billion on armaments would magically generate R110 billion in offsets to create sixty-five thousand jobs. That they not only heavily promoted the idea but then also blocked all efforts to expose the associated corruption implies that they were both criminally negligent and accessories to crime.

South Africa and South Africans suffered incalculable damage because of their actions. Hundreds of thousands of people have died of HIV/Aids-related causes because weapons procurements were given priority instead of anti-retroviral drugs. With unemployment rates of approximately forty per cent, South Africa's future as a constitutional democracy has been severely imperilled.

The education system has been 'dumbed down' so that politicians can boast of improving matriculation pass rates, yet many school graduates are so functionally illiterate that they are unqualified either for university entrance or for the job market. An entire generation of school leavers is essentially unemployable.

Hundreds of teachers' and nurses' training colleges around the country were closed down, meaning that South Africa's economic and social recovery will be hugely problematic. As with the Aids catastrophe he inflicted upon the country, Mbeki simply would not listen to church and community leaders. At his direction, his health minister, Manto Tshabalala-Msimang – whose husband, Menzi Msimang was Treasurer of the ANC – prescribed beetroot, olive oil and lemon juice instead of highly effective anti-retroviral drugs.

The 'chapter nine institutions' and other checks and balances established by the Constitution all kowtowed to Mbeki. Predictably, and as was eventually admitted, the offset proposals proved a dismal failure. British government officials had been seconded to South Africa, ostensibly to ensure the success of the offset programme but, in reality, to cover up irregularities and wrongdoing and to block investigations.

Parliamentarians and the Auditor General's Office who demanded details of the offsets were fobbed off with the excuse that the programmes were 'commercially confidential', and that their disclosure was prohibited. This is a standard ploy, which is incorporated into the wording of all BAE contracts to circumvent the commitment of the British government to the provisions of the OECD Bribery Conventions.

A press release in September 1999 listed twenty-one possible Swedish offset projects linked to the BAE/Saab Gripen contract. About half of them were linked to Billy Rautenbach's Wheels For Africa Group, which held the franchise rights for Volvo and Saab in Africa south of the Equator. Wheels For Africa went bankrupt about a year later. Rautenbach was wanted for murder in South Africa, and was also alleged by the United Nations to be one of the financial brains behind the ongoing war in the Democratic Republic of Congo.

Rautenbach's assets in the United States were frozen by the US Treasury in November 2008. In short, Saab's intended partner in the offset projects was a man identified as one of the main role players in the Congolese war in which an estimated ten million people have died. Rautenbach testified a year later at Selebi's trial just how his business partner had met Selebi and Agliotti in 2005 to discuss his legal troubles, amongst them charges of fraud and tax evasion.

The online *Daily Maverick* reported:

> Rautenbach's business partner reported success after that meeting telling him: 'Agliotti has a contact and we may be able to take this forward to the next level.' Taking it to the next level meant handing over US$100 000 in cash to Agliotti a few days later. The prosecution says US$30 000 of that ended up in Selebi's hands.
>
> Agliotti had previously sold Rautenbach on the reach and extent of his contacts. Rautenbach implied that he had little choice but to hand over the US$100 000 because 'prosecuting authorities at that time had closed the door', and there was no other way to make the arrest warrant hanging over his head go away.
>
> If Rautenbach's version of events is true, then he didn't exactly get value for his money. He eventually agreed in September 2009 to pay R40 million to have the charges against him dropped, so Selebi clearly didn't do much for his case.[11]

With the collapse of Wheels for Africa, the Department of Trade and Industry (DTI) selected Diesel Management Systems (DMS) in Durban as one of the flagship offset projects. DMS had developed a process to drastically reduce diesel pollution. Against an agreement with BAE/Saab, DMS increased its premises and staff. Loan facilities were negotiated from ABSA bank, which were guaranteed by BAE.

Once the BAE/Saab agreements were signed, BAE demanded an eighty per cent share of the company's equity. Understandably, the directors refused to give away their business. BAE then withdrew its guarantees and, consequently, ABSA withdrew its loan facilities. The company almost went under. It sued ABSA some years ago, but the judge has since 'forgotten' to give his judgement.

Mbeki, Manuel, Erwin and Modise made a mockery of constitutional commitments to open, transparent and accountable governance. That they then rigorously suppressed all investigative efforts into the arms deal scandal warrants full legal penalties against them, such as thirty years' imprisonment in terms of the Prevention of Organised Crime Act (1998).

Just what is the point of passing such legislation if politicians believe that they are immune from its provisions? Even worse, however, have been the roles of European governments, most especially the British, in pressuring an inexperienced South African government to buy armaments the country did not need and could not afford. The British in particular have long experience of the consequences of unleashing corruption in newly liberated societies.

Affidavits that I held explain how and why a group of well-connected British agents linked to Margaret Thatcher created BAE's front companies such as Red Diamond Trading Company. It was Thatcher's lawyers who established the structures through which Fana Hlongwane, John Bredenkamp and others received bribes of £115 million.

Six months before Jacobs died, in March 2008 the *Mail & Guardian* revealed in a story entitled 'Arms Probe Reopened':

> If late defence minister Modise is the ghost at the arms-deal banquet, Hlongwane is the guest who got it all.
>
> Hlongwane, Modise's close adviser at the Defence Ministry, is private and does not answer allegations about the tens of millions that BAE allegedly paid him for 'consulting'. But the very high walls obscuring his Hyde Park, Johannesburg, mansion have not contained the rumour about an alleged extravagant lifestyle. A contributor to an online discussion group wrote last year: 'There is a Playboy mansion in Hyde Park.
>
> 'The guy is a black multimillionaire like Hugh [Hefner] and the girls are just as pretty and blonde. One of them drives a Ferrari, another a Porsche and the list goes on; they wear Gucci this, Fendi that and they travel around the world just for shopping ... The guy's name is Fana Hlongwane [so I've heard].'
>
> Modise, who died in 2001 aged seventy-two and Hlongwane were regarded as very close during Modise's term at the Defence Ministry. Both, it is alleged,

got improperly close to BAE during that time.

In 1997 already, Modise secretly got shares in the Conlog/Log-Tek electronics group, which stood to benefit substantially from arms-deal offset agreements, including with ABB, a sister company of BAE partner Saab.

The known high-water mark of Modise's alleged batting for BAE was his 1998 intervention to urge a 'visionary' approach, excluding cost considerations, which led to BAE's Hawk jet trainer being short-listed and ultimately selected over Aermacchi's much cheaper offer.

Hlongwane, meanwhile, was advising not only Modise but also BAE. Investigations by the SFO have revealed that BAE agreed to an annual retainer of £1-million with Hlongwane in 2002 and a 'settlement' in 2005 to pay him $8-million (now about R64-million) 'in relation to work done on the Gripen project'.

The South African Institute For Race Relations (SAIRR) joined my application as an amicus of the court, and in their documents declared that the president's arguments were:

> … misconceived and suggested a contempt for the Constitution. The President is legally obliged to uphold the Constitution at all times. In addition, the President must act reasonably and rationally in exercising his constitutional powers. The scourge of corruption threatens everything we hold dear and precious in our hard-won constitutional order.[12]

The only logical explanation that can be deduced for the arms deal and its cover-up is that with the collusion of the British government huge kickbacks were paid to the ANC through various front men, including Hlongwane and Bredenkamp. Not only is Bredenkamp a highly placed British intelligence agent, but he has also been the money-man behind Robert Mugabe as well as numerous scams in the Congo.

The US Treasury froze his assets in the US in November 2008, describing him as:

> A well-known Mugabe insider involved in various business activities, including tobacco trading, gray-market arms trading and trafficking, equity investments, oil distribution, tourism, sports management and diamond

extraction. Through a sophisticated web of companies, Bredenkamp has financially propped up the regime and provided other support to a number of high ranking officials. He also has financed and provided logistical support to a number of Zimbabwean parastatal entities.[13]

Consequently, Standard Bank blacklisted Bredenkamp and closed his accounts in South Africa, a decision upheld by the Supreme Court of Appeal in May 2010.[14] The National Prosecuting Authority (NPA) tried every conceivable ploy to avoid prosecuting either Hlongwane or Bredenkamp.

Authorities in Liechtenstein had frozen Hlongwane's bank accounts, but the director of the NPA, Menzi Simelane, in 2010 decided that there was insufficient evidence of corruption to seize the funds. In an investigation that she chaired, the former Speaker of Parliament Frene Ginwala had previously described Simelane as 'unfit to hold public office'.

That, however, had not deterred Zuma from appointing him, presumably so that Simelane could then protect both Zuma and other 'black diamonds' from prosecutions. The *Sunday Times* newspaper in March 2010 reported:

> Explosive allegations in court documents, hidden from the public until now, contradict the reasons given by National Prosecutions boss Menzi Simelane for dropping the case against the man central to the decade-long arms deal scandal.
>
> Simelane claimed that he had abandoned an attempt to freeze flamboyant playboy Fana Hlongwane's foreign bank accounts because of a lack of evidence against him. Documents in the *Sunday Times*'s possession show he was indirectly paid more than R200 million by British defence company BAE – cash suspected to have been used to bribe officials.
>
> The closely guarded court file includes a one hundred and six page affidavit from deputy director of Public Prosecutions Billy Downer in which he details how Hlongwane was paid £4.9 million between October 1999 and July 2001 by a company set up by BAE to pay 'commissions' for the arms deal.
>
> More than eight hundred pages of new evidence have emerged from a criminal probe into Hlongwane by Liechtenstein prosecutors in the past two years, all of which was shared with the NPA in October 2009.[15]

The Constitution requires that government decisions must be rational. While visibly irritated that Zuma's legal counsel had not bothered to prepare themselves for the Constitutional Court, Chief Justice Sandile Ngcobo bent over backwards to be 'even-handed'. Quite logically, Ngcobo argued that both sides should be heard in an issue of such gravity as the arms deal scandal.

We could have insisted there and then that Morume, as the president's legal counsel, 'had made his bed and must now lie in it'. Sensing, however, that we could push our luck too far, we agreed to a four-month postponement. Both parties were admonished to supplement their papers.

Whether that was what Ngcobo intended, it was just the opportunity we wanted. We could now offload more than one thousand, five hundred pages of documents into the court records. These included affidavits in my possession which detailed why BAE had established Red Diamond Trading Company and other front organisations in the British Virgin Islands, to whom BAE paid bribes of over £115 million, and even into which bank accounts in South Africa the bribes had been paid.

As cabinet ministers with oversight over the arms deal, it was blatantly obvious that Mbeki, Manuel and Erwin had colluded with BAE and the British government on the payment of bribes to frontmen such as Hlongwane and Bredenkamp. How those bribes were paid to the ANC as 'donations' is incidental.

We set to work immediately, even before flying home to Cape Town. First, we offered the president's counsel what we termed an 'open tender' for a judicial commission of inquiry modelled after the Truth and Reconciliation Commission. We suggested that to save the presidential dignity and the embarrassment of full-blown exposure at the Constitutional Court:

- a judicial commission of inquiry into the arms deal must be agreed by the end of May 2011,
- at least five commissioners must be appointed from the ranks of retired judges, and they be given adequate resources to conduct an investigation in an open, transparent and accountable fashion,
- the commissioners must be given power to grant indemnity from prosecution against full and frank disclosure,

- the commissioners must specifically be tasked with the possibility of cancelling any arms deal contract that was tainted by fraud, corruption or any other wrongdoing,
- all proceedings must be conducted in an open, transparent and accountable fashion.[16]

The thought of impunity from prosecution for corruption is legally repugnant. Nonetheless, I was prepared to make the suggestion in the hope that South Africa would at least learn from Mbeki, Erwin and Manuel what pressures were exerted by the European governments and arms companies. The president's lawyers, however, rejected the proposal. Just days later, a memo written in September 2010 by General Hans Meiring of the Hawks was leaked by the *Mail & Guardian* newspaper, and set the proverbial cat amongst the pigeons.

It is a bizarre and extraordinary document motivating why the arms deal investigations should be abandoned. After confirming that the volume of evidence against BAE is so massive that 'approximately four hundred and sixty boxes of documents and 4.7 seven million pages of documents must be perused and analysed', Meiring argued that:

- the right to a speedy trial might have been compromised by the passage of time,
- companies, witnesses and evidence were no longer available,
- a proper investigation would be resource-intensive,
- some suspects had died,
- parallel foreign investigations had closed, and
- it is difficult to get witnesses and evidence from abroad.[17]

In emphasising the difficulties, Meiring declared that 'three suspects in the BAE leg in South Africa have all passed away' and, 'some of the suspects are now residing in other countries and extraditions will have to be applied for'.

Meiring's suppositions were patently not true. Indeed, the beneficiaries of the bribes detailed in BAE affidavits, with one exception, are all still alive and are resident in South Africa for most or at least part of the year.

Hlongwane is certainly alive and well, and living in the ritzy Hyde Park area of Johannesburg.

Another recipient of the BAE bribes, Richard Charter died in 2004 in highly suspicious circumstances, but his widow Janet lives in Hermanus, and continues to 'run the business'. She is now reportedly in a romantic relationship with no less than Bredenkamp, who frequently flits in and out of South Africa and has many businesses and properties in this country.

In addition, investigations against BAE in the US and Sweden are still continuing. We submitted our supplementary affidavit to the Constitutional Court with so much additional detail that we feared we might overload the judges. Richard Young of c2I2, Andrew Feinstein, Gavin Woods, John Hunt and even the cartoonist Zapiro also provided supporting affidavits. Then another bombshell erupted in Sweden.

Swedish TV4's Kalle Fakta (Cold Facts) programme had approached me in April 2011 for assistance in making a documentary to be broadcast in May. I agreed and was interviewed, but I also provided some documents including the BAE bribery affidavits detailing the involvement of Sanip (Pty) Ltd with Hlongwane. The resulting ructions continue. Saab's chief executive officer, Häkan Buskhe confirmed three weeks later that BAE had fraudulently misused Saab's accounts to pay an amount of R24 million to Hlongwane.

It also transpired that BAE, which in 1995 bought a fifty per cent interest of the Gripen project and responsibility for international marketing, had just a few weeks earlier sold off its remaining equity in Saab. Buskhe was now free to spill the beans, and was highly embarrassed by the corruption scandal that Saab had been sucked into because of its associations with BAE. Could there now be a 'falling out amongst thieves'?

I wrote to Buskhe suggesting that he might provide the Constitutional Court with an affidavit

> … detailing how and why Saab allowed itself to be associated with a company that, bluntly, is organised crime on a scale that makes the Italian mafia look like amateurs. Now that BAE no longer holds an equity interest in Saab, I look forward to your candid revelations together with your proposals for substantial restitution to the people of South Africa so grievously afflicted.

South Africa's celebrated transition to democracy is now imperilled by the corruption that BAE and Saab jointly unleashed.[18]

The *Sunday Independent* newspaper editorialised:

> As a country, we are left with no choice. President Jacob Zuma has no option but to authorise and capacitate investigators to look, unencumbered by political interference, into the cesspit that is the arms deal, which has not only muddied our politics, but also caused us shame every time there is a revelation in some part of the globe about shenanigans that are linked to this deal.
>
> But, in all honesty, we must ask: How can we expect a man who almost did not become a president because of the arms deal to launch a thorough investigation into the same deal?
>
> Whatever the answer, it does not appear that the monstrosity that is the arms deal will disappear any time soon. For our politicians to move from one townhall to another, promising to root out corruption while ignoring the putrid stench of the arms deal is hypocrisy of the highest order.[19]

In agreeing to a postponement, the Constitutional Court instructed President Zuma's legal team to supplement their papers by August 1, 2011. Two days before that deadline, his lawyers requested another six weeks' delay which took the matter to September 15, by which time the president's legal advisers still could not refute the mountain of evidence.

Faced with these realities, the president announced he would appoint a commission (not yet a judicial commission as announced later) of inquiry. A few weeks later he announced the terms of reference, and gave the Commission two years to complete its work. There are six provisions in the terms of reference, three of which deal with offsets.

1. The rationale for the Strategic Defence Procurement Packages (SDPP)
2. Whether the arms and equipment acquired in terms of the Strategic Defence Procurement Packages are underutilised or not utilised at all
3. Whether job opportunities anticipated to flow from the Strategic Defence Procurement Packages have materialised at all and
   - if they have, the extent to which they have materialised, and

- if they have not, the steps that ought to be taken to realise them
4. Whether offsets anticipated to flow from the SDPP have materialised at all and
   - if they have, the extent to which they have materialised, and
   - if they have not, the steps that ought to be taken to realise them
5. Whether any person/s, within and/or outside the Government of South Africa, improperly influenced the award or conclusion of any of the contracts awarded and concluded in the SDPP procurement process and if so
   - whether legal proceedings should be instituted against such persons, and the nature of such legal proceedings
   - whether in particular there is any basis to pursue such persons for the recovery of any losses that the State might have suffered as a result of their conduct
6. Whether any contract concluded pursuant to the SDPP procurement process is tainted by any fraud or corruption capable of proof, such as to justify its cancellation, and the ramifications of such cancellation

Judicial commissions of inquiry are internationally notorious as a place to park political hot potatoes, and I immediately smelt many rats. My intended submission to the commission will be that offsets fail South Africa's constitutional requirements for governmental procurements, and that the arms deal was therefore both unconstitutional and illegal right from inception.

If it is accepted that the arms deal is unfixable, what South Africa needs is remedial action including cancellation of the contracts. The politicians and their bribery bagmen who sucked South Africa into the mess need to be held accountable. The financial consequences of cancellation then would fall to the British and German taxpayers who guaranteed the loan agreements that financed the arms deal.

to be continued in *Eye On The Gold*

Endnotes

1. Shaun de Waal: 'Alms (and arms) for Oblivion?' *Mail & Guardian*, October 10-16, 2008.
2. Constitutional Court case 103/2010.
3. Ilham Rawoot: 'Conflict Rocks State Diamond Buyer: Zuma Ally Accused Of Breaching Kimberley Accord By Buying Zimbabwe Stones', *Mail & Guardian*, June 10, 2011.
4. Kevin Bloom: 'Paul O'Sullivan: And I'm Also Going After Thabo Mbeki', *Daily Maverick*, July 6, 2010.
5. 'Cecil Rhodes's Funeral, Imposing Ceremony Yesterday At Cape Town', *The New York Times*, April 3, 1902.
6. Dean Andromidas: 'BAE Money Trail Leads To Thatcher', *EIR*, December 2008.
7. Jenny Cargill: *Trick Or Treat*, Jacana Media (Pty) Ltd, Cape Town, 2010.
8. Section 2 of the Constitution.
9. Ernest Mabuza: 'Zuma To Answer Arms Deal Claims', *Business Day*, May 6, 2011.
10. Albie Sachs: *The Soft Vengeance Of A Freedom Fighter*, Souvenir Press, UK, 2011, pp 241 and 242.
11. Mark Allix: 'Billy Rautenbach Damns Selebi, Clears Ngcuka (Mostly)', *Daily Maverick*, November 19, 2009.
12. SAIRR press release, May 5, 2011.
13. US Treasury statement, November 25, 2008.
14. Supreme Court of Appeal, Case 599/09.
15. Rob Rose: 'How arms deal man escaped with R200m', *Sunday Times*, March 21, 2010.
16. Letter to the State Attorney's Office, Cape Town dated May 10, 2011 written at my instructions by my attorneys, Abrahams Kiewitz.
17. Stefaans Brummer: 'The Memo That Sank The Arms Probe', *Mail & Guardian*, June 3, 2011.
18. Letter to Häkan Buskhe, Saab, dated June 21, 2011.
19. 'Will Zuma Do The Right Thing On Arms Deal?' *Sunday Independent*, June 26, 2011.

LIST OF ACRONYMS

ACR	African Consolidated Resources
AIPAC	American Israel Public Affairs Committee
ANC	African National Congress
BCCI	Banque du Credit et Commerce Internationale
BDS	Boycott Divestment and Sanctions (campaign)
BEE	Black Economic Empowerment
BSA	British South Africa Company
CAAT	Campaign Against Arms Trade
CIA	(United States) Central Intelligence Agency
DRC	Democratic Republic of the Congo
EAPPI	(World Council of Churches) Ecumenical Accompaniment Programme for Palestine and Israel
ECC	End Conscription Campaign
ECGD	(British) Export Credit Guarantee Department
EO	Executive Outcomes
FARC	Revolutionary Armed Forces of Colombia
FBI	(United States) Federal Bureau of Investigation
ICC	International Criminal Court
ICJ	International Court of Justice
ICAHD	Israeli Committee Against House Demolitions
Idasa	Institute for Democracy in South Africa
IDB	Illicit Diamond Buying
Ifaisa	Institute for Accountability in Southern Africa

ISC	International Signal Corporation
JCI	Johannesburg Consolidated Investments
MK	Umkhonto we Sizwe
MPLA	Popular Movement for the Liberation of Angola
NATO	North Atlantic Treaty Organisation
NEC	National Executive Committee (of the ANC)
NPA	National Prosecuting Authority
NIS	New Israeli Shekel
Numsa	National Union of Metalworkers
OECD	Organisation for Economic Cooperation and Development
OPEC	Organisation of Petroleum Exporting Countries
PNAC	Project for the New American Century
RDP	Reconstruction and Development Programme
RPF	Rwandan Patriotic Front
RUF	(Sierra Leone) Revolutionary United Front
SACC	South African Council of Churches
SADF	(pre-1994) South African Defence Force
SAZF	South African Zionist Federation
Scopa	Standing Committee on Public Accounts
SFO	(British) Serious Fraud Office
Swapo	South West African People's Organisation
SWIFT	Society for Worldwide Interbank Financial Telecommunication
TRC	Truth and Reconciliation Commission
UAE	United Arab Emirates
UDF	United Democratic Front
UNHRC	United Nations Human Rights Council
Unita	National Union for the Total Independence of Angola
WDC	World Diamond Council
ZDI	Zimbabwe Defence Industry
ZMDC	Zimbabwe Mining and Development Organisation

SELECTED INDEX